THE BEST
OF
ITALIAN COOKING

AN  BOOK

WAVERLEY ROOT

THE BEST
OF
ITALIAN COOKING

GROSSET & DUNLAP
Publishers   New York

CONTENTS

THE SPIRIT
OF A GREAT CUISINE

Modern Italy is Renaissance Italy with a little of its gilt rubbed off by the erosion of half a millennium of troubled times; modern Italian cooking is therefore, inevitably, Renaissance cooking, with some of its extraneous excrescences planed down, which is all to the good. If you want to know why Italians eat the way they do, look to the Renaissance.

Renaissance: rebirth. A rebirth of what? What could it have been, if not that of the classical Greco-Roman civilization which had been carried in the knapsacks of the Legions to all of Western Europe, to Asia Minor, and to North Africa, until it died in 476 A.D. when the last Roman Emperor, Romulus Augustulus, Augustus the Little, was deposed by the Barbarians?

But it was an Italy which preferred the sober spirit of the Greeks to the unrestrained indulgence of the Romans, and thus escaped retrogression to the gastronomic excesses of Imperial Rome, which had coarsened and eventually eliminated whatever finesse Roman cooking had possessed originally. Degeneracy, whether in the kitchen or in the seats of government, was not in tune with the character of reawakened Italy. The senile model of a Roman Empire which was running down did not appeal to a youthful Renaissance which was speeding up, in government, in philosophy, in literature, in painting, in cooking. The first cookbooks published in Italy after the classical period were, it is true, reissues of those of ancient Rome; but Platina warned against the excesses of Apicius. The dishes of ancient Rome which survived through the drought of the Dark Ages were basic and elemental, the simple foods of the poor, which had been capable of maintaining themselves through the centuries of want which followed the collapse of Roman luxury—polenta, pasta, brodetto.

The gastronomic heritage which Renaissance Italy received from ancient Rome had been purged of its unhealthy elaborations, and there was no enthusiasm for reviving them. By the fifteenth century, the cuisine of Italy was the best of the Western world.

That great cultural, intellectual, artistic, scientific and spiritual explosion which we call the Renaissance, whose revivifying flame was to light all Europe and end a thousand years of Dark Ages, was born in Italy; its capital was Florence. Why Italy? Perhaps simply because Italy was where it was, geographically, in the path of a cultural wind ready to blow from East to West. When darkness settled over Europe, the centre of civilization shifted to the Arab world, prepared to receive it because it had imbibed Hellenic culture from the Greek colonies which had found hospitable territory on the soil of Asia Minor. Nor had the Arabs neglected gastronomy. They possessed foods Europe had lost or had never known—exotic herbs and spices, sugar cane, coffee, spinach, rice—and they had learned how to make sherbet and to distill alcohol.

When the uncouth Crusaders of the West took it upon themselves to try to wrest the Holy Land from the more refined Saracens, they rediscovered civilization and reimported it to their own world. In the process they passed, coming and going, through Italy, the handiest way station, which consequently became the first beneficiary of the revivifying current from the East. Venice, Genoa and Pisa all furnished fleets for the Crusades, and the Venetians and the Genoese set up and maintained trading counters in Asia Minor from which they imported heady ideas and precious goods; the latter were the basis for the accretion of wealth which was a necessary condition for the flowering of Renaissance art—and the development of Renaissance cooking.

It is the crass fact that neither the fine arts nor gastronomy can develop without a minimum threshold of prosperity; somebody has to be rich enough to pay the painters and the pastry cooks; nor is a country living at the margin of bare survival much interested in the quality of what it eats; it will settle for quantity. If the arts flourished in Renaissance Italy, it was because there was enough wealth to permit some citizens to abandon material production and devote themselves to artistic production; if the kitchen flourished in Renaissance Italy it was because there was enough wealth to fill the pantry.

When we look back to the cooking of the Renaissance, we should take care not to miss the essential because we are dazzled by the brilliance of the exceptional, like the spectacular banquets of Duke Borso d'Este or Lorenzo the Magnificent. The glittering feasts of the Estes and the Medicis captivate the attention, but they were no more typical of the normal life of those times than are the occasional ostentatious and expensive antics of the newly rich of ours; nevertheless these phenomena were not rare, for the prospering Italy of the Renaissance was broken up into a bewildering mosaic of kingdoms, principalities, dukedoms, counties, Imperial and Papal fiefs and even republics, each with a court or a seat of government, an urge to outshine the others, and money to spend in the attempt to do so—on architects, sculptors and painters to build and decorate magnificent palaces, even writers to sing their patrons' praises or merely to reflect glory upon them by their more or less respectful attendance—or on food, flunkies, and cooks for the sumptuous banquets which attested to the wealth, the power and the splendor of the hosts.

This ducal feasting may well recall the orgies of Imperial Rome; but the extravagances of Rome and the extravagances of the Renaissance were staged against very different backgrounds.

Beneath the level of the courtly feasts of the Renaissance, the foundations were much more solid. A handful of superlatively rich patrons, of artists and of cooks, is all very well, but the very mighty can never be sufficiently numerous to support a significant school of art or to provide wide enough scope for the development of a deep-rooted national or racial or regional cuisine. But when, as in the Renaissance, there is a well-to-do middle class numerous enough to patronize not only a few selected geniuses, but a large body of artists, and to patronize not only a small clique of master cooks but a whole population of ordinary cooks, both art and cooking can expand to dimensions which assure their survival.

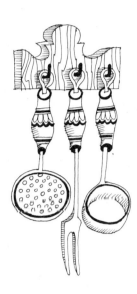

The middle class of the Renaissance was made up of employers' associations called "the guilds", which controlled the exploding economy of Florence: they made up a true bourgeoisie. The bourgeoisie is frequently excoriated for being commercially minded: and so, no doubt, it was during the Renaissance. So much the better. Self-interest brought about a much more general distribution of wealth through the different classes of society than had ever been achieved in antiquity. Under the bourgeoisie of the Renaissance, the means for distributing wealth was the modern one of the employer-employee relationship. Money thus filtered down from the wealthy to the industrial and commercial workers, to the artisans and the suppliers of personal services in sufficient quantity to make of them significant consumers of goods, including food; a large population of customers living above bare subsistence level is necessary to pay for the development of an important cuisine. Some of the general wealth seeped down even to the peasants, the ultimate producers of food, who were thereby enabled and encouraged to offer a more varied choice of foodstuffs to a market which was demanding it.

Economically, the Renaissance was ready to accept and support, and because of its aesthetic awakening, to appreciate, a great cuisine. It therefore received one. Without a solid base, a great cuisine can not be created or developed. The comfort-loving burghers of Renaissance Italy demanded plain food—sound, simple, unsurprising but perfectly prepared. Around this "cuisine bourgeoise" or "cucina casalinga" were built dishes of such refinement as to eventually require true gourmets to appreciate them.

The wealth of the Renaissance, which, seeping down through all layers of the population, made it possible for Italy to eat better food than it had known for centuries—than it had ever known, perhaps, if the whole mass of the population and not simply the upper crust is taken into account—was to a large extent created, in a spiral far from vicious, by food itself. It was not only the bankers of Lombardy and the weavers of Tuscany who were bringing money into the peninsula, relatively much richer in comparison with the rest of the world than it is today, it was to an even greater extent the importers of Genoa and Venice, who were supplying all Europe with the fragrant herbs and biting spices of the Orient, upon which Europeans fell avidly to give character to a diet which for several centuries had been drab, unexciting and tasteless. The palaces of Venice were founded financially on spices. True, the capital of the Renaissance was not Venice, but Florence, but the spice-born wealth of Venice flowed over the borders of the Veneto at least as far as to Tuscany. Venetian shipowners and exporters needed capital and the Florentines were bankers.

Enormous fortunes were made in spices. They were as good as money, sometimes better, and in that case were a substitute for it. In a period when every great city had its own coinage, and often cheated on its content of precious metal—a pound of nutmeg was a more reliable unit of foreign exchange than a pound of silver. Pepper had been worth its weight in gold under the Roman emperors; it was worth its weight in gold again during the Renaissance.

Spices are exotic and luxurious additions to the larder; they might have been expected to encourage excess in the style of the ancient Romans—and, indeed, in the first exuberance of their rediscovery, some sensationally over-seasoned dishes appeared; but their vogue, at least outside of the high-level banquets, was short (a penchant for indiscriminately over-spiced dishes lasted longer in some other European countries than in Italy). Instead of ladling all available seasonings into every dish as the ancient Romans had been prone to do (thus making all foods taste alike), Renaissance Italy quickly settled down to the subtler technique of flavoring each food only with the herb, spice, or combination of herbs and spices which accorded best with its own nature. Under the Romans the function of seasonings had been that of drowning and disguising natural flavors; under the Renaissance it was that of enhancing or accompanying them.

Another influence for restraint which may have helped prevent Italians from going overboard about their new seasonings was the fact that there lay, more or less unnoticed, behind the romantic glitter of the exotic imports, other down-to-earth materials—like one which had begun to build up the wealth of Venice even before the Oriental seasonings made their appearance. It was a seasoning too, but one which seemed thoroughly unspectacular, even humdrum. It was an item one never thinks about unless it is lacking—salt. Venice had a monopoly of salt in its own area, and deep into the valley of the Po. There was also among the new imports a food indubitably important, but sobering in comparison with spices—rice.

One event which might have inspired overweening fantasy in Renaissance cooking failed to do so—the discovery of America. True, most of the new foods of the New World were exotic only in the sense that they were strange because unknown and that they came from distant unexplored countries, not in the sense that they were curious or provocative or exciting—maize and the potato are not quite stimulants. There were, of course, some among the new discoveries which thoroughly deserved the adjective "exotic", vanilla and chocolate for instance; but Italy would not become conscious of them for a long while; and their dissemination was retarded, in the case of chocolate at least, and probably in that of vanilla also, by the fact that the Spaniards who had first discovered and first imported them kept the secret of their origin for 100 years, to maintain their monopoly.

New foods in any case are normally very slow in making their way into areas previously unacquainted with them. Few habits are more resistant to change than eating habits. Unfamiliar dishes are regarded warily and with suspicion, and are seldom adopted before long periods of probation. The few innovations which escape the operation of this rule manage it precisely because they do not seem totally unfamiliar. The one American food which began to be eaten in Italy during the Renaissance (though not very widely at the beginning) was the haricot bean, sufficiently similar to the European broad bean so that Italians were not afraid to swallow it. On the contrary, a food without which it is difficult to imagine Italian cooking today, the tomato, required two or three centuries to become naturalized.

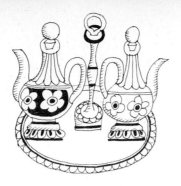

The products of any society, whether they are machines, produce, fabrics, ideas, furniture, hair styles, or desserts, are in harmony with each other. It cannot be otherwise. In the unending milling together of the myriad separate elements which make up the mass of artifacts, material and spiritual, of that society, anything extraneous is broken off or rubbed down or altered in tone. Allow a little time and everything, by interaction, has come into tune. Manifestations of the human spirit which spring from the same source cannot be inconsistent one with another. The art of cooking (cooking is certainly an art, if a minor one; that depends on what you consider to be minor) cannot be otherwise than in harmony with the noble arts, since both were born at the same time from the same spirit, and developed together during the same era.

Renaissance architecture is characterized by exteriors notable for their sobriety, and at the same time for the grace of their proportions, restrained and without extravagance; but within they are decorated with a warmth, a color, and a richness which few ages have equalled, and certainly none with such taste. The architecture of the Renaissance kitchen is built upon such solid, basic, simple and unpretentious materials as, for instance, pasta, or (chronologically a little later) rice. But they are then transfigured by their decoration, the sauces whose ingenuity and piquancy turn them into a series of tingling experiences which, nevertheless, avoid, sometimes by a hair's breadth, the extravagances which would carry them beyond the limits of good taste. This fragile analogy can also be carried into painting, as noted by the art critic, Bernard Berenson. Writing of the Umbrian School, Berenson described Pinturicchio's later work as "an *olla podrida* rich and savory, but more welcome to provincial palates than to the few gourmets. And when such an opulent and luxurious half-barbarian as Pope Alexander VI was his employer, then no spice nor condiment nor seasoning was spared."

The correspondence between cooking and painting holds true throughout Italy: Tuscan cooking differs from Venetian cooking as Tuscan painting differs from Venetian painting. It was the food of Florence which led the way in Renaissance Italy, and it was the School of Florence which dominated Italian painting from the beginning to the end of the Renaissance, with Giotto in the Trecento, Fra Angelico and Botticelli in the Quattrocento, Leonardo and Michelangelo in the Cinquecento. These were the great founders of solid artistic values, the serious creators of a body of work which required no superficial artifice and was, therefore, in that sense—the best sense—simple. It is precisely in the native Tuscany of Giotto, Fra Angelico, Botticelli, Leonardo da Vinci and Michelangelo that Italian food is most solid and most simple. It is the only region which eats much beef. It is the home of *arista*, a superbly-flavored loin of pork—and probably also originally of *porchetta*, a whole roast suckling pig, though Rome today claims this as its own. Its favorite vegetable is the unspectacular but nourishing bean.

The School of Venice is airy, cerulean, imbued with color—color luminous rather than violent, no doubt inspired by the constantly flickering effect of rippling water against subtly-colored stone. The cooking of Venice is light and airy too. If it depends largely upon fish, that is not only by accident of geography (of course geography may have been

decisive in shaping the Venetian spirit itself) but to an inborn resistance of Venetians to stolid food. Venice does not much care for meat, and when it is eaten there at all, it rarely appears in large assertive pieces (steaks, roasts, chops) but cut up in stews or hashed. The only native Venetian meat dish that comes immediately to mind is *Fegato alla veneziana*, calf's liver (cut as delicately thin as possible) with chopped onions, sauteed in butter. Nowhere else do cooks manage to bring it off with the lightness achieved in Venice, just as elsewhere cooks make a rather soggy mess out of that other famous Venetian specialty, *risi e bisi*, rice with young peas from the vegetable gardens of the Venetian lagoon. Neither of these dishes sounds particularly subtle, but as produced in Venice, they are ethereal, like the Venetian painting of Giorgione, Titian or Tintoretto.

If the cooking of Italy is in harmony with its painting, another art form springs immediately to mind. Is there no parallel between that most Italian of arts, Grand Opera, and Italian cooking? True, when modern Italian cooking was born, at the time of the Renaissance, opera did not exist, neither in Italy nor anywhere else; nevertheless the Renaissance was a dramatic period, and it was to be drama—the very stuff of opera—which would dominate everything else in Italian music. The Italian musical genius, when it developed, would turn almost entirely in this direction. There was no lack, among Italian composers, of the harmonic skill or melodic invention or dexterity in handling the orchestra which in other countries would lead to the development of the symphony; they turned away from the symphony, whose drama is incidental to its main purpose, and turned to opera, of which drama is the main purpose. It is the major concern of Italian music, and is ever present also in the Italian kitchen. The strident shrilling of wild mint in Roman cooking is like the high notes of the trumpet, the caress of myrtle in Sardinia like a soft murmur in the chalumeau register of the clarinet.

Drama, drama, drama! The Italian meal itself is an opera, its cymbal clashes ringing where the composer would put them, at the beginning and the end. The incisive bite of the strings, the shrilling of woodwinds, or the trumpeting of the brass which, opening the overture, silences the audience and whets its appetite for what is to come, is exactly paralleled by the antipasti, whose function is to shock, to excite, to arouse the attention, like a peal of bells, festive, creating a mood. What is the content of the overture? Most often tidbits of the highlights of the music that will be heard later, an anticipatory promise which sets the nerves tingling pleasantly. What is the content of the antipasti? Samplings from the full repertory—morsels of fish, fresh, pickled, preserved, or smoked; of shellfish or crustaceans; of vegetables, fresh or preserved provocatively in vinegar, unctuously in oil; of spicy cured meats; of tiny tasty salads; of bite-sized pizzas, subtle canapes or little pancakes rolled around surprising stuffings. The other predictable summit of the opera, whatever may have happened in between, comes at the closing climax, with the entire cast crowding the stage shouting its heads off while the kettledrums explode in the orchestra pit. The object now is no longer to arouse the appetite, but to sate it; and this is the function performed by the rich Italian desserts, dramatized to the limit, like luscious creamy Roman chocolate cake, drenched in subtle liqueurs, as barbarically exotic as the Grand March from *Aida*.

The example of courts which were brilliant but potentially corruptive might also have operated to push Renaissance cooking towards the spectacular, the extravagant, the artificial or the precious, and thus to cut it off from the mass of the population, whose constant daily participation in the preparation of a nation's cuisine is required to keep it alive and durable. The courts provided a culture medium in which the unhealthy bacteria of excess might have flourished, as in Rome, but they did not. A little stranger, perhaps, is that the courts, in spite of their elaborate feasts, did not give Italy the *haute cuisine* which would develop later in France. Italy, after all, was earliest in the field of gastronomy, and gave to France the first lesson in culinary finesse. But counter-influences were operating within the courts themselves, and they held Italian cooking on the admirable course which it is still pursuing today.

The *haute cuisine*, stylized, meticulously regimented, requiring almost as much education for its appreciation as for its creation, was not in tune with the expansive spirit of the Renaissance, which was above all certainly not regimented. The *haute cuisine* was a cuisine of luxury, of subtlety and of refinement, but the glittering courts of the Italian Renaissance were, in their gastronomic aspect, magnificent rather than refined, striking rather than subtle, lavish rather than luxurious. The lords of the Renaissance were often swashbucklers, barely out of brigandage, like the Sforzas, former *condottieri*. The cooking they subsidized was not rarefied, it was virile and stemmed from the peasantry. Nobles paid for the feasts, but peasants executed them; and it was the taste of peasants (usually trustworthy in matters of food, since it is they who produce it and consequently they who know it best), not the taste of aristocrats, which formed the Italian cooking we enjoy today. The nobles, to tell the truth, were only incidentally interested in cooking, aside from its functions of display and of conviviality; they were content to give their cooks a free hand, as long as they fed them lavishly and maintained a reasonable level of palatability. They achieved a good deal more than a merely reasonable level.

Thus Italian cooking, despite the ostentation of the courts, was from the beginning based on the sound unspoiled standards of the peasants (or along the coasts of the fishermen, those peasants of the sea). The dominant factor in the Italian cuisine today is that, however intricate and however sophisticated it may sometimes become under the ministrations of the fine Italian hand, it remains fundamentally peasant cooking, home cooking, *la cucina casalinga*. A national cuisine might conceivably be based soundly in the peasantry, as it is in Italy, and widely accessible to all social and economic strata of the population, as it is in Italy, and still be monotonous. A great cuisine cannot develop within narrow limits. It needs to draw inspiration from a variety of sources. This is the case for the great French cuisine, made up, as I wrote in *The Food of France*, of the contrasting contributions of all the regional differences.

Regional differences are even more important in Italy than in France. When the Roman Empire collapsed, Italy broke up into small pieces which changed masters with kaleidoscopic versatility; each had its separate history and has today its distinctive person ality. The United States, in the New World, is older than Italy, one of the oldest European

nations of the Old World, so far as political unity is concerned; the United States achieved it in 1776, Italy in 1861. The arrival of unity was important—for cooking as well as for other things.

For diversity is not enough to make a great cuisine either. Alone, it could be chaotic, anarchic. Italy has a Tuscan cuisine, a Venetian cuisine, a Sicilian cuisine (indeed, *three* Sicilian cuisines!) and a score of others, but if they merely co-existed side by side, unintegrated, isolated, on the same peninsula, Italy would still possess only a parochial Tuscan cuisine, a parochial Venetian cuisine, and so forth and so on, a sort of mosaic of separate pieces which had never been put together into a coherent pattern. Diversity, yes—but diversity within a disciplining unity, capable of binding the separate elements together, so that while each region might still retain its individuality, they would all share a common spirit which would compose from a number of petty cuisines a single great national cuisine. Within it, every regional school of cooking displays more likenesses with the others than differences, and more likenesses with other Italian schools than with foreign schools (with certain exceptions, such as that of the Teutonic cooking of the Alto Adige which, however, has not remained untouched by the overlying Italian spirit).

In Italy the disparate elements have been knit together by the major dominant pattern of the Italian language and the Italian culture—a process which, indeed, began long before the politicians caught up with it and welded Italy into a single state. The dominant pattern was composed of the Tuscan language and the culture of the Renaissance. If it was Tuscan which was destined to replace Latin and become Italian, that was because Tuscany was the cradle of the Renaissance, and it was the mighty expansive sweep of the Renaissance which carried a common culture throughout Italy.

Since Italy was a country even more diverse than France, it required, to arrive at an equally happy balance between diversity and unity, in culture and in cooking, a stronger unifying centripetal force to counteract the also stronger centrifugal force of its disparities. That force was present, in an element France did not possess—a unity of nature. France is a congeries of contrasting climates (they provide one of the factors of its diversity) but Italy is climatically as homogeneous as any country of its size and shape could possibly be. With minor exceptions, the climate throughout Italy, a natural geographic unit, is much the same; the proportions of water, lowlands and mountains not too different, the flora and the fauna (the raw materials of food) remarkably consistent in kind. Eating habits develop largely as a function of the types of food available and the climate in which they are eaten (peoples of cold countries eat very differently from peoples of warm countries), and in Italy there was no natural obstacle to the evolution of similar habits of eating. The separate regional cuisines, at the same time that each retained its own individuality, were nevertheless fused together into a whole with a common spirit which made it recognizable, from Treviso to Bari, from Syracuse to Turin, as Italian.

I cannot think of any exception, anywhere in the world, to the rule that all great cuisines are based fundamentally on the cooking of peasants. It may be, then, that a measure of the extent to which a country's cooking has remained uncorrupted and true to its

sources is to be found in the degree of importance granted in that country to the four simple elementary foods which everywhere go into the knapsack of the peasant or the woodsman or the shepherd setting out for work in the fields or the forests or the pastures for a day or a week or a month—bread, cheese, sausage and (wherever the climate is propitious) wine. These foods are so fundamental and so important, they have been labored over in every locality with so much care and so much devotion, that each has developed its own preferred varieties and bestowed upon them proudly the names of the places which produced them. The most consistent example of this identification of food with the name of the place which created it is provided by wine (Beaune, Orvieto), followed closely by cheese (Camembert, Gorgonzola), then by sausage (frankfurter—Frankfurt, boloney—Bologna) and less rigorously by bread (Vienna bread, Italian breadsticks).

I am sometimes tempted to wonder whether there is not a significant co-relationship between decline in the quality of a country's cooking and increase in its willingness to accept factory-made bread. It is too much to expect housewives today to produce genuine homemade bread. The individual baker has, alas, practically disappeared from the United States and nearly so in Britain. He still struggles on in France, which is why Anglo-Saxons visiting that country are so unanimously loud in their praise of French bread, but, unfortunately, even in France the number of the local bakeries is dwindling under the baneful influence of the supermarket; more and more "bakeries" do not bake, but act simply as middlemen between their customers and the monstrous mass manufacturers of a standardized and tasteless product. I suspect that this is one of the reasons why the French, once considered the greatest bread eaters of the Western world, are eating less and less of it.

If the Frenchman is not now the greatest breadeater, who, in comparable Western countries, is? No doubt the Italian—*certainly* the Italian if you class pasta as a form of bread. It would also be my guess that among all the industrialized Western countries, it is in Italy that the greatest proportion of bread is homemade. Get out of the cities and into the countryside—especially, naturally, the poorer countryside—and you will come upon that precious product of the past, homemade bread. Here it is still the staff of life.

I remember sitting in the not too relentless heat of a September sun in the garden of a small farm in Sicily, bathing in the fragrance flowing from the primitive outdoor oven from which my hostess was drawing, one after the other, a score or more of steaming fat round loaves, some of which would feed her family, while the rest were destined for the fortunate village bakery, ten miles or so away. These simple round loaves are probably the most common form of bread, or at least of homemade bread, everywhere in southern Italy. Sometimes they are scored across the middle, so that they may easily be broken in two; sometimes instead the scoring facilitates breaking them into four or six, or, to provide individual portions, even eight parts. These loaves are identical in size and shape, and akin in ingredients too, with the loaves found in the oven of a Pompeian bakery 1,700 years after the baker had shoved them in and closed the oven door. It was an ancient type of bread even then. Hesiod described the same loaf as the familiar food of the farm worker

of ancient Greece; if my memory is exact, it was the eight-scored loaf he mentioned; one-eighth of the whole, probably accompanied by a bit of onion, was considered a sufficient midday ration for the abstemious Greek peasant, who might help it down with a little wine from a goatskin, but more probably with cool pure water from a mountain stream, a drink much appreciated by the Greeks, for whom springs and water courses were divinities.

One might expect that bread proper would have dwindled to minor proportions in Italy, where any meal is likely to include pasta—and what is pasta but a form of bread? Bread and pasta both are made from dough of basically the same ingredients—in the simplest version, flour, water and salt (of course, the type of flour used is often different). One might be tempted to suggest that the chief distinction between them is that bread contains yeast, or some other raising ingredient, and pasta does not; but there are types of bread which contain no yeast, and types of pasta which do. Bread is less closely dependent on wheat flour than is pasta, but pasta is not invariably made from wheat flour—there are buckwheat pastas in the Alps. In general it is nutritionally, if not gastronomically, true that bread and pasta are the same food; and since Italy eats a great deal of pasta, it would be logical for it to eat very little bread. Let us concede that the Italian is not logical; he eats a great deal of bread all the same.

Sicilians, for instance, are great pasta eaters; they are great bread eaters too; the same is true for Apulians. Sardinians actually *prefer* bread to pasta. They have their own cherished unique variety, "music-paper bread", made without yeast. It does not take the form of loaves but of what looks like very thin pancakes—"music-paper" either because the circles of bread are paper thin, or because they develop long parallel cracks which recall the lines of the musical staff, or both. Sardinia also goes in for ring-shaped loaves as well as the solid round ones which are common to all southern Italy, though in Sardinia they are looked upon almost contemptuously, as the sort of bread any housewife can produce offhand when she is not in a mood to give real care to her work. Neapolitans, with characteristic attention to decoration, may glaze their bread with egg white and decorate it with conventional designs. Ferrara is noted for its *ciupeta*, of curious form—a sphere whose crust is drawn up into four detached points at the top, like a crown, but whose outstanding virtue is not its shape but the quality of the fine white *soglia* flour from which it is made, a specialty of the region. The Paduan countryside also claims superiority for its bread; this is another region where it is often homemade. The Valle d'Aosta dotes on black bread of mixed barley and hard wheat flours, Lombardy's Valtellina makes buckwheat bread; and in the Alto Adige, the neighborhood of Merano also mixes barley and wheat. The Alto Adige makes several types of bread whose dough has been kneaded so violently that it is said to have been "beaten"—*Vorschlagbrot, Tralendalbrot, Schüttelbrot* (which means, literally, "shaken-up bread"). In Apulia, not only is the bread often homemade, the yeast is also; that means slower rising than if shop yeast were used, and more elbow grease is required for the kneading, but the result, Apulians think, is worth the extra trouble. Sicilians, on the contrary, do not knead the dough at all for their homemade *casareccio* (it must be admitted that it sometimes lies heavily on the stomach). The mountainous section of the province of Modena prefers fried breads, one of which, *tigella*, may go back to prehistoric times. It is cooked between two disks; Stone Age man, before he had devised cooking vessels which could be placed over a fire, cooked his crushed, moist grain between two heated stones.

This list is far from exhaustive, but it should suffice to prove that, if the existence of a variety of breads and the persistence of homemade bread is a barometer to the integrity of a national cuisine, then Italy unquestionably passes the test.

The most venerable cheeses of the Italian mainland are presumably the two the ancient Latins made from sheep milk, even before the founding of Rome; they are both still favorites of that city today. One is the creamy *ricotta*, a sort of cottage cheese, and the other the hard *pecorino*. *Pecorino* is today the most popular cheese of Italy, accounting all by itself for one-seventh of the country's total cheese consumption. *Pecorino romano*, after nearly 3,000 years of trial, is still considered the best, but the Sardinian version, *pecorino sardo*, is a close second; the two together provide one-half of the total production of this cheese, though it is made almost everywhere throughout the country. It is possible that Sardinia possesses a cheese even older than the ancient Latin ones, for its salty white goat-milk *fetta* is virtually identical with the Greek *feta*, which antedates Roman times.

Probably not so old, but in any case old enough, is the *fontina* of the Valle d'Aosta, the one used for making its famous melted-cheese dish, *fonduta*. The earliest written reference to it of which I know, *"Vallis Augusta casei boni sunt"* ("in the Valle d'Aosta the cheeses are good") dates only from 1477, but cheese in this area certainly goes back much farther than that. The statement, being in the plural, can cover other cheeses as well as *fontina*, and the region is rich in them: *sero*, a common cottage cheese, which when hardened for keeping is called *cacio magro*, and when enlivened by the dried flowers of aromatic herbs and bits of pimento, *salignon*; *reclèque*, a cream cheese eaten with sugar for dessert; *tome*, whose richness is ascribed to the fact that it is made from the milk of cows who have grazed throughout the summer on the fragrant herbs of the high Alpine pastures, 4,000 feet above sea level. *Tome* has a reddish color and is described locally as having "three virtues: it sates hunger, quenches thirst, and cleans the teeth". The Abruzzi region has a high-altitude cheese too—*scamorsa*, firm as to crust but creamy within, also from the milk of cows which graze at 4,000 feet.

The Italian cheese most widely known to foreigners may well be Parmesan, which, grated, is sprinkled freely over pasta and into minestrone; it may come as a surprise to some that it is also first-rate eaten on its own, in solid slices. Parmesan is no youngster either, 2,000 years old they say in Parma, though documentary evidence does not seem to go farther back than the fourteenth century, when Boccaccio referred to it, in a fashion which indicated that it was already well established and widely known. Parmesan is made with as much care as is bestowed on wine, from selected milk produced only between April 15 and November 15, when the grass is at its lushest. It is aged lengthily, for, like wine, the older it is, within reasonable limits, the better it is. If you want it for eating rather than grating purposes, look for *vecchio*, old (two years); or, better, *stravecchio*, extra old (three years); or, best, *stravecchione*, extra *very* old (four years up to as much as 20). Again as in the case of fine wines, Parmesan can only be sold under this name if it comes from a restricted area rigidly defined by law. Excellent grating cheese of the same type is made elsewhere, but it cannot be labelled Parmesan; it is called *grana*. First-rate *grana* comes from a number of other places, Ferrara, for instance; and Lodi, in Lombardy, makes more *grana* than Parma does—so much that Alexandre Dumas wrote confidently but erroneously that Parmesan did not come from Parma at all, but from Lodi.

If Parmesan is not the Italian cheese best known abroad, then either Gorgonzola or Bel Paese must be. Both come from Lombardy. Many persons think of Gorgonzola, a "blue" cheese, as a creamier Roquefort, but there is an important difference between them: Roquefort is made from sheep milk, Gorgonzola from cows' milk. So is Bel Paese, soft, yellow and bland. Some foreigners are aware of *provolone* also, a cheese so hard that it is not easy to cut. The same name is often tagged to different cheeses in various places, so *provolone* in the Campania may mean also a type of cheese unknown elsewhere in Europe and certainly strange to the United States—buffalo-milk cheese. There are other buffalo cheeses too—*caciocavallo*, (another usurped name, for it means something else everywhere except in Pescocostanza), *provola*, *provatura* and above all the classic buffalo-milk cheese, *mozzarella*. *Mozzarella* is a Neapolitan specialty, and if you want to eat it as Neapolitans do, you will have to go where it is made. It is eaten very fresh, preferably the day it is produced, when it is soft and creamy, swimming in its own buttermilk. However it is also hardened, formed into various fanciful shapes, and shipped to distant markets; but even then it should be eaten young.

What *caciocavallo* (literally, horse cheese) means everywhere except in perverse Pescocostanza, is a cows'-milk cheese shaped like a figure eight with its upper loop much smaller than the lower one. One explanation given for the name is that in nomadic times it was made of mare's milk, but the real reason is implicit in its shape and the fact that these cheeses are sold in pairs. *Caciocavallo* was originally designed to be carried on horseback. Make slipknots at the two ends of a short length of cord, tighten each around the narrow section of one of the two cheeses, and sling the cord over the neck of your horse, with one cheese dangling on each side, in convenient reach of a hungry rider. It is probable that no one treats *caciocavallo* in this fashion nowadays, for the horse, except for racing, is becoming obsolete; but the cheese is not.

Nobody knows how many other kinds of Italian cheeses there may be, but only a few need be mentioned. *Groviera italiano* means Italian Gruyere, and is Lombardy's imitation of the famous Swiss cheese. Liptauer, popular in Trieste, brings a breath of Central Europe into Italy—it is really not one cheese, but two, Gorgonzola and *mascarpone* crushed together with butter, plus various piquant flavorings—crushed anchovy fillets, caraway seeds, chopped leeks, mustard, paprika, capers, onion. (*Mascarpone* is a Lombardy cream cheese usually eaten sugared for dessert.) To round off the list, I give you the prettily named Flower of Sardinia, *fiore sardo*, handmade by shepherds on the high plateaux where they are isolated among their sheep for months at a time; sharp in taste, it is usually grated for

sprinkling over pasta. I think it is safe to say that the Italian cuisine passes the cheese test.

Turn to the subject of sausage and you enter a realm of limitless complexity. *Salumeria*, which includes not only sausage but other preserved pork products as well—ham, head cheese, cured shoulder, belly meat, rolled pigs' cheeks, the air-cured pork of Umbria—is an important item in the Italian larder. Not only every region, but every province, every city, every town, every hamlet, if not every family, seems to have its own special variety of sausage. When you try to identify their many sorts, you are apt to be frustrated by a carefree interchangeability of names—the word applied to one kind of sausage in Village A is attached to another in Village B, the same sausage has one name in Village C and another in Village D.

The chief city of Emilia is Bologna, hence boloney, which in reality is mortadella, whose foreign cousin is bland almost to the point of tastelessness; but the Italian original is studded piquantly with whole peppercorns (or in Prato, a Tuscan city, flavored delicately with fennel). A sharply spiced variety breathing of garlic is made from the exceptionally tasty pork of the pigs which feed on the high pastures of the mountains of Abruzzi's Teramo region. The fine smooth texture of *mortadella* was in the beginning achieved by crushing its ingredients into a sort of paste by hand in a special mortar, the "mortar for pig's meat"—*mortaio della carne di maiale*, or, for short, *mortadella*.

The mildness of mortadella is in contrast to the flavorfulness of most Italian sausages, which tend to be highly spiced, especially in the South—like the fat flattened *soppressato* of the Basilicata, tingling with ginger; or Sardinia's smoked *sartizzu*, which contains a lively mixture of fennel, cinnamon and pepper; or the *capocello* of Apulia, also packed with sharp spices; but even in Italy's farthest North the seasoning is high, as in the hard air dried sausage of the Valle d'Aosta, of mixed lean beef and pork, where bay leaf, garlic and pepper are assisted by a variety of other spices, even including the incisive clove.

Italy does not lack examples of what is often described as the world's oldest sausage, blood pudding, supposed to have been invented in Tyre by the Phoenicians. Its name varies with the region; it is *el busecchin* in Milan, *boudin* in the Valle d'Aosta, but most often *sanguinaccio*—for instance in Lecce, whose version of it is reported, erroneously, to have been bartered with Brindisi for one of the terminal columns of the Appian Way, which stands today in the Piazza Sant' Oronzo of this city which the Roman highway never reached.

Another family of sausages usually thought of as Teutonic (and hence called liverwurst in English) is indeed represented in the Germanic Alto Adige, but pig's liver sausage is indigenous to several other regions of Italy as well—*mazzafegato* in Umbria, where the liver flavor almost disappears beneath the heady tang of coriander, pepper and garlic; *mortadella di fegato* in Sondrio, where it is smooth and unctuous; and the baroquely flavored *salsicce di fegato* of the Abruzzi, which contains garlic—and orange peel! The Abruzzi is nothing if not original. It also offers two other liver sausages, served together for contrast: sweet liver and crazy liver: the first is flavored with honey, the second with the hottest of hot pimentos.

An Italian asked to name Italy's most distinctive sausage might, if he were capable of putting local pride aside, plump for Modena's *zampone*, so called when its envelope is an emptied pig's foot; when the same stuffing goes into other casings it may be *sassolini*, *cotechino* or *cappello da prete* (priest's hat, because of its shape), a favorite of Rossini. *Cotechino* plays a festive role in Rome, where, cooked with lentils, it is a fixture of the New Year; Bologna combines sausage and lentils for the New Year.

For the whole world the most famous ham of Italy is that of Parma, whose quality depends in part on the fact that it is as lightly salted as possible, so that the delicate flavor of its air-cured meat will not be submerged beneath the bite of salt; but Italian gourmets rate another kind of *prosciutto*, virtually unknown outside the peninsula, as equal or better. This is the ham of San Daniele di Friuli, which, if you run across it, may put you off by its rustic lack of finish. Parma ham is boned and shaped, but the San Daniele product leaves the whole leg on, and is covered with an unappetizing crust of what appears to be ashes. However you need not worry overmuch about the danger of missing a treat because of the prejudices of your eyes; they are unlikely ever to fall upon a San Daniele ham. Its production is small, and connoisseurs usually buy it all up before it can reach the general markets. Both Parma and San Daniele hams are cured in mountain air, and so are several other notable specimens, for instance that of the Abruzzi, which is strikingly similar to the Spanish *jamon serrano*, probably because the Spaniards once ruled this country, or the flavorful Sardinian ham, from acorn-fed pigs. (Sardinia also makes wild boar ham, but this is becoming scarce, along with the wild boar.) In the Alps you have *Speck*, which in the Alto Adige is usually smoked bacon, but can also be smoked ham, for which the principle is to do the smoking as slowly as possible. In the Valle d'Aosta, *lo speck* is always ham, only partly smoked, so that it must be boiled before eating.

If the ubiquity of sausage is proof that a peasant-based cuisine is holding its own, then Italy need have no fears for its *cucina casalinga*.

You have often heard it said (and probably never heard it disputed) that French wine is superior to Italian wine. This is an axiom. Nevertheless I shall venture to demur.

To begin with, I have never seen any necessity for making such comparisons. Which is better, coffee or tea? What is your favorite color, red or green? These, I feel, fall into the category of silly questions. The supposition seems to be that two elements can be isolated from their environment and compared in a vacuum. They can't be.

Wine certainly is not appreciated in a vacuum, except perhaps by professional wine tasters, who get no benefit from it since they spit it out instead of swallowing it. Wine is properly drunk with food. The relationship between wine and food is so important to the taste of both that gourmets regularly get into heated arguments about which wines go best with which foods—arguments which often degenerate into simple snobbishness. The preciosity of many wine-food dicta notwithstanding, there *is* a basic kinship between certain sorts of food and certain types of wine, but you do not have to become entangled in the esoteric lore of the wine experts to appreciate it; just pay attention to the messages of your taste buds. So: Is French wine better than Italian wine? Yes—with French food. But Italian wine is better than French wine with Italian food. Would it occur to you to order a

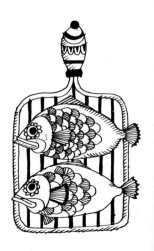

Chateau Lafite with a plate of *tagliatelle alla bolognese*? French wines and Italian wines are different; their merits—nobody, surely, will deny that both possess them—are therefore different also.

The nature of the contents of a wine bottle depends in part upon the acts of man, in part on the bounty of nature. In French wines, it may well be that the major contribution is that of man; in Italian wines, it is surely that of nature. Italian wine is in essence home-made—*casalinga*, like Italian food. It is precisely this which I appreciate in Italian wine, as in Italian food—its naturalness, its comparative lack of artifice; this does not prevent me from appreciating French wines too, for qualities almost exactly opposite.

So let us forget about French wine and concentrate on Italian—not in a vacuum, but in its context.

I had better now not name any "favorite" wines; I should then be skirting the area of silly questions myself. Let me indicate warily certain areas in Italy which produce vintages which indisputably rise about the average.

Between Piedmont's Langhe hills to the south and Monferrato hills to the north, lies a region at first bordered and then crossed by Piedmont's very own river, the Tanaro; it has been particularly favored by Bacchus. Here grows Barolo, a full rich wine which on occasion has reminded me of Bordeaux. Julius Caesar liked it—or rather he liked its ancestors, for modern Italian wines, mercifully, do not much resemble the wines the ancients grew on the same soil; the Romans manhandled them. Barolo is made from the Nebbiolo grape, and so are two other notable vintages of this area, Barbaresco and Nebbiolo itself. Three others are produced here too, the excellent Barbera, made from the grape of the same name, and the less estimable Dolcetto and Moscato d'Asti. The last is made from the same grape which, a little farther north, produces a wine most foreigners know, Asti Spumante, often described rashly as Italian champagne. I am no fancier of sparkling wines myself, but if you must have one, you can possibly do better than Asti by seeking out a wine few foreigners know—Ferrari di Trento Riserva, which comes from Venezia Tridentina.

On the opposite side of the peninsula from Piedmont, stretching eastward from Lake Garda into the Veneto, is another notable wine area, which produces the excellent Bardolino, Valpolicella and Valpantena reds and the Soave white.

South of the Piedmont and Veneto vineyards, in Tuscany, is the domain of a wine every foreigner knows—Chianti. The familiar bulbous straw-covered bottle is almost a trademark of Italy. It is picturesque and folkloric, but to tell the truth if your Chianti comes in straw-covered bottles you aren't getting the best. It is only run-of-the-mill Chianti that goes into such bottles (run-of-the-mill Chianti isn't bad), for a very simple reason: wine is hardier than straw. The lesser Chiantis are drunk young; they can be wrapped in straw. But a major Chianti may be five years old or more before it is drunk; and if it were kept that long in straw-covered bottles, the straw would have rotted unappetizingly away before the wine was ready to drink.

These are the three major table wine areas of Italy, but I have a personal weakness for a fourth, whose wines are undoubtedly minor, but are apt to be served to you in the most

delightful of settings, under a velvet blue night sky on a warm evening in the garden behind a Trastevere *trattoria*—those of the Castelli Romani, south of Rome. In such a setting, a Frascati, a Nemi or an Albano slips so easily and refreshingly down the throat that its memory remains forever synonymous with all the charm of Italy.

For an appreciator of Italian wine, I find myself often oddly at variance with the taste of the Italian majority. For instance, many Italian localities produce "pasta wines", designed specifically to be drunk with pasta. They are usually white. Yet for my palate, nothing goes better with pasta than a sturdy red wine, preferably a little coarse. In Emilia I am out of step with the Bolognese or the Modenese who boast proudly of the region's Lambrusco; I find it a rather thin sour wine, and I wonder why it is preferred over, say, Sangiovese, a local vintage too. The folklore of Naples exalts the depressingly dark red Gragnano, although within easy reach are Falerno, either red or white (the descendant of the Falernium Horace praised so highly) or Capri (white). Perhaps my lack of enthusiasm for Lambrusco and Gragnano stems from a personal prejudice against sparkling red wines; neither of them is a real sparkler, but both fizz up momentarily as they are poured, reminding me unpleasantly of American bottled strawberry or raspberry pop. In the Naples area I have been disappointed also by the prettily named Lacrima Christi (Tear of Christ); but there is a great deal of imitation Lacrima Christi about, and it may be that I never managed to taste the real thing. I tend in any case to distrust wines with picturesque names (or wines put up in fancifully shaped bottles). They are attended with the odor of the merchandising wizard, conniving to persuade you to spend your money on a fancy label because the contents of the bottle which bears it are too poor in quality to sell on their own merits. Beware, unless in a particular case you happen to know better, of bottles labeled Sorriso di (Smile of) somewhere or other; it is a frequently encountered name which tells you nothing about the wine you are buying, except that it dare not depend upon an honest place name. In a different category, however, are the many curious or folkloric wine names which do identify a known quality, and which are therefore often worth trying despite the whimsy of their titles—Tear of the Arno in Tuscany; Crazy Water (a sparkler) on Elba; Est! Est!! Est!!! in Lazio, whose story is too well worn to bear retelling here; Devil Chaser in Umbria; Charley's Whiskers, Firebug and Blood of Judas in Lombardy; Hell's Wine in the Valle d'Aosta; Divine Fury from the Amalfi Coast; Halfway Up Etna (a designation of quality, since Etna wines grow stronger as you progress uphill, and the medium strength is the best); Crow, also of Sicily. Get away from the big cities and you may discover wines which have no names at all, for they are not made for sale. The fortunate owner of a farm which contains a small vineyard makes wine for his own use, and when he has a surplus, he sells what he doesn't need, unlabelled and unidentified. Such modest wines are almost always agreeable. They are completely natural, homemade with a vengeance. I remember fondly such anonymous bottles which I sampled in Perugia, in Todi, and in Vico Equense.

What do you drink before your meal in Italy? Vermouth, of course (except in Sardinia, where you drink wine, but a Sardinian wine tastes like an apéritif anyway). And after? *Grappa*, the distillate which comes closer to brandy than any other in Italy, if you

can support it; otherwise any of an endless list of digestives and liqueurs, ranging from the sharp bitter medicinal Centerbe (Hundred Herbs) to the delicate anisette called Sambuca, with a crunchy coffee bean dropped into the clear sweet liquid.

Would a few Italian wine terms be useful? *Bianco*, *rosato* and *rosso* are, of course, white, rose and red respectively. *Secco* is dry, *amabile* is sweet. *Spumante* is a sparkling wine, usually made so artificially, *frizzante* is only barely sparkling, generally so created by nature. *Passito* wines are made from grapes dried in the sun until they are practically raisins, which produce a liquerish sweet wine, Italy's answer to France's Sauternes; its richest manifestation is Vino Santo, for which the grapes are usually dried indoors. *Vino cotto*, cooked wine, means one whose volume has been reduced by gentle heating; it has probably been subjected to other operations as well, such as blending or fortifying with spirits, producing beverages which, like Malaga, are suitable for drinking either before or after a meal—or between meals, for that matter. Finally, if your bottle bears a label identifying the year the wine was grown, put it down to snobbishness, an attempt to please customers by aping the practice of France, where the year does made a difference, whereas in Italy dating has little significance; most wines are drunk too soon after they are made for vintage years to have much importance. Italy has had great years on occasion, however, for instance the Opimian year, 121 BC; but the last bottle of its wine seems to have been drunk by Pliny, who described it as "rough honey". What an Italian label *should* tell you is the alcoholic content of the wine: in general, the higher the content the better the wine, of its kind; but this is far from an invariable rule.

Thus stands Italy's record for the four simple elemental touchstones of a nation's cooking (you could also call them the cornerstones if you want)—bread, cheese, sausage, wine. All have remained what they should be—sound, healthy, sturdy, pure, uncorrupted and natural. Therefore it follows almost necessarily that the Italian cuisine has preserved these virtues too.

Indeed, natural is the most true adjective to encompass the essence of Italian eating. It is not in Italy that you are deprived of the delight of witnessing the yearly renaissance of the fruits of the earth, one after the other, not in Italy that your senses are dulled to novelty and freshness by the senseless insistence that all foods should be always present during all the months of the year. Italy prefers to wait, with the tingle of anticipation, for the drama of nature to unfold. "Everything is eaten fresh and in its proper season, when it is at its absolute best," Luigi Barzini writes in *The Italians*. "No fruit or vegetable comes from the hot house, with the damp paper taste of artificial products. Nothing is picked before its time and allowed to ripen in storage. Nothing is frozen, nothing is chemically preserved." Amen!

Here once again we have the stamp of a *natural* cuisine. It respects its materials, it prefers not to tamper with them. It is on this basis that Italy has built one of the Western world's two greatest cuisines. France has staked its reputation on complication—and won. Italy has opted for simplicity—and won too. The spirit of the Italian cuisine, hospitable, open widely to us all, is that of peasant cooking, of home cooking, of amateur cooking—amateur, from *amare*, cooking with love.

ANTIPASTI

Among the unpublished works of Gioacchino Rossini is an opus described as *56 Semi-Comic Pieces for the Piano*, which includes "The Four Hors-d'œuvre: (1) Radishes; (2) Anchovies; (3) Pickles; (4) Butter." Possibly Rossini had in mind the hors-d'œuvre of France, where he died, rather than the antipasti of Italy, where he was born, for this selection would constitute a rather serious underestimate of the appetizers of a country which seems to conceive them as a series of tiny gustatory explosions—especially from a man whose father was a meat inspector, whose mother was a baker's daughter, and who might himself have been famous as a gourmet if his gastronomic talents had not been surpassed by his musical genius.

The tingling challenges of Italian appetizers are so pronounced that even a hurried housewife with no time to do more than open a few cans or bottles can produce in a few minutes a platter as colorful as a painter's palette from the least complicated items of the rich store of antipasti. Sardines or tuna glisten with golden olive oil; a slab of scarlet preserved peppers adds Oriental luster; ripe olives are purple-black, pickled ones light green, with or without a vermilion core; anchovies present their tart promise coiled around capers or lapped in tomato sauce; large circles of pale mortadella are flanked by small circles of dark red salami; and, if one takes the trouble to slice a tomato and dust it with chopped herbs and hard-boil an egg or two, the juicy bright slices of the first, the golden-centered rings of the second, enhance the gaiety of the mouthwatering design. This assault of color on the eye is followed at the first nibble by the tingle of vinegar rising in the nose or the seductive caress of olive oil on the tongue. Or, alternatively, fragrant orange melons can be cut in halves and served with paper-thin slices of delicate Parma ham, a combination honored in Italy since at least the fifteenth century.

In both these cases, the meal is off to a perfect start, and without effort. But effort is well worth expending when there is time for it; and actually, not a great deal is necessary. A minimum of preparation, a minimum of ingenuity, goes a long way in the titillating domain of Italian antipasti, designed to captivate all eaters at the first bite.

Marinata per verdure

Vegetable marinade

Enough for marinating
2-1/4 lbs. vegetables
Difficulty *
Time: 30 minutes

3 cups water
7 tbsp. oil
Juice of 2 lemons
Bouquet garni of celery,
parsley, fennel, thyme, bay leaf
8 peppercorns
8 whole coriander seeds

In a saucepan combine water, oil, lemon juice, bouquet garni, peppercorns and coriander. Bring to a boil and simmer for about 1/2 hour. Remove from heat. Marinate cooked vegetables in this for 2 or 3 days before using them cold as a vegetable or salad.

Marinata per verdure

Avocados con gorgonzola

Avocado and Gorgonzola spread on toast

Serves 4
Difficulty *
Time: 1 hour

2 avocados
4 oz. (1/2 cup) Gorgonzola cheese
4 slices bread

Cut avocados in half lengthwise and remove seed. Scoop out and press avocado through a sieve or a food mill or crush with a fork. Put avocado puree in a bowl and beat in Gorgonzola cheese until creamy. Cut bread slices in half diagonally and toast. Spread avocado and Gorgonzola cream on toast and serve at once.

Seafood, meat, eggs and even unsweetened pastry all have their place on Italian antipasti platters, but they are still dominated by vegetables. A few olives (technically the olive is a fruit, but it behaves like a vegetable), green or black, are likely to turn up with the appetizers even when they are not on the menu, like an unannounced sprig of parsley with a sliced tomato; however the olive can easily be promoted to a featured position if you feel like it. Such versatile vegetables as the tomato (or is that a fruit too?), the pepper or the eggplant are capable of appearing in a protean variety of disguises. Sometimes they appear with other taste ticklers on a platter of *antipasti assortiti*, sometimes they take on such substantial form they open the meal by themselves.

Antipasto d'estate

Summer hors-d'œuvre

Serves 4
Difficulty *
Time: 1 hour

4 large cucumbers
4 eggs, hard-cooked
4 fillets salted herring, chopped
1 small onion, chopped
1 tbsp. prepared mustard
Pepper
1 tbsp. olive oil
8 tsp. horseradish

Cut the ends off cucumbers. Cut them in half lengthwise and scoop out, leaving a boat-shaped shell about 1/2-inch thick. Cook for 5 to 6 minutes in boiling water, drain and dry well. Separate whites from yolks. Put the yolks through a sieve or mash with a fork. Mix sieved yolks with herring fillets and onion, mustard and a pinch of pepper. Add oil and mix well. Use this mixture to fill cucumber boats. Garnish each cucumber with 1 teaspoon grated horseradish and arrange them on a platter. Chill until ready to serve.

Funghi del "gourmet"

Gourmet Mushrooms

Serves 4
Difficulty *
Time: 1-1/2 hours

3/4 lb. cultivated mushrooms
3 artichoke hearts, sliced thin
Juice of 1 lemon
1 very white celery heart, cut into strips
1/2 lb. shrimp, cooked, shelled and deveined
16 asparagus tips, cooked and drained
3/4 cup homemade mayonnaise (see page 34)
2 tbsp. olive oil
2 ripe tomatoes, peeled and pressed through a sieve
Salt

Mushrooms are excellent arousers of the taste buds, and (a tip for weight watchers) they perform that service without adding any fattening elements to the meal. They are rich in vitamins and proteins, but contain no sugar and practically no fats.

Peel mushroom caps, simmer for 15 minutes in water to cover. Drain them well. Sprinkle artichoke hearts with half of the lemon juice to keep them from darkening. Put mushrooms, artichokes, celery, shrimp and asparagus in little piles in a large glass bowl. Chill. Mix mayonnaise with oil, remaining lemon juice and tomato pulp. Add salt to taste. Serve this sauce with vegetables.

Funghi del "gourmet"

Funghi alla trasteverina

Mushrooms Trastevere style

Serves 4
Difficulty *
Time: 2 hours

1-1/2 lbs. small button mushrooms
7 tbsp. olive oil
1 small onion, chopped
1 clove garlic, chopped
2/3 cup white vinegar

3 cups chopped tomato pulp, skin and seeds removed
A bouquet garni (bay leaf, parsley and thyme)
Salt, pepper

Remove stems from mushrooms. Use for soups or gravies. Saute caps in half of the oil for 5 minutes. In a separate pan saute onion and garlic in remaining oil. Add white vinegar. Simmer 10 minutes. Add chopped tomato pulp and bouquet garni and salt and pepper to taste. Bring to a boil and simmer over moderate heat for about 20 minutes. Discard bouquet garni, add mushrooms and simmer for 5 minutes. Serve cold as an hors-d'œuvre.

Olive farcite alla catanese

Stuffed olives Catania style

Serves 4
Difficulty *
Time: 1 hour plus time required to marinate olives

2 cans (5-3/4 oz. each) pitted black olives, colossal size
2 tbsp. salt
1 tsp. fennel seed

2/3 cup capers
1/2 a 2 oz. can flat anchovy fillets
Olive oil

Cover olives with water. Add salt and fennel seeds. Let marinate at room temperature for 10 hours. Drain olives. Chop capers with anchovies until very finely chopped. Use a cone of waxed paper to stuff olives with mixture. Put olives in a jar and cover with oil. Marinate for several hours before serving.

Olive nere all'umbra

Umbrian black olives

Serves 4
Difficulty *
Time: 30 minutes, plus time required to marinate olives

1 cup olive oil
1 tsp. salt
1 clove garlic, mashed
1/2 bay leaf, pulverized
Grated rind of 1/2 orange
2 cans (5-3/4 oz. each) giant black olives

Mix oil, salt, garlic, bay leaf and grated orange rind. Wash olives, dry, put them in a small bowl. Cover them with oil mixture. Let them marinate at room temperature for at least 24 hours, stirring occasionally, before serving.

Olive nere all'umbra

Funghi marinati

Marinated mushrooms

Serves 6
Difficulty *
Time: 1 hour
Chill 24 hours

1-1/2 lbs. cultivated mushrooms	4 cloves garlic, minced
Juice of 1/2 lemon	1 bay leaf
Salt	1 sprig thyme
1 cup vinegar	2 tbsp. chopped parsley
7 tbsp. olive oil	8 cumin seeds

Remove and reserve stems of mushrooms, rub buttons with a clean cloth to remove earth. Put mushrooms in a saucepan with cold water containing lemon juice and a little salt; bring to a gentle boil and simmer for 10 minutes. Drain and transfer to a bowl. Combine remaining ingredients in a saucepan and simmer over low heat for about 1/2 hour. Pour this marinade over the mushrooms and refrigerate for at least 24 hours. Drain off the marinade before serving.

Insalata di riso alla romana

Rice salad Roman style

Serves 4
Difficulty *
Time: 1 hour

1 cup (8 oz.) rice	1/3 cup diced lean prosciutto crudo
2/3 cup uncooked cannellini beans	4 slices (4 oz.) slab bacon
2 cloves garlic	1 can (2 oz.) flat anchovy
1/2 tsp. red pepper flakes	fillets, rinsed with cold
1/2 cup soft bread crumbs	water
soaked in 1/4 cup beef broth	8 large green olives
and squeezed dry	2 tbsp. coarsely chopped
1/2 cup oil	fresh basil leaves
3 tbsp. red wine vinegar	2 tbsp. coarsely chopped
1 tsp. salt	fresh marjoram

Cook rice and beans separately in lightly salted water until tender. Drain and cool. Grind garlic and hot pepper in a mortar, add squeezed bread crumbs and beat in oil, wine vinegar and salt. Put rice and beans in a salad bowl. Add prosciutto. Cut bacon into thin strips and saute in 1 tablespoon oil until crisp. Drain bacon and add to salad bowl. Stir in bread sauce. Roll anchovy fillets around olives and arrange them on top of salad as decoration. Sprinkle with basil and marjoram cut into rather large pieces. Chill. Serve either as a luncheon dish or as antipasto.

Insalata di riso alla romana

Insalata alla moda contadina

Salad country style

Serves 4
Difficulty *
Time: 1 hour

4 large potatoes, boiled and sliced
2 cups cooked cut green beans
1-1/2 cups cooked beans and chick peas
2 half-ripe tomatoes, sliced

2 young onions, sliced and separated into rings
2 tbsp. chopped fresh basil leaves
3/4 cup oil
1/4 cup vinegar
2 tsp. salt
1/4 tsp. pepper

In a salad bowl mix potatoes, green beans, beans and chick peas. Place tomato slices as a garnish around edge of bowl. Sprinkle onion rings and chopped basil over surface. Place remaining ingredients in a jar with a tight lid. Shake until well blended. Pour over salad and toss. Chill until ready to serve.

Insalata di tagliolini

Thin noodle salad

Serves 6
Difficulty *
Time: 1 hour plus time for refrigeration

8 oz. fine egg noodles
1/2 cup olive oil
1 clove garlic, chopped
1 tbsp. chopped fresh basil
1 can (7 oz.) tuna, drained and flaked

1/3 cup sliced sour gherkins
1 green pepper, diced
1/2 cup chopped pickled mushrooms
1-1/2 cup (6 oz.) strips Gruyere or Provolone

Cook noodles in boiling salted water until just tender but still firm. Drain and rinse with cold water. Drain and pour into a salad bowl. Heat oil and saute garlic and basil until very lightly browned. Cool oil. Mix oil, noodles and remaining ingredients until well blended. Chill until ready to serve.

Insalata Isabella

Isabella salad

Serves 4
Difficulty *
Time: 2 hours

1 cup (8 oz.) rice
2 zucchini, sliced
2/3 cup (4 oz.) fresh lima beans
1 eggplant (aubergine)
3/4 cup olive oil
1 plump red bell pepper
2 tomatoes, sliced

1 cucumber, sliced
1 tbsp. chopped fresh basil
1 tbsp. chopped fresh oregano
Juice of 1 lemon
1 tsp. salt
1/4 tsp. pepper
1 clove garlic, mashed

Boil rice, drain while still *al dente* and cool. Boil zucchini and beans. Chop eggplant into small pieces and saute in one-third of the oil. Singe pepper over high heat and rub to remove skin. Cut into strips. Combine rice, zucchini, beans, pepper, eggplant, tomatoes and cucumber. Sprinkle with finely chopped basil and oregano. Beat remaining oil, lemon juice, salt and pepper until thick. Stir in garlic. Pour over salad and toss.

The salad became an appetizer in Italy thanks to the Emperor Domitian. Before his time it was served at the end of the meal; Domitian moved it to the beginning. Italians, (unlike the French, whose salads contain only one vegetable at a time), let themselves go when they deal with salads, producing a wide variety of ingenious, tasty and sometimes complicated combinations.

Insalata alla buongustaia

Insalata
alla buongustaia

Gourmet salad

Serves 4
Difficulty *
Time: 30 minutes

1 green pepper
1 heart of celery
1 tomato
1 cucumber
3 cups chicory, in bite-size pieces
1 cup (4 oz.) cooked cut green beans

1 cup (strips) white meat
of boiled or roasted chicken
1/4 cup (strips) boiled ham
1/4 cup (strips) Swiss cheese
1/3 cup oil
2 tbsp. vinegar
1/2 tsp. salt
1/4 tsp. pepper

Cut all vegetables into strips. Place into a salad bowl and add chicory, green beans, meats and cheese. Toss with salad dressing. To prepare dressing combine oil, vinegar, salt and pepper and shake in a covered jar until well blended.

Involtini di mortadella

Cipolle farcite
con purea di tonno

*Stuffed onion appetizer
with tuna puree*

Serves 4
Difficulty **
Time: 1-1/2 hours

8 medium-sized onions
1 cup cider vinegar
1 cup white wine
1/4 cup olive oil
6 sprigs parsley, thyme, bay leaf
(bouquet garni)

1 clove garlic, minced
Salt
1 can (7 oz.) tuna, drained
and sieved

Place onions in a saucepan and add vinegar, wine, oil, parsley, thyme, bay leaf, garlic and a good pinch of salt. Cook over low heat until onions are done, about 15 to 20 minutes or until tender. Drain, reserving cooking liquid. Scoop out onions leaving a shell 1/2-inch thick. Fill with tuna puree. Arrange stuffed onions on a serving dish. Chop onions removed and add to reserved cooking liquid. Boil until one-half its original volume. Press through a sieve and spoon over stuffed onions. Chill and serve.

Formaggio tonnato

Cheese and tuna appetizer

Serves 4
Difficulty *
Time: 20 minutes plus time for
refrigeration

1/2 cup (4 oz.) canned drained
tuna
1 cup (8 oz.) ricotta cheese

1/2 cup (2 oz.) grated Parmesan
cheese
1 cup (1/2 pint) heavy cream

Press tuna and ricotta through a sieve. Mix them in a bowl with grated Parmesan until smooth. Whip cream until stiff and fold into the mixture. Heap into a mound on a platter for serving. Chill.

Involtini
di mortadella

Bologna rolls

Serves 2
Difficulty *
Time: 30 minutes

2 slices mortadella di
Bologna (Italian bologna
sausage)

1 canned roasted pimento pepper
6 pickled gherkins
6 pitted black olives

Cut each piece of mortadella into three strips. Cut roasted pepper into strips. On each piece of mortadella place 1 strip of pepper. Place 1 gherkin at one end of strip. Roll up slices and spear on a toothpick. Spear olive on top of bologna roll.

Basic Recipe for Mayonnaise

Makes 1 cup
Difficulty **
Time: 30 minutes

2 egg yolks
Salt
Pepper

1-1/4 cup salad oil
Juice of 1 lemon

Put egg yolks into a small mixing bowl with a pinch of salt and pepper. Beat steadily with a whisk or electric mixer while adding oil, drop by drop, until it thickens. When mayonnaise begins to thicken beat in a few drops of lemon juice. Continue beating in, alternately, oil and lemon until mayonnaise is smooth and thick.

Insalata di pesce come piace a me

Fish salad as I like it

Serves 4
Difficulty **
Time: 2 hours plus time required to marinate fish
Oven Temp. 350° F.

4 sole fillets or 4 small flounder fillets
9 tbsp. olive oil
Salt
Pepper
1/2 cup chopped parsley
2 lemons
1 tsp. prepared mustard
1 tsp. vinegar
2 small zucchini
1-1/2 cups diced potatoes
2 cups cauliflowerets

1-1/4 cups 1-inch pieces green beans
1 cup tiny shelled peas
2/3 cup mayonnaise
1 can (2 oz.) flat anchovy fillets
2 hard cooked eggs
1/2 cup whole pitted black olives
1 tbsp. mustard butter
4 very small hearts of Boston lettuce (cabbage lettuce)
1/4 cup sliced sweet gherkins
1 tbsp. capers

Arrange fillets in a baking dish greased with 1 tablespoon olive oil. Sprinkle with salt, pepper, parsley, 2 tablespoons oil and juice of 1 lemon and bake in a preheated oven (350° F.) for 20 minutes. In a cup or small mixing bowl prepare a marinade by beating together remaining oil, juice of second lemon and mustard mixed with vinegar. When fish is cooked, drain and remove to a separate platter. Pour marinade over it and marinate for about 2 hours. Cook all vegetables separately, cool and dice. Drain fillets, reserve marinade, and place fillets on a platter. Set aside. Mix marinade with vegetables. Stir in 2 tablespoons of mayonnaise and 2 anchovy fillets, finaly chopped. Place mixture into a salad bowl. Top with remaining mayonnaise and garnish with hard cooked egg wedges, pitted olives, anchovy fillets curled and stuffed with mustard butter, see recipe below. Add fillets alternated with lettuce hearts. Sprinkle with gherkins and capers. Chill salad until ready to serve.

Burro di mostarda piccante

Mustard butter

Makes 2/3 cup
Difficulty *
Time: 20 minutes

10 tbsp. (5 oz.) butter
1-1/2 tbsp. sharp mustard

1 tsp. Worcestershire sauce
Cayenne pepper

Cut butter into pea-size fragments, soften and whip to a cream. Beat in mustard, Worcestershire sauce and a generous pinch of Cayenne pepper. This mustard butter is particularly good for canape sandwiches and similar dishes.

Antipasto capriccioso

Serves 4
Difficulty **
Time: 2 hours

Herb mayonnaise:

Basic Recipe for mayonnaise
Olive oil
1/2 lemon
1 tsp. tomato ketchup

1 tsp. Worcestershire sauce
Salt
Pepper

Appetizer:

1-1/2 lbs asparagus
1/2 lb. small mushrooms
2 tbsp. butter
4 oz. cooked, shelled and deveined shrimp
2 artichokes
Juice of 1 lemon

1 celery heart cut into strips
1 barely ripe, solid tomato (in part still green)
1/2 a 7 oz. can tuna, drained
8 anchovy fillets, rinsed with cold water
1/2 cup pitted black olives

Herb mayonnaise: Follow procedure given in the mayonnaise basic recipe. When mayonnaise is ready, dilute it with 1 tbsp. olive oil beaten in a separate bowl with lemon juice, ketchup and Worcestershire sauce. Season to taste with salt and pepper. Chill mayonnaise until ready to serve.

Preparation of appetizer: Peel asparagus, wash in cold water and tie them into bundles of a few stalks each. Cook them in boiling salted water until tender but still firm. Drain. Cut off stems and chill tips until ready to use. Clean mushrooms and remove stems. Peel them and cook them for 15 minutes with a little lightly salted water into which you have put butter. Slice mushroom caps. Chill mushrooms and shrimp.

Detach all hard leaves and choke from artichoke, leaving the tender heart. Cut hearts into thin slices. Place artichoke hearts in a bowl and cover them with cold water containing lemon juice. A few minutes before serving, arrange on a hors-d'œuvre plate, in small piles as shown in the illustration, the asparagus tips, mushroom slices and shrimp; garnish with celery strips, tomatoes and raw artichoke hearts. Add tuna, anchovy fillets and black olives. Serve with mayonnaise on the side.

Antipasto capriccioso

Uova tonnate

Eggs with tuna

Serves 4
Difficulty **
Time: 45 minutes plus time for
refrigeration

9 eggs
Juice of 1 lemon
7 tbsp. olive oil
Salt, pepper
4 oz. canned tuna

1 tbsp. capers
1 tbsp. vinegar
4 anchovy fillets
4 pickled gherkins, sliced

Beat 1 raw egg yolk with 2 teaspoons lemon juice. While beating, drip in oil one drop at a time until thick. Mix with remaining lemon juice and add salt and pepper to taste. Sieve tuna and stir into mayonnaise with capers. Heat frying pan of salted water 1-1/2 inches deep to which vinegar has been added and bring to a simmer. Break remaining eggs, one at a time and slip into frying pan and poach four minutes. As soon as they are set, place them in a pan of cold water to stop the cooking. Remove with a slotted spoon. Drain on absorbent paper and trim ragged edges of eggs with a knife and arrange on a serving platter. Spoon mayonnaise over eggs. Garnish with anchovy fillets cut in half and with gherkins. Chill until ready to serve.

Aringhe salate all'italiana

Italian herring salad

Serves 4
Difficulty *
Time: 1 hour, plus time required
to marinate herring

4 salted herrings
Milk
7 tbsp. oil
3 tbsp. wine vinegar

1 tsp. French mustard
1/4 cup chopped fresh basil
4 pickled gherkins, chopped

Singe skin on herring under a broiler (or grill). Skin and fillet herring, cutting on either side of the backbone. Arrange fillets in a deep dish. Cover with milk and soak for 2 to 3 hours, changing milk at least once. Beat oil and wine vinegar together with a fork, add mustard and continue to beat with fork or whisk. Add chopped basil and gherkins and mix again. Drain herring fillets, dry with a kitchen towel, arrange in an hors-d'œuvre dish and pour oil and vinegar dressing over them.

Aringhe in insalata alla rovigina

Herring salad Rovigo style

Serves 4
Difficulty *
Time: 30 minutes, plus time required
to marinate herring

4 salted herrings
Milk
2 onions, sliced

2 tbsp. capers
1/3 cup olive oil

Prepare herring fillets as in Aringhe salate all'italiana above. Soak onions in cold water for at least 1 hour (this will cause them to lose a little of their flavor and will also make them more digestible.) Drain herring, dry with a clean kitchen towel, then arrange them in a salad bowl and cover them with onion rings and capers. Toss with oil and serve.

Sardine sott'olio alla veneta

Canned sardines Venetian style

Serves 4
Difficulty *
Time: 30 minutes

**12 canned skinless and boneless sardines
1 jar (4 oz.) pimento, drained and cut into strips
4 hard cooked eggs, chopped
1/2 cup butter
2 tbsp. tomato puree
1 clove garlic, chopped
A few fresh sage leaves, chopped
Salt, pepper**

Arrange sardines on a serving platter. Garnish with pimento strips and chopped eggs. Cream butter until very soft. Stir in tomato puree. Stir in garlic, sage leaves. Season to taste with salt and pepper. Spread this sauce over the sardines. Serve at once.

Sardine sott'olio alla veneta

Cozze in antipasto

Mussels hors-d'œuvre

Serves 4
Difficulty **
Time: 1 hour plus time for refrigeration

**2 lbs. mussels
1 cup dry white wine
2 egg yolks
3/4 cup olive oil**

**Juice of 1 lemon
Salt, pepper
1 tbsp. chopped parsley
2 red or yellow sweet peppers**

Wash mussels thoroughly, brush them and remove beards. Put them in a saucepan. Add wine and put over high heat until shells open. Drain, reserving liquid. Shell mussels and put them in a stemmed glass of type used for shrimp cocktail. Beat egg yolks and beat in oil, drop by drop, alternating with a few drops of lemon juice, until a thick mayonnaise. Reduce liquid from mussels to 1/3 cup. Cool and stir into mayonnaise. Stir in salt and pepper to taste and parsley. Pour sauce over mussels. Roast peppers over high heat. Rub off skin. Remove seeds and cut into strips. Use pepper strips for garnish. Chill until ready to serve.

BASIC RECIPE

Frittata al formaggio

Cheese frittata

Serves 4
Difficulty *
Time: 1/2 hour

6 eggs
1/4 cup (1 oz.) shredded Gruyere
1/4 cup (1 oz.) grated Parmesan cheese
Salt
Pepper
5 tbsp. butter

In a bowl beat eggs just enough to blend whites and yolks. Fold in Gruyere, Parmesan, salt and pepper to taste. Brown butter in an omelet frying pan or iron skillet. Pour in egg and cheese mixture and at first stir vigorously with a wooden spoon. Then cook without stirring. As soon as frittata begins to set, shake omelet pan or skillet slightly to free frittata from bottom of pan. When bottom is brown, place a cover or a plate large enough to cover pan over frittata. Turn pan upside down to turn frittata onto plate. Slide it from the plate back into pan (adding a bit of butter if needed) and brown on other side. When done, frittata should be soft on inside and golden brown on outside. Serve immediately while piping hot.

Frittata di spinaci fantasia

Italian spinach omelet

Serves 4
Difficulty *
Time: 1 hour

What can you do to nationalize an egg? It might seem that soft-boiled eggs (*uova mollette*) could hardly be differentiated from one country to another, or that hard-boiled eggs (*uova sode*) must be the same whether you are in the United States, Great Britain, France or Italy (but it took an Italian, the Renaissance historian Benedetto Varchi, to achieve the *tour de force* of writing a whole book devoted solely to hard-boiled eggs). Despite the vocation of the egg for neutrality, the Italian cook manages to impart an Italian quality to the Italian egg. It is true that he has centuries of experience behind him. The ancient Romans may have concentrated on eggs because they neglected the egg producers; for several centuries Romans kept chickens solely for eggs. The scrawny birds which laid them were unattractive for the table—until the Greeks taught Rome how to breed and fatten poultry. In the meantime they invented the omelet.

The omelet entered the Italian menu via the dessert course, if we may trust one account of the origin of its name. This reports that the ancient Romans beat eggs together with honey, calling the result "honeyed eggs" *ova mellita*, which was telescoped into "omelet". Unromantic modern dictionaries want us to believe that "omelet" comes from *lamella*, a thin metal plate, represented as being essential for cooking omelets. Perhaps; but in ancient times omelets were cooked in earthenware dishes.

Omelets, in their limitless variety, should be more or less the same everywhere; but do not underestimate the inventiveness of the Italian temperament. Imagine six people sitting down to dinner in a restaurant almost anywhere in the world—and all of them ordering omelet. What would the chef do almost everywhere? He would spring joyously to the occasion and produce an enormous omelet for six, to be carried steaming to the table in all its bulky majesty. But what does the Roman cook do? He makes six small individual omelets, finishing each of them in a sauce of tomatoes, bacon, olive oil, garlic, bay leaf, sweet basil, and that Roman trademark, wild mint. In this case, seasoning is the secret which differentiates Italian egg dishes from those made elsewhere.

1-1/2 lbs. fresh spinach	**2 tbsp. milk**
6 tbsp. butter	**6 eggs**
Salt	**2 tbsp. (1 oz.) grated Parmesan**
Pepper	**cheese**
2 tbsp. (1 oz.) diced Fontina cheese	

Clean spinach and boil in a very small amount of salted water. Drain well, pressing out all liquid. Sieve and heat briefly in a saucepan with 1/3 of the butter. Add salt, pepper to taste, Fontina cheese and milk. Heat until cheese is melted. In another bowl beat eggs with Parmesan cheese and a pinch of salt and pepper. Stir in spinach mixture until ingredients are well mixed. Heat remaining butter in omelet pan or skillet. Cook frittata as described in Frittata al formaggio.

Frittata di spinaci fantasia

Frittata fredda alla rustica

Cold frittata country style

Serves 4
Difficulty *
Time: 1 hour

3 artichokes
Juice of 1 lemon
1 small eggplant (aubergine),
peeled and cut into 1/2-inch
thick pieces
1/2 cup olive oil
2 peppers
6 eggs
Salt and pepper

Frittata fredda alla rustica

Remove and discard hard outer leaves of artichokes. Cut artichokes into slices, putting them immediately into cold water containing lemon juice (this keeps the artichoke slices from darkening). Drain well on absorbent paper. Sprinkle eggplant with salt. Let stand 1 hour, then drain and pat dry. Heat half of the oil in a skillet or frying pan, and when it is hot add artichokes and eggplant. Cover and cook for 30 minutes or until very tender, adding a little water if needed. Singe peppers over high heat, remove skin, then remove seeds and membrane and cut into thin strips. Beat eggs in a bowl with a pinch of salt and a little pepper. Drain artichokes and eggplant well on absorbent paper. Chop them and add to eggs with pepper strips. Mix well.
Heat remaining oil, until it sizzles, in another 10" frying pan. Pour in egg and vegetable mixture and cook as in Frittata al formaggio (page 38). Turn frittata out on a serving platter. Cool and then cut into small wedges. Serve cold.

Uova alla fiorentina

Eggs Florentine

Serves 6
Difficulty *
Time: 1 hour
Oven Temp. 400° F.

1/2 cup (4 oz.) butter
3 tbsp. flour
2 cups milk
Salt, pepper
7 eggs
2/3 cup (5 oz.) ricotta cheese
3 tbsp. grated Parmesan cheese

Prepare a bechamel in following manner: Melt half the butter in a saucepan. Stir in flour. When flour is slightly browned, gradually stir in milk. Stir constantly until sauce bubbles and thickens. Season to taste with salt and pepper.
Hard cook 6 of the eggs. Shell and cut each egg lengthwise in half. Using a spoon, remove yolks without breaking whites. Put yolks through a sieve into a mixing bowl. Press ricotta through sieve and stir into egg yolks with 2 tablespoons of the Parmesan cheese, remaining butter, softened, 1 raw yolk, and salt and pepper to taste. Mix ingredients well and stuff egg whites with the mixture. Put stuffed eggs side by side into a shallow baking pan. If any stuffing is left over, spoon it into baking pan. Spoon over bechamel. Sprinkle with remaining Parmesan. Bake in a preheated hot oven (400° F.) for 20 minutes or until eggs are slightly browned. Serve piping hot.

Asparagi lessati sul crostone

Poached eggs and asparagus on toast

Serves 4
Difficulty **
Time: 2 hours
Oven Temp. 350° F.

1 bunch asparagus, tough ends trimmed
4 slices toast
1/2 cup butter, melted
4 slices prosciutto cotto (boiled ham)

2 tbsp. white vinegar
4 eggs
4 slices Fontina cheese
1/4 cup grated Parmesan cheese
Salt, pepper

Cook asparagus in boiling salted water 15 minutes. Drain and cool. Spread toast with some of the melted butter, cover with slices of ham. Top with asparagus tips. Pour some of the melted butter over each. Fill a large saucepan with water, add vinegar and bring to a boil. Lower heat until simmering. Break eggs, one at a time into saucer or plate. Slide them, also one at a time, into poaching water. Cook in simmering water for 3 minutes over moderate heat. Remove eggs with slotted spoon and trim off ragged edges of egg whites.

Top toast with egg and a slice of Fontina cheese. Bake for 10 minutes in a preheated oven or until cheese melts slightly. Sprinkle with grated Parmesan, salt and pepper. Arrange on a hot serving platter.

The recipe entitled mozzarella in carrozza *all'italiana*, deftly sidesteps the danger of carnage between two cities both of which claim it as their own. Romans list mozzarella in carrozza as one of their specialties, thus arousing Neapolitans to fury. The internal evidence, as literary critics would put it, is in favor of Naples; the dish is thoroughly Neapolitan in character. It is nourishing but cheap (Naples is poorer than Rome); it is rustic (Naples is not much given to citified food); and it has been decked out with a resounding name (Neapolitan showiness). Mozzarella in carrozza means "buffalo cheese in a carriage". The carriage is the two slices of bread between which the mozzarella is spread; on the same principle you might call a ham sandwich "ham in a carriage".

Mozzarella in carrozza all'italiana

Toasted mozzarella sandwiches

Serves 4
Difficulty *
Time: 30 minutes

2 balls, 8 oz. each, mozzarella cheese
8 slices firm type white bread, crusts trimmed
Milk, about 1-1/2 cups
Flour
2 eggs
Salt
2 tbsp. butter
1/3 cup olive oil

Slice mozzarella into 1/2-inch thick slices. Dip slices of bread into milk removing them quickly so that they are barely softened. Place a slice of mozzarella between each pair of bread slices and press gently between your hands. Cut each sandwich into 2 rectangles. Flour sandwiches lightly and then dip into eggs beaten with a pinch of salt. Fry sandwiches in butter and oil in a large frying pan; wait until oil and butter are very hot before you put sandwiches in. Fry until brown, turn and brown on other side. Remove and drain on paper towels. Serve on a preheated platter covered with a napkin. This "mozzarella in carrozza" can be made more zestful by including pieces of anchovy fillets between mozzarella and bread.

Fave crude alla romana con pecorino

*Raw fava beans
Roman style
with Pecorino cheese*

Serves 4
Difficulty *
Time: 20 minutes

**1-1/2 cups shelled raw fava beans
Grated Pecorino cheese
Rough country bread**

Serve fava beans as an antipasto, with Pecorino cheese and country bread.

Mozzarella a sorpresa

*Mozzarella cheese
surprise*

Serves 4
Difficulty *
Time: 30 minutes

**2 tbsp. chopped parsley
3 cups (12 oz.) grated mozzarella cheese
3/4 cup light cream
3 tbsp. milk
3/4 lb. pork sausage, cooked until brown**

Wash and chop parsley. Shred mozzarella. Mix mozzarella in a saucepan together with cream and milk. Stir until smooth and melted. Remove from heat and cool. Remove sausage casing and cut into thin slices. Place sausage on serving platter and spread cheese over it evenly before it hardens. Sprinkle with parsley and serve at once.

Fave crude alla romana con pecorino

42

Crema di formaggio fritta

Fried cheese cream

Serves 4
Difficulty **
Time: 3-1/2 hours, including refrigeration

10 tbsp. (5 oz.) butter
1 cup sifted all-purpose flour
2-1/4 cups milk
3 eggs
1-1/2 cups (6 oz.) grated Gruyere cheese

1/4 cup heavy cream
Worcestershire sauce
Salt, pepper
Dry bread crumbs

Melt 3 tablespoons butter in a saucepan. Stir in 1/2 cup of the flour. Gradually stir in milk. Stir constantly until sauce bubbles and becomes very thick. Beat in 2 egg yolks, cheese, cream, a few drops of Worcestershire sauce and salt and pepper to taste.
Pour into an 8-inch square pan and chill at least 2 hours. Cut into small diamond-shaped pieces. Dip into remaining flour, then into remaining beaten whole egg and then into bread crumbs. Fry pieces in remaining butter until brown on both sides. Drain on absorbent paper and serve immediately.

Grated cheese is ubiquitous on the Italian table, spread thickly over pasta, submerged in minestrone, or, less often, sprinkled over rice or eggs, *after* the dish to which it is added has been cooked. Perhaps that is why there are comparatively few Italian dishes in which cheese, cooked together with other ingredients, is the principal element. When cheese does form the basis for such dishes, it is often of a kind largely unknown outside of Italy—buffalo-milk cheese, whose commonest manifestation is the creamy mozzarella. The buffaloes which provide it are not, as some foreigners are prone to think, simply misnamed cows. They are genuine buffaloes, imported from India about 600 A.D., now completely acclimated in Italy. You are likely to come across them, massive, white and calm, grazing anywhere along the coast of the Campania, which has become for them a native land.

Mozzarella ai ferri

Grilled mozzarella

Serves 6
Difficulty *
Time: 30 minutes

2 balls, 8 oz. each mozzarella cheese

Slice mozzarella cheeses into 1/2-inch thick slices. Heat a lightly greased flat grill or heavy skillet until surface is almost red hot. Put on mozzarella slices. On contact with hot grill mozzarella will form a golden brown crust. Have a spatula ready to turn mozzarella quickly. Leave on grill until a good crust is formed and then remove (after 3 to 4 minutes). Serve hot, perhaps with boiled finocchio seasoned with salt and butter.

Pizza Margherita

Serves 4
Difficulty **
Time: 2 hours, plus time required for dough to rise
Oven Temp. 400° F.

Dough

4-1/2 cups sifted all-purpose flour
1 tsp. salt
1 envelope active dry yeast
1-1/2 cups lukewarm water

Filling

1 lb. peeled and cored tomatoes, chopped
1 lb. mozzarella cheese, sliced
2 tsp. crumbled oregano
2 tbsp. oil

Put flour and salt into a bowl. Dissolve yeast in 1/3 of the lukewarm water. Make a hollow in flour. Pour in yeast. Stir adding more water until you have a soft dough.
Beat dough until it has become smooth. Turn out on a floured board. Lift up from mixing board and slap down against board, repeating operation until dough, even while remaining soft, comes off the board easily and does not stick to the hands; by this time it should be smooth and elastic. Form dough into a ball and cut a cross into top to help dough rise. Place into a greased bowl, cover and let rise in a warm place until double in bulk. This will take about 3 hours. Put it back on mixing board and knead again, following same procedure as before.

Preparation of pizza: Roll out dough directly on baking sheet (which should be of metal), which should first be greased with a little olive oil, into a 14-inch round. Pinch up edges to form a rim. Spread tomato pulp evenly over dough. (Canned peeled Italian tomatoes can also be used.) Place mozzarella cheese slices over tomatoes. Sprinkle pizza with oregano and sprinkle with oil.
Instead of making a large pizza, you may wish to make 2 small pizzette. In that case, divide the dough into halves and roll out two rounds 8 inches in diameter.
Bake in a preheated oven (400° F.) for 30 to 40 minutes. Serve piping hot.

Pizza Margherita

Pizza con funghi

Pizza with mushrooms

Serves 4
Difficulty **
Time: 1-1/2 hours, plus time required for dough to rise
Oven Temp. 400° F.

Pizza dough (see recipe for Pizza Margherita on page 44)
1 lb. tomatoes cut into strips
1 lb. mushrooms, trimmed and sliced
4 oz. grated Parmesan cheese
Salt and pepper to taste
3 tbsp. olive oil

Prepare pizza dough as directed. Roll out pizza dough directly on a greased baking sheet to a 14-inch round. Pinch up edges to form a rim. Sprinkle tomatoes and mushrooms evenly over dough. Sprinkle with Parmesan cheese and salt and pepper to taste. Sprinkle oil over surface of pizza and bake in a preheated oven (400° F.) for 30 to 40 minutes. Serve immediately.

In ancient Rome, a favorite snack—often the Roman breakfast—was "bread with a relish". The "relish" was anything that might be at hand to make a slice of dry bread more palatable (there was no butter in those days), usually something light and simple—a bit of leftover cabbage, a few caraway seeds, often a little onion—or the bread might simply be moistened with olive oil. Eventually it occurred to someone to turn up the rim of the bread, which by now had become round, so that it would hold the relish more easily; pizza had been invented. In Genoa, "pizza", when it stands alone without further definition, still means only the empty shell, at the most spread with cheese (the relish), it becomes more complicated when it is called *pizza alla genovese*, for instance, which indicates a filling containing mussels, mushrooms and chopped ham.

Pizzas of various kinds are made all over Italy, sometimes masquerading under other names (*pitta* in Calabria is pretty close, but who would suspect that the *sardenaira* of the Riviera di Ponente is a pizza?) The undisputed capital of pizza today, however, is Naples, where it goes back a long way; the inhabitants of Pompeii were already eating a pizza very much like the kind we know now. The varieties of pizza in Naples are limitless, but the classic *pizza alla napoletana* is made from the same coarse bread the Romans used, moistened with olive oil as in ancient Rome, and filled with the richest of relishes—diced buffalo-milk cheese, bits of fresh tomato or tomato paste, assertive herbs, usually anchovy fillets, and often garlic.

Pizza rustica

Pizza country style

Serves 4
Difficulty **
Time: 2 hours, plus time required for dough to rise
Oven Temp. 400° F.

2-3/4 cups sifted all-purpose flour
Salt
1/2 cup butter
Water (about 1/2 cup)
1/2 cup (4 oz.) chopped prosciutto
1-1/4 cups (5 oz.) diced mozzarella cheese
1/2 cup (4 oz.) diced smoked mozzarella cheese or Provolone
1/3 cup (3 oz.) chopped salami (about 3 slices)
2 eggs and 1 egg yolk
1/4 cup milk
Pepper
1/2 tsp. crumbled oregano

Mix flour and a pinch of salt. Cut in butter until particles are very fine. Add water gradually and stir until dough cleans the bowl. Knead it vigorously on a floured surface and shape into a ball. Place in a floured mixing bowl, cover with a dish towel and let it rest for 1/2 hour. Divide dough into 2 parts, one slightly larger than the other. Roll each part on a floured surface into a 12-inch round and a 10-inch round, 1/8-inch thick. Use larger sheet to line bottom and sides of 10-inch round pan which has been buttered and floured. Layer prosciutto, two different kinds of mozzarella and salami in lined pan. Beat 2 of the eggs with milk, salt and pepper to taste until smooth. Pour over mozzarella and salami. Sprinkle with oregano, then cover with second sheet of dough. Pinch two sheets at the edges to seal. Beat egg yolk and brush surface of pizza. Bake in a preheated oven (400° F.) for 30 to 40 minutes. Serve hot.

Pizza Napoletana

Neopolitan pizza

Serves 4
Difficulty **
Time: 1-1/2 hours, plus time for raising pizza dough
Oven Temp. 400° F.

1 recipe pizza dough (see Pizza Margherita, page 44)
2 cups chopped tomato pulp (skin and seeds removed) or 1 can peeled Italian tomatoes, drained, seeds removed and chopped

1 lb. mozzarella cheese
1 can (2 oz.) anchovies or 4 salted anchovies
1 tsp. crumbled oregano
1/4 cup olive oil

On a greased baking sheet stretch out dough large enough to make a 14-inch round. Pinch edge to make a rim. Cover with chopped tomato and slices of mozzarella. Arrange anchovies like a lattice on top of cheese. Sprinkle on oregano and oil. Bake in a preheated oven for 30-40 minutes. Serve piping hot from the oven.

Sandwiches di melanzane

Eggplant sandwiches

Serves 6
Difficulty *
Time: 1-1/2 hours

1 eggplant (aubergine)
1/2 lb. ricotta
1/2 cup diced spiced tongue
1 cup grated Gruyere cheese
1/2 cup grated Parmesan cheese
1 hard-cooked egg yolk, sieved

6 sprigs parsley, chopped
Salt, pepper
Flour
2 eggs, well beaten
Dry bread crumbs
2 tbsp. butter
1/4 cup oil

Cut ends off eggplant, peel and cut into 12 round slices 1/4-inch thick. Let stand for 1 hour at room temperature and then drain off juice. Dry slices well. Sieve ricotta into a mixing bowl and add tongue, Gruyere, Parmesan, sieved egg yolk, parsley and pepper and salt to taste; mix well.
Make sandwiches with this filling and slices of eggplant. Flour sandwiches, dip in eggs (lightly salted) and then in bread crumbs. Heat frying pan with butter and oil and when oil is hot fry sandwiches to a golden brown on both sides. Drain on paper toweling, transfer to a serving platter and serve hot.

Sandwiches di polenta

Polenta sandwiches

Serves 4
Difficulty *
Time: Prepare polenta the day ahead. 30 minutes

For polenta:

6 cups water
1 heaping tbsp. salt
1 lb. cornmeal

For filling and frying:

8 oz. Gruyere cheese, sliced rather thick
6 oz. sliced baked or boiled ham
2 eggs
1 tsp. salt
Flour
Dry bread crumbs
1/4 cup olive oil

Cook polenta (see Polenta p. 81) ahead of time so that it has time to cool and harden. Cook and remove from heat and pour into a moistened 9-inch square pan. Cover pan tightly and let polenta cool. When polenta is cold and firm, cut it into thick 3-inch rounds. Cut each thick round into 1/4-inch thick rounds. Cut slices of Gruyere and ham to the same diameter as polenta rounds. On half of the polenta rounds place 1 slice Gruyere and 1 slice ham. Cover with remaining rounds to make sandwiches; press gently to close them well. Beat eggs in a bowl with salt. Roll the sandwiches, only on their edges, first through flour then through beaten eggs, then through bread crumbs so that when sandwiches are fried filling does not fall out. Fry in hot oil until they are a golden brown on both sides. Drain on absorbent paper and eat piping hot.

Erbazzone reggiano

*Spinach,
bacon and cheese pie,
Reggio Emilia style*

Serves 6
Difficulty **
Time: 3 hours
Oven Temp. 400° F.

Pastry

2-3/4 cups sifted all-purpose
flour
1/4 cup butter
1 tbsp. oil
Salt
Water

Filling

2 pounds fresh spinach
2 tbsp. oil
2/3 cup (5 oz.) chopped bacon
1/4 cup chopped parsley
1 clove garlic, chopped
1 egg
2/3 cup grated Parmesan cheese
Salt

Preparation of pastry: Put flour on mixing board, make a hollow at top of pile. Into hollow place butter, softened, together with oil and a pinch of salt. Mix it, adding water as needed to form a dough the consistency of pie crust. Knead a few times on a floured surface until smooth. Wrap and chill 1 hour.

Preparation of filling: Cook and drain spinach, pressing it to remove as much water as possible. Chop it, then saute it with oil and most of bacon, reserving 2 slices for top of pie. Stir in parsley and garlic. Remove from heat and mix in egg and Parmesan cheese.

Preparation of final dish: Roll out 2/3 of dough into a layer about 1/4-inch thick and with it line a 9-inch pie pan. Spoon in filling. Roll out remaining dough into a circle big enough to cover pan. Seal pie by pinching edges together with tines of a fork. Trim edges. Prick airholes into top layer of dough. Sprinkle rest of chopped bacon over pie crust and bake in a preheated oven (400° F.) for about 1 hour. Serve either as a hot or cold antipasto; it is equally delicious either way.

Croste con cotechino al marsala

*Cotechino canapes
with Marsala*

Serves 4
Difficulty *
Time: 1 hour
Oven Temp. 400° F.

8 slices of bread
about 1-1/2 inches thick
Olive oil
1-1/2 cups chopped cooked
cotechino or Italian sausage

2 tbsp. rendered pork fat (or lard)
1/4 cup Marsala wine
2 tbsp. butter
1 tbsp. lemon juice
6 sprigs parsley, chopped

Trim crusts from slices of bread. Place slice cut side down on a board. With a sharp knife cut around edge, making a shell 1/2-inch thick. Remove center section in one piece. Brush shell and piece removed on all sides with olive oil. Bake in a preheated oven on a baking sheet for 15 minutes or until golden brown. Keep hot. In a frying pan brown sausage in pork fat and 1 tablespoon oil. With a slotted spoon remove sausage pieces. Drain fat from pan. Pour Marsala into frying pan and boil until 1 tablespoon remains. Put sausage back into pan. Add butter and saute for a few minutes. Add lemon juice, parsley and remove from heat. Spoon sausage ragout into fried-bread "boxes". Replace lids and serve at once.

Erbazzone reggiano

PASTA

Whatever else happens during an Italian meal, it is very close to a certainty that it will include pasta, in one form or another—and the forms are infinitely variable—or a reasonable facsimile thereof.

The one thing everybody knows about pasta is that it was introduced into Italy by Marco Polo; but the one thing everybody knows isn't so. The Marco Polo story started with a mistranslation of a sentence in his memoirs which, as it was published, seemed to say that he had "discovered" pasta in China. What he really wrote was that he had seen in China noodles "which are like ours." He was simply comparing a Chinese dish to one already familiar to him at home. But even without Marco Polo's own evidence, we would have known that Italy did not wait for his return from China to learn about pasta. Marco Polo left for China in 1271; he returned to Venice in 1295. There are documents in the archives of Parma which refer to both lasagna and ravioli; they are dated during the time he was away. The first cookbook to appear in Italy since ancient Roman times—an anonymous work which has remained in manuscript—contained recipes for three different kinds of pasta; it was written some time between 1260 and 1290—at least five years before Marco Polo's return, and perhaps even before his departure. The Spaghetti Historical Museum at Pontedassio contains decrees establishing standards of quality for pasta; they are dated at a period in the twelfth century preceding Marco Polo's voyage. In Emilia-Romagna, records dating from the same time refer to the practice of making gifts of tortellini to priests and monks at Christmas. The very word "macaroni" entered the language somewhere around 1200, if we can believe the story that Frederick II was served this form of pasta by a woman whose name has come down to us only as Giovanella, though she was so gifted a cook that Frederick II, the story goes, described her pasta as "*makaria*," which was the Greek word for the particularly rich food served at wakes. Before him, William the Hermit had already written of the pasta he ate near Naples—the capital of macaroni and spaghetti today.

But all this is *modern* history; we can go much farther back. The ancient Romans knew lasagna, which Apicius included in his cookbook. They called it *laganum*; it is still *lagana* in Calabria today. But even this is not our earliest date for pasta. Pasta shapers have been found in Etruscan tombs. They looked like knitting needles. Dough was rolled around them, and when it was cooked, the result was very much like our macaroni today. We know too that the Etruscans grew a special type of grain for pasta—hard wheat, for which Clusium was noted; in Pisa it was ground into semolina flour like that used for pasta now.

Pasta is one of the most protean of foods. In an attempt to impose some sort of order on the chaos created by the sheer number of kinds of pasta, various categories have been set up; in the South, for instance, they are sometimes sorted out into long pasta (*paste lunghe*) or short pasta (*paste corte*). This is not very satisfactory, since the length of a piece of pasta bears very little relation to its essential qualities. More valid is the distinction between Southern pasta and Northern pasta. In the South, the pasta archetype is typified by spaghetti or macaroni, hard brittle manufactured products usually bought packaged in a shop. In the North, the norm is a limper dough-like kind—tagliatelle, for instance—which can also be bought in a shop if you want, but which is frequently made at home; it has a sub-class of stuffed pasta (tortellini, ravioli), made from the same dough, often referred to as *pasta tirata*, which I suppose could be translated as meaning pasta which has had lengthy acquaintance with the rolling pin. Northern pasta usually has egg in the dough, Southern pasta usually not, but there are numerous exceptions on both sides of the pasta frontier—which, curiously, is identical with the political frontier which separated the Northern culture from the Southern culture from ancient Roman times until 1861.

Pasta all'uovo casalinga

Pasta refers to a paste made of flour, water and salt. Very often eggs and oil are added to make the pasta more palatable. This paste is then rolled or shaped into the many shapes we are familiar with such as spaghetti, macaroni, shells, ziti, rigatoni, etc. Most of these shaped pastas require special machinery and are not often prepared at home. But the thinly rolled paste can be made into noodles, linguine, lasagne or shaped and stuffed to make ravioli, cannelloni, manicotti. These can be prepared at home and taste best when freshly made. The plain pastas are usually boiled and served with a sauce, butter or cheese to make them tastier and easier to eat. Some pastas are boiled and then layered into casseroles and baked with sauces. Pastas can also be stuffed and served or baked with sauces. Then pasta cookery becomes a fine art with flavors intermingled to make a tantalizing combination for the taste buds.

For the uninitiated there are a few basic rules to observe when buying or making pasta. Purchase your pasta from a reputable company or freshly made from your local Italian pasta maker. The shapes and sizes are endless and many of them can be used interchangeably in many of our recipes. However, when you go to the trouble of making your own pasta, buy only the best ingredients. The best flour to use for pasta is semolina flour which can be purchased from a pasta maker's supply house or from your local Italian pasta maker. This is a hard wheat flour (known as durum or Graham wheat) with a very fine grain that makes a dough that has the plastic quality needed to roll out to paper thinness. All-purpose (plain) flour can be used but produces a dough that cannot be rolled as thin. Also, do not make pasta on a hot humid day since it does not dry well and produces a pasta that is soft and mushy after cooking.

To cook pasta properly use 6 to 7 quarts of water to every pound of pasta. Place the water into a large kettle or stock pot. The type of pot, enamel, stainless steel or aluminum, makes no difference. Add 2 tablespoons salt to the water and bring it to a full rolling boil. Add a tablespoon of olive oil to prevent sticking. Drop the pasta slowly into the boiling water so that the boiling does not stop. Make sure all the pasta is slowly pushed under the boiling water. Stir gently several times during cooking to keep pasta from sticking to the bottom and to keep it from clumping together. Cook at a boil until the pasta is *al dente*—"to the tooth." This means the pasta has the right chewy consistency and is not mushy. This may mean a different consistency for each person, chewier for some than others. It should suit your personal taste. Of course this does not mean cooking to a state of soggy mushiness which makes the pasta tasteless. The pasta should be firm enough to resist the teeth. It is important to realize that pasta sold in the stores and pasta made at home cook in different lengths of time. The store bought pasta takes longer to cook since it has had more moisture removed and is drier. Drain the pasta quickly in a colander and rinse with very hot water, making sure all the excess starch is removed. Then pour the pasta quicky into a bowl and toss gently with the sauce. Do not let the pasta cool, but work quickly to keep it piping hot. And keep the guests waiting while you are tossing, as pasta only tastes great when eaten fresh and hot.

Most of the sauces in this book are typical of good Italian cuisine. They require little cooking and are not thick, but are light flavorful coatings made only to enhance the taste of the pasta.

Throughout the entire section on pasta, you will see chopped or sieved tomato pulp being used. To prepare the pulp, use only the reddest, ripest tomatoes – regular or Italian plum tomatoes. Spear them on a fork and heat over high heat or dip into boiling water for a few seconds until skin blisters. Peel off skin and then cut out core. If chopped pulp is required, quarter the tomatoes and remove the seeds and juice. Chop the remaining pulp, measure it and then use as stated in the recipe. To prepare sieved pulp, put chopped pulp in a food mill, sieve or blender and press or whirl until tomatoes are a fine pulp. Measure pulp and then use as stated in the recipe.

Basic pasta

Makes about 1-1/2 pounds

3-1/2 to 4 cups all-purpose
flour or semolina flour
1-1/2 tsp. salt
4 eggs, well beaten
1 tbsp. olive oil
1 tbsp. lukewarm water
**(For ravioli add 1 extra egg to be
used for brushing dough)**

The simple pastas can be prepared at home according to this recipe. All types of noodles—lagane, laganelle, fettuccine, pappardelle, trenette, taglierini, lasagne, and stuffed pasta such as ravioli and cannelloni—are easy to prepare with this basic recipe. The more complex pastas are difficult and require special flour and special machines for shaping. These pastas should be purchased from a good local pasta maker for the best flavor and quality. These include bucatini, linguine, fusilli, macaroni, crestoni, penne, rigatoni, spaghetti, ventoline and vermicelli. For those who only want to buy their pasta, substitute an equal weight in purchased pasta. In cooking the pasta remember the commercially made pasta is drier than the homemade pasta and will require more cooking time.

Mix flour and salt in a bowl. Make a hollow in the flour. Add eggs, olive oil and water. Stir until a soft clay-like ball of dough is formed. Place dough on a floured surface and knead until smooth and elastic, about 10 minutes. Cover and let rest 1 hour. Cut dough into 4 pieces and roll out each piece on a lightly floured surface to paper thinness, the thinner the better. For noodles, cut dough after it is rolled to make it easier to cut into strips the width needed in the recipe. Toss noodles to separate and let dry at least 1 hour to several hours on a clean dry towel. Cook and serve as directed in recipe.

1/3 recipe	2/3 recipe	1-1/2 recipes
1-1/3 cups flour	2-2/3 cups flour	5-3/4 to 6 cups flour
1/2 tsp. salt	1 tsp. salt	2 tsp. salt
1 large egg	2 large eggs	6 eggs
1 tsp. olive oil	2 tsp. olive oil	1-1/2 tbsp. olive oil
1 tsp. water	2 tsp. water	1-1/2 tbsp. water

Basic spinach
or green noodles

Makes about 1-1/2 pounds

3/4 lb. spinach, trimmed
and washed
3-1/2 cups all-purpose flour
or semolina flour
1 tsp. salt
3 eggs, well beaten
1 tbsp. olive oil

Cook spinach with water clinging to leaves until tender. Cool. Squeeze out all excess moisture. Puree spinach in a food mill. Mix flour and salt in a bowl. Make a well in the centre and add eggs and spinach. Continue preparation for Basic Pasta. Cut and dry as for noodles. Serve as directed in recipe.

2/3 recipe	1-1/2 recipes
1/2 lb. spinach	1-1/4 lbs. spinach
2-1/4 cups flour	5-1/4 cups flour
1/2 tsp. salt	1-1/2 tsp. salt
2 eggs	4 large eggs
2 tsp. olive oil	1-1/2 tbsp. olive oil

Bucatini alla carbonara

Bucatini (spaghetti)
Carbonara

Serves 4
Difficulty *
Time: 1 hour

4 egg yolks
Salt, white pepper
6 tbsp. heavy cream
1/2 cup (2 oz.) grated Pecorino
or Parmesan cheese

1/2 cup (4 oz.) diced bacon
2 tbsp. butter
3 tbsp. olive oil
1 lb. bucatini

Beat egg yolks in a large bowl until foamy. Season with salt and pepper. Stir in cream and Pecorino cheese. Saute bacon in butter and oil, removing pan from heat as soon as bacon is brown. Cook spaghetti, drain when al dente and rinse with hot water. Toss spaghetti vigorously in beaten egg mixture until well covered with sauce. Finally, add hot bacon and pan drippings. Toss again and serve at once.

Fusilli con sugo di verdure

Fusilli
with vegetable sauce

Serves 6
Difficulty *
Time: 1 hour

1 onion, chopped
6 tbsp. olive oil
2 tbsp. butter
2 carrots, chopped
2 celery ribs, chopped
1/2 cup chopped fresh basil

1 can (1 lb.) Italian peeled
tomatoes, drained
Salt, pepper
1-1/2 lbs. fusilli (spiral
spaghetti)
1/4 cup grated Parmesan

Saute onion in oil and butter until wilted. After a few minutes add carrots, celery and basil and saute briefly. Add tomatoes, 1 cup water and simmer sauce for 40 minutes over moderate heat, stirring occasionally. Season to taste with salt and pepper. The sauce is ready when it has thickened.
Cook fusilli al dente, drain and rinse with hot water. Drain and toss in a bowl with the vegetable sauce and sprinkle with grated Parmesan.

Lagane alla basilicatese con fagioli

Noodles Basilicata style
with beans

Serves 4
Difficulty ***
Time: 2 hours excluding time
for drying pasta

1 recipe Basic Pasta
1 lb. fresh baby lima beans
2 tbsp. lard (or bacon fat)
1 tbsp. olive oil

3 cloves garlic, chopped
1 tbsp. hot red pepper,
dried, crushed
Freshly ground black pepper
Salt

Prepare pasta. Cut dough into 1-inch wide broad noodle strips (lagane). Separate strips on a floured board and let them dry.
Boil beans in salted water to cover and leave them in water until pasta is cooked. Cook pasta in lightly salted boiling water, drain while still al dente and rinse with hot water. Put them in a deep dish. Drain beans and add them to pasta. Heat lard and oil and saute garlic cloves until golden. Sprinkle with crushed red pepper, salt, freshly ground black pepper and mix with pasta and beans.

Lagane alla basilicatese con fagioli

Laganelle con acciughe e pomodoro alla pugliese

Thin noodles with tomato and anchovies Apulian style

Serves 4
Difficulty ***
Time: 2 hours excluding time to dry noodles

Laganelle con acciughe e pomodoro alla pugliese

1 recipe Basic Pasta

3 garlic cloves, chopped
3 anchovies (soaked in cold water and then rinsed)
7 tbsp. oil
3-1/2 cups chopped tomato pulp (skin and seeds removed)
Salt, pepper
2 tbsp. chopped parsley

Prepare pasta. Cut pasta dough in strips 1/2-inch wide. Dry for 1-1/2 hours on a clean towel.
Chop garlic, mash anchovies to a paste in a mortar. Heat oil and saute garlic until golden. Add anchovies, tomatoes, season with salt, plenty of pepper (or dried red peppers), and cook for 10 to 12 minutes. Cook pasta in boiling salted water. Drain while still al dente and toss with sauce. Garnish with chopped parsley and serve.

Lasagne alla cacciatore

Lasagne hunters' style

Serves 4
Difficulty *
Time: 1-1/2 hours

1 lb. lasagne, broken into squares (2/3 recipe Basic Pasta)
A young rabbit, cut into serving pieces
1/4 cup oil
2 tbsp. butter
2 cloves garlic, chopped
1/2 cup (4 oz.) chopped lean bacon
1 onion, chopped

1 cup dry white wine
3/4 lb. small onions, left whole
2 lbs. tomatoes peeled and diced (or 1 can—1 lb. 14 oz.—Italian peeled tomatoes)
Salt, pepper
2 tbsp. minced parsley
1 tbsp. minced carrot
2 tbsp. minced celery

Prepare pasta. Cut dough into 2-inch wide strips. Clean and wash rabbit pieces, rub with salt and place in a covered pan over very low heat for about 10 minutes. When rabbit has lost a bit of its water, drain and add oil, butter and garlic. Saute until brown on all sides. Add bacon and onion and cook for another 10 minutes. Pour in wine, simmer 5 minutes. Add onions and tomatoes, peeled by scalding in boiling water for a moment. Lower the heat, cover and cook for about 40 minutes or until rabbit is tender. Season to taste with salt and pepper and add minced parsley, carrot and celery. Cook without cover for 10 minutes. Cook and drain pasta while al dente and rinse with hot water. Put on a serving platter and place rabbit pieces on top. Spoon over vegetables and cooking juices.

Fettuccine is, so far as I know, identical with tagliatelle; it is simply the Roman name for it. Rome deserves having a private name for this form of pasta, however, because of the skill with which she presents it, using the simplest possible sauce, butter (plus, of course, the grated cheese sprinkled over almost all pasta dishes). Rome uses such excellent butter and applies it so lavishly, turning and returning the hot pasta in its melting golden goodness, that the effect is as rich as that of a complicated sauce.

Fettuccine verdi al funghetto

Green noodles with mushrooms

Serves 4
Difficulty *
Time: 1 hour

12 oz. green noodles
(1/2 recipe Spinach Noodles)
1 green onion
1/2 cup (4 oz.) butter
1 tbsp. olive oil
1 pound mushrooms
Salt, pepper
7 tbsp. dry white wine
2-1/2 cups chopped tomato
pulp (skin and seeds
removed)
Nutmeg
3/4 cup (3 oz.) grated Parmesan

Fettuccine verdi al funghetto

Prepare pasta. Cut dough into 1/4 inch wide strips. Chop onion and saute in 3 tablespoons of the butter and oil until onion is transparent. Dice mushrooms, season with a pinch of salt and pepper and add to onions with wine. Let wine evaporate almost completely, then add tomato pulp and grate in a little nutmeg. Stir and continue cooking at moderate heat for about 15 minutes. Cook green noodles in lightly salted boiling water. Drain while still al dente and rinse with hot water. Season with remaining butter, half the grated Parmesan and half the tomato and mushroom sauce. Mix well and serve, passing the rest of the sauce and Parmesan.

Linguine con seppie e pisellini

Linguine with cuttlefish or squid and peas

Serves 4
Difficulty **
Time: 2 hours

1 lb. cleaned squid or cuttlefish
2 cloves garlic, minced
7 tbsp. olive oil
7 tbsp. dry white wine
2 cups chopped tomato pulp (skin and seeds removed)
1-1/2 cups small peas, cooked and drained
Salt and pepper
1 lb. linguine or trenette
1/4 cup chopped parsley

Linguine con seppie e pisellini

Clean squid or cuttlefish removing bone and ink sac. Cut into thin strips. At high heat brown garlic in oil, add squid or cuttlefish. Add wine and simmer until it has evaporated. Add tomato pulp; continue cooking, adding a bit of hot water if necessary until sauce is thick enough to spoon over pasta, about 15-20 minutes. Shortly before cooking is completed, add peas. Season with salt and pepper (or dried red pepper, if preferred).
Cook linguine or other pasta in lightly salted, boiling water and drain while still al dente. Rinse with hot water. Put pasta in a deep serving platter, cover with squid and peas sauce. Sprinkle parsley over it. Grated cheese is not used in this dish.

Linguine con olio e aglio alla napoletana

Neapolitan linguine with oil and garlic

Serves 4
Difficulty *
Time: 1 hour

1 lb. linguine (or lingue di passera or trenette)
2/3 cup olive oil
2 or 3 cloves garlic, sliced
1 tbsp. chopped hot red pepper
Salt
1/2 cup chopped parsley

Cook linguine in boiling salted water until tender but still firm. Five minutes before draining, pour oil into shallow 1-1/2 quart casserole, add garlic and saute gently until slightly browned; add red pepper, a pinch of salt, 3 tablespoons of pasta cooking water and parsley. Simmer gently for 4 to 5 minutes. Drain linguine and rinse with hot water. Add linguine to sauce, mix well, leave it on heat for another 2 to 3 minutes and serve.

Maccheroni alla marinara

Macaroni with marinara sauce

Serves 4
Difficulty *
Time: 1 hour

2 cloves garlic, minced
1 tbsp. chopped Italian *peperoncino*
(These are little Italian
green peppers, 1-inch long,
quite hot but edible.)
2 tbsp. olive oil
2 lbs tomatoes,
skin and seeds removed,
and sieved
1/2 cup ripe Italian
or Greek olives,
pitted and halved
1 tbsp. small capers
Salt
1 lb. bucatini macaroni
1 tbsp. chopped parsley

Maccheroni alla marinara

Saute garlic and peperoncino in oil. Add tomato pulp, bring to a boil, then lower heat and simmer for 15 minutes. Add olives and capers. Season to taste with salt. Break macaroni into pieces about 3 inches long, cook until al dente in lightly salted boiling water. Drain and rinse with hot water. Put macaroni in bowl and pour in sauce and chopped parsley. Mix well and serve.

Maccheroni al mascarpone

Macaroni with mascarpone and meat sauce

Serves 6
Difficulty *
Time: 30 minutes

1 small onion, sliced
1/4 cup butter
1/4 lb. ground (minced) beef
1/4 lb. (bulk) sausage meat
1/2 cup dry white wine
Beef broth
Salt

1-1/2 lbs. grooved macaroni
2/3 cup grated Parmesan
3/4 lb. mascarpone (an Italian cream cheese) or other soft, unripened cheese (triple creme, boursin, neufchatel)

Saute onion in half of the butter. Add ground beef, sausage and wine. Simmer until meat is brown and crumbly. If sauce seems too thick, add a little beef broth. Season to taste with salt. Cook macaroni in boiling salted water until al dente. Drain, rinse with hot water and transfer to serving bowl. Toss with meat sauce, remaining butter and mascarpone broken into small pieces. Toss until pasta and sauce are well blended. Sprinkle with grated Parmesan and serve.

Pappardelle alla toscana con la lepre

Broad noodles, Tuscan style in hare sauce

Serves 4
Difficulty **
Time: 3 hours, plus time
to marinate hare

1 recipe Basic Pasta
2-1/2 lbs. hare or rabbit
2 cups dry red wine
1 small onion, chopped
1 piece celery, chopped
Pinch of thyme
Bay leaf
Salt, peppercorns
4 slices lean bacon, chopped
1 small carrot, chopped
2 tbsp. olive oil
Nutmeg
1/4 cup (2 oz.) butter

Pappardelle might be described as lasagna cut into squares, but its dough is likely to be heavier. That depends a little on where you encounter it, for the different regions of Italy are not always in agreement about what pappardelle means. In its coarser versions, it is a particularly appropriate accompaniment for heavy dishes with thick sauces, like game; a favorite combination is pappardelle with hare.

Prepare pasta. Cut dough into strips about 3/4-inch wide and 7 to 8 inches long. Let dry several hours.

Cut hare into pieces, cover with red wine, add half the onion, celery, thyme, bay leaf and a few peppercorns. Marinate for 2 hours, stirring occasionally. Saute bacon, remaining onion and carrot in oil. Drain hare and add pieces to the pan, add salt and a little nutmeg and brown pieces on all sides. Continue cooking over moderate heat basting from time to time with a little of the marinade, about 1-1/2 hours. When hare is tender, put pan juices through a fine sieve and keep both hare and sauce hot.

Cook pappardelle (broad noodles) al dente in boiling salted water. Rinse with hot water. Toss with sauce and pieces of butter. Serve with grated Parmesan if desired. Serve hare meat separately as a second course.

Penne all'arrabbiata

Penne Enraged

Serves 6
Difficulty *
Time: 1 hour

1/2 lb. mushrooms
4 slices bacon, cut into strips
3 tbsp. butter
1 tbsp. olive oil
1 clove garlic, halved
1-1/2 lbs. ripe tomatoes
(or 1 can (1 lb.) Italian
peeled tomatoes, drained)
A sprig of basil
1 small hot dried pepper,
chopped
Salt
1-1/2 lbs. penne (quill-like pasta)
1/2 cup (2 oz.) grated Pecorino
cheese

Clean mushrooms and cut off lower ends of stems. Rub mushrooms with a damp cloth and slice both stems and tops. Cut the bacon into strips and cook in half the butter and oil. When bacon is crisp, remove pieces and reserve. Brown garlic in drippings then discard garlic. Saute mushrooms in same pan, raising heat to allow water contained in them to evaporate. Stir to prevent sticking. Put crisp bacon pieces back in pan with mushrooms, keep at high heat for 2 to 3 minutes, then remove from heat. Peel, seed and chop tomatoes (or drain and remove seeds from canned tomatoes, then chop them.) Put the tomatoes in another saucepan together with basil and red pepper. Cover and cook at low heat, stirring often for 15 minutes. Add mushroom and bacon mixture and cook for 5 minutes longer to thicken sauce and to blend flavors. Season to taste with salt.

Cook pasta al dente, drain and rinse with hot water. Toss with mushroom sauce. Dot with remaining butter and sprinkle on grated Pecorino. Grated Parmesan may also be used. Toss gently to blend. Serve immediately.

Pappardelle alla toscana con la lepre

Spaghetti alla puttanesca

Spaghetti harlot-style

Serves 4
Difficulty *
Time: 30 minutes

1 lb. spaghetti
2 cloves garlic
2 tbsp. olive oil
Small hot red pepper, minced
6 anchovy fillets, chopped finely
1 cup pitted black olives, sliced
2 tbsp. capers, chopped
1 lb. meaty ripe tomatoes, peeled and thinly sliced
Salt
1/2 cup chopped parsley

Cook spaghetti al dente in lightly salted boiling water. While pasta is cooking, saute whole garlic cloves in oil, add hot pepper and anchovies. Add olives, capers and tomatoes. Season to taste with salt. Simmer 10 minutes or until very hot. Remove garlic. Drain spaghetti, rinse with hot water and toss with sauce. Sprinkle with parsley.

Spaghetti alla puttanesca

Spaghetti, which, because of its shape, takes its name from *spago*, cord, is a type of pasta so universally known that it often stands for pasta in general; so does macaroni, for that matter. Both belong to the same pasta family, of which Naples is the capital. They are usually factory made, from dough without egg, bought hard and brittle, in sharp contrast to the limp doughy types of pasta preferred in northern Italy, which are more apt to be homemade. An early American appreciator of spaghetti was Thomas Jefferson, who in 1787 brought a spaghetti-making machine from Italy to the United States.

Spaghetti con polpettine di carne

Spaghetti and meatballs

Serves 6
Difficulty *
Time: 1 hour

1/2 lb. ground (minced) beef
6 sprigs parsley, chopped
1 large slice salami, chopped
1/2 cup grated Parmesan cheese
Salt
Nutmeg

1 egg
1 lb. ripe tomatoes
1 small onion, chopped
1/4 cup butter
1/4 cup olive oil
1-1/2 lbs. medium spaghetti

Mix beef, parsley, salami, Parmesan, salt, a little freshly grated nutmeg and egg. Stir until all ingredients are thoroughly mixed. From mixture make small meatballs the size of a cherry and set them aside on a plate. Peel tomatoes, remove seeds and chop fine. Saute onion in butter and oil until wilted. Stir in tomatoes and salt to taste. Simmer over very low heat for 30 minutes, stirring from time to time. Add meatballs and cook over low heat for another 15 minutes. While the meatballs are simmering, cook the spaghetti in boiling salted water and drain when al dente. Rinse with hot water. Toss with meatball sauce and serve.

Spaghetti alla bucaniera

Spaghetti buccaneer-style

Serves 4
Difficulty *
Time: 1-1/2 hours

2 cloves garlic, chopped
1 tsp. dried red pepper flakes
7 tbsp. olive oil
Salt, pepper
1 lb. tomatoes, chopped
3/4 cup *each* chopped raw
octopus and chopped raw shelled
and deveined shrimp
1/2 cup chopped raw clams
1 lb. spaghetti
1/4 cup chopped parsley

Spaghetti alla bucaniera (pirates' spaghetti) belongs to a category of pasta (like spaghetti alla zappatora, ditchdiggers' spaghetti, and maccheroni alla carrettiera, teamsters' macaroni) whose names indicate that their spicing is so hot or their garlic content so insistent that only he-men can be expected to cope with them.

Saute garlic and red pepper in half of oil, with a pinch of pepper. Add tomatoes, salt to taste and continue cooking for about 15 minutes. In another saucepan put octopus, together with shrimp and clams and remaining oil. Saute for 15 minutes and add them to tomato sauce. Cook spaghetti, drain while still al dente and rinse with hot water. Sprinkle with parsley and mix with sauce.

Spaghetti all'Amatriciana

Spaghetti Amatrice

Serves 4
Difficulty *
Time: 30 minutes

1/2 small onion, chopped
3 tbsp. olive oil
3/4 lb. ripe tomatoes, skin
and seeds removed
1 piece dried hot red pepper
Salt
9 slices bacon (lean) in strips
1 lb. medium spaghetti
or bucatini
1/2 cup (2 oz.) grated Pecorino
cheese

Saute onion in oil. When onion is transparent, add tomatoes and red pepper. Add salt to taste. Cook over high heat for 5 minutes, stirring constantly. Add bacon strips and simmer another 5 minutes. When sauce is done, it should be fairly thick, but tomatoes should not become mushy. Cook spaghetti in boiling salted water and drain while still al dente. Rinse with hot water. Mix with hot sauce and sprinkle generously with Pecorino cheese.

Spaghetti alla bucaniera

Spaghetti all'amatriciana, as it is spelled here, is the correct name of this dish, but you will find it about half of the time masquerading on Italian bills of fare as spaghetti alla matriciana. This is an error perpetrated by those unacquainted with the origin of the dish. It is a preparation which was developed in Amatrice, a town of Lazio.

Tagliatelle di lusso

Noodles de luxe

Serves 6
Difficulty*
Time: 30 minutes

**1-1/2 lbs. medium egg noodles
(tagliatelle all'uovo,
or 1 recipe Basic Pasta)
1/2 lb. baked or boiled ham,
sliced fairly thick
1/2 cup (4 oz.) butter
2 egg yolks
Salt
1/2 cup (2 oz.) grated Parmesan
1 black or white truffle**

Prepare pasta. Cut dough into 1/4 inch wide strips. Cut 1/3 of the ham into strips and the rest into 3/8-inch squares. Cook noodles al dente in boiling salted water. Drain and rinse with hot water. Melt butter in a fairly large frying pan (big enough to hold finished pasta.) Add squares and strips of ham and toss briefly in melted butter (which should be foaming). Remove pan from heat for a moment and remove strips (not the squares) of ham. Set aside. Put pan back on the heat and pour in drained noodles. Stir noodles around in butter and ham for a few minutes, making sure to mix all the noodles thoroughly with ham. (To avoid breaking noodles, use two forks to swirl them.) Beat egg yolks with a fork, adding a pinch of salt and Parmesan. Remove pan from heat and pour beaten yolks over noodles. Toss gently. Transfer pasta to serving platter and shred truffle over noodles. Garnish with ham strips and serve. Note: If you wish a creamier sauce, add 1/4 cup warm cream to beaten yolks, then add to noodles.

> Tagliatelle, flat ribbon-shaped pasta whose dough ordinarily contains egg, is typical of the northern pastas whose capital is Bologna; Bologna itself claims its paternity. The story goes that the Bolognese cook of Giovanni II of Bentivoglio invented tagliatelle in 1487 in imitation of the long flaxen hair of Lucrezia Borgia. It makes a pretty story, but in all probability tagliatelle existed long before Lucrezia did.

Trenette con pesto

Trenette with pesto sauce

Serves 4
Difficulty *
Time: 30 minutes

**1 lb. trenette
(or 2/3 Basic Recipe)
1/2 cup (4 oz.) chopped basil
1/2 clove garlic
Salt
2/3 cup grated Parmesan cheese
1/4 cup olive oil**

Prepare pasta. Cut dough into 1/8-inch wide strips. Wash and dry basil leaves, chop them fine, together with garlic. Put chopped basil and garlic in a bowl, add a pinch of salt and Parmesan. Gradually stir in olive oil. It is better to grind basil mixture in a mortar using a pestle. Strain through a sieve. This mixture can also be whirled in a blender until smooth.
Cook noodles or linguine al dente, drain, rinse with hot water and toss in a bowl with basil sauce, which is called pesto.

> I have heard trenette described as nothing more than the Genoese name for the same type of pasta called tagliatelle in Bologna and fettuccine in Rome; but, as I recall the trenette I have eaten in Genoa has always been a trifle narrower and a trifle thinner than the other two. The chief function of trenette is, modestly, not to call attention to itself, but to bring out the full flavor of that distinctive Genoese sauce, pesto (which also goes into minestrone). Some foreigners would perhaps prefer that the full flavor of pesto should *not* be brought out; to unaccustomed palates it sometimes seems unpleasantly harsh and sharp. However, almost every Ligurian town has its own variant of pesto, so if the uninhibited Genoese original strikes you as too violent, look around for a blander version—for instance, that of Nervi, only seven miles south of Genoa, which tones it down by adding cream to the Genoese recipe.

Pesto di formaggio

Basil and cheese sauce

Makes 1-1/3 cups
Difficulty *
Time: 20 minutes

1/4 cup finely chopped fresh basil
3 cloves garlic
Salt

1/2 cup (2 oz.) grated Sardinian pecorino cheese
1/2 cup (2 oz.) grated Parmesan cheese
1 cup olive oil

Mash basil in a mortar together with garlic and a pinch of salt, adding pecorino and Parmesan cheese a little bit at a time. Finally, beat in oil very slowly until well blended. Can also be made in a blender using the same method as for mortar.

Pesto
Basil Sauce

Use basil, garlic, salt and oil and prepare as above. Makes enough sauce for 1 lb. cooked spaghetti.

Vermicelli piccanti alla calabrese

Sharp vermicelli Calabrian style

Serves 4
Difficulty *
Time: 1 hour

1 lb. vermicelli
1 clove garlic, chopped
2/3 cup olive oil
1 tsp. dried red pepper flakes
1 can (2 oz.) fillets of anchovy (desalted and reduced to a paste in mortar)
1 tbsp. chopped parsley
Salt

Cook vermicelli in lightly salted, boiling water. Drain them al dente, rinse with hot water and turn them onto a serving platter. While pasta is cooking, prepare this simple sauce: Saute garlic in oil, add hot pepper, anchovies and parsley. Pour over drained vermicelli, mix well and serve. Season to taste with salt. No Parmesan required.

Vermicelli, which comes in fine threads, is often trusted with the function of adding interest to consommé. Its name would hardly conjure up appetizing visions for most persons, but fortunately few eaters are aware of what vermicelli means—"little worms". It is probably not because of their appearance on the plate that vermicelli are so called; the name was probably suggested to the workers who make it because, during the process, dough is pressed through the holes of a sort of colander; and as fine threads emerge squirming from the holes they might easily evoke the image of minute worms.

Vermicelli piccanti alla calabrese

> The cooking of pasta necessarily begins by boiling; but it may finish otherwise. The most elaborate pasta dishes end in the oven, usually, after the preliminary boiling, buried under rich sauces. A favorite for such treatment is lasagna, but almost any sort of pasta can be so treated, adding an extra dimension to the basic dish.
>
> Cannelloni are among the largest of the tube-shaped pastas—the very word means "big tubes." Their caliber lends itself admirably to stuffing, in one luscious fashion or another; thus enriched, they are often first boiled, then confided to the oven to end up as baked pasta.

Cannelloni alla laziale

*Cannelloni from
the Roman countryside*

Serves 4
Difficulty **
Time: 2-1/2 hours
Oven Temp. 400° F.

1 recipe Basic Pasta

For filling:

1/2 small onion chopped
1/2 carrot, chopped
1/2 celery stalk, chopped
3 tbsp. butter
9 oz. lean ground (minced) beef
1/4 cup (2 oz.) diced
prosciutto crudo
1 package (1 oz.) dried
mushrooms, soaked and chopped

1 small lamb's brain, boiled
until firm and skinned
7 tbsp. white wine
1 tbsp. flour
1 cup (7 oz.) chopped tomato
pulp (skin and seeds removed)
Salt, pepper
Nutmeg

For meat sauce:

1 small onion, chopped
1/4 cup butter
2 tbsp. olive oil
1/4 lb. ground (minced) beef
2-1/2 cups sieved tomato pulp
(or 1 can (1 lb.) Italian
canned peeled tomatoes)

6 whole basil leaves
Salt, pepper
3 tbsp. heavy cream
2/3 cup grated Parmesan
cheese

Prepare pasta. Cut dough into 4x4 inch squares.
Preparation of filling: Simmer chopped vegetables in butter in a saucepan. Add meat, prosciutto, mushrooms and chopped brains. Add wine, flour and tomato pulp. Cook until liquid is thick, about 30 minutes. Season to taste with salt, pepper and nutmeg.

For meat sauce: Saute onion in butter and oil until wilted. Add beef and cook until brown and crumbly. Add tomato pulp, basil leaves and a little salt and pepper. Cover and continue cooking over very low heat for 15 minutes. When thick remove basil leaves. Stir in cream.

Cook pasta in boiling salted water until tender but still firm. Drain and set to cool on a kitchen towel. Spread filling on dough and roll to form cannelloni. Spoon a thin layer of sauce into a buttered 1-1/2 quart shallow baking pan. Arrange cannelloni in a single layer, seam side down on top of sauce. Dot layer with butter and cover with meat sauce and sprinkle with Parmesan. Place in preheated oven for 30 minutes or until brown and crusty.

Pasticcio di lasagne

Lasagna pie

Serves 6
Difficulty ***
Time: 2 hours, excluding time
for drying pasta
Oven Temp. 350° F.

1 recipe Basic Pasta

For final preparation:

**6 slices baked or boiled ham
3/4 lb. ricotta cheese
2 eggs
Salt
1 cup (4 oz.) grated Parmesan
1/4 cup butter**

For sauce:

**1/2 green onion, minced
1/4 cup butter
2 tbsp. olive oil
2 cooked chicken breasts
(or same quantity of chicken
leftovers) skinned, boned
and chopped**

**4 chicken livers, chopped
1/2 cup dry white wine or broth
1 tbsp. tomato paste
Salt, pepper**

Prepare pasta. Cut dough into rectangles of lasagna 2 x 5 inches. Let dry for several hours.

For sauce: Saute onion until transparent in butter and oil. At this point add chicken breasts and livers to pan. When all ingredients are well browned, add wine or broth mixed with tomato paste. Cover and cook over gentle heat, stirring from time to time. Season to taste with salt and pepper. When finished, the sauce should be good and thick.

For final preparation: Grease a shallow baking dish well. Roll up slices of ham and arrange them in the bottom of the baking dish in the form of a star. Cook the lasagna in boiling salted water until al dente. Drain and rinse with hot water. Dry in a towel and place a layer of them on top of ham. Follow this with a layer of sauce and ricotta mixed with eggs, a pinch of salt and some of the grated Parmesan. Continue putting in layers in this order until all ingredients have been used, ending with Parmesan cheese. Dot top with butter. Bake in preheated oven for 30 minutes; remove when the surface is well browned. When you are ready to serve, turn baking dish over on a serving platter and remove, revealing the pie decorated with the ham star.

Lasagne alla ferrarese

Lasagna Ferrarese

Serves 4
Difficulty **
Time: 2 hours, excluding time
for drying pasta
Oven Temp. 375° F.

1 recipe Basic Pasta

**1 cup (4 oz.) mixed chopped
blanched almonds and walnuts
7 tbsp. oil**

**2/3 cup milk
Salt, pepper**

Prepare pasta. Cut dough into rectangles measuring 1-1/2 x 4 inches. Let dry on a floured board in a single layer for several hours. Prepare sauce by grinding nutmeats in a mortar or meat grinder until very fine and mushy. Add oil to make a paste and finally milk, adding salt and pepper to taste. Cook lasagna in boiling salted water until tender. Drain, rinse with hot water and arrange them in layers in shallow 1-1/2 quart baking dish. Pour sauce on each layer and brown in preheated oven for 20 to 25 minutes or until lightly browned.

Lasagna must be the ancestor of all the other forms of pasta. Whatever variety you intend to make, you have to begin by rolling the dough into a sheet; and if you stop there, you have lasagna. The ancient Romans knew this type of pasta and gave it its name, from *lasanum*, a cooking pot. It lends itself more happily than any other pasta to the addition of spinach to its dough, producing green pasta. It appears most often in baked dishes.

A particularly rich version of baked lasagna is vincisgrassi, whose name is so mysterious that it baffles most of the cooks who make it (particularly in the Abruzzi, where it is called pincisgrassi, a corruption of the original word which loses touch completely with its meaning). Vincisgrassi is a complicated variation on Bolognese baked lasagna created in the Marches in the early nineteenth century to honor the commander of the Austrian occupation forces there— Prince Alfred zu Windischgrätz. Vincisgrassi immortalizes him—but nobody knows it.

Lasagne verdi casalinghe

Home-made green noodles

Serves 6
Difficulty **
Time: 1-1/2 hours, excluding time for drying pasta
Oven Temp. 375° F.

For meat sauce:

1 small onion, chopped
2 tbsp. butter
2 tbsp. olive oil
1/2 lb. ground (minced) beef
1/4 lb. (bulk) sausage meat
Salt, pepper
1/2 cup dry white wine or broth
1 can (1 lb.) peeled Italian tomatoes, chopped
2 basil leaves, chopped
1 can (8 oz.) peas, drained

For bechamel sauce:

1/4 cup butter
1 cup (4 oz.) all-purpose flour
1 quart milk
Nutmeg

1-1/2 recipes Spinach Noodles

For garnish:

1 cup (4 oz.) grated Parmesan cheese

4 slices Gruyere
2 tbsp. butter

Prepare spinach noodles. Cut dough into small 1-1/2-inch rounds or 1 x 2-inch rectangles, reserving a few of them for garnishing finished dish. Let dry at room temperature for several hours.

For meat sauce. Saute onion with butter and oil. Add beef and sausage, season with salt and pepper and saute. Pour wine or broth over meat and cook until it evaporates. Put tomatoes through a food mill or sieve and add to sauce, together with basil. Simmer over low heat for 10 minutes. Add peas and cook another 5 minutes.

For bechamel sauce: Melt butter and stir in flour. Add hot milk slowly. Season to taste with salt and a pinch of nutmeg. Stir over low heat until smooth and thick.

Cook pasta and pieces reserved for garnishing until al dente. Drain pasta, rinse with hot water and drain well. Set aside pasta for top of casserole. Grease a 3-quart baking dish with a little of the meat sauce, spoon in a layer of bechamel, a layer of pasta and a layer of some of the grated Parmesan. Continue layering in this way until pasta and sauces are all used. Cover the last layer with Gruyere. Top with reserved pasta and remaining Parmesan. Dot with butter and bake in a preheated oven for 20 minutes.

Ravioli alla panna gratinati

Ravioli–in cream sauce– au gratin

Serves 4
Difficulty **
Time: 3 hours, excluding time for drying pasta
Oven Temp. 400° F.

Ravioli, those little envelopes of dough stuffed with infinite variety, which are familiar to everybody all over the world, are supposed to have been invented by Genoese sailors. The story is that in the days of sailing ships, when the length of voyages, which depended upon the fickle favors of the winds, was unpredictable, nothing could be wasted of the limited stores of food aboard; hence, at the end of each day all leftovers were chopped up together and wrapped in dough for the next meal. "Ravioli" is supposed to be derived from the Genoese dialect word, "rabiole", meaning scraps of little value—in this case, leftovers.

1 recipe Basic Pasta

For filling:

**2 tbsp. chopped onion
3 tbsp. butter
3/4 lb. sweet Italian sausage, casing removed and crumbled
1/4 cup dry bread crumbs
Salt, pepper
2 egg yolks
2 tbsp. grated Parmesan cheese**

For sauce:

**1/2 cup (4 oz.) butter
3/4 cup (3 oz.) grated Parmesan cheese
2/3 cup heavy cream**

For filling: Saute onion in butter until wilted. Add sausage and saute until cooked. Drain excess fat. Add bread crumbs and season with salt and pepper to taste and continue cooking for about 5 minutes. Put cooked sausage mixture into a mixing bowl. When it has cooled, add egg yolks and Parmesan and mix well.
Prepare basic pasta. Roll out half of the dough at a time. Place a teaspoon of the filling in mounds, 1-1/2 inches apart, on top of dough. Roll out second half of dough and brush with extra beaten egg. Place dough egg side down over filling and cut apart with a fluted pastry cutter. Dry 1-1/2 hours to several hours on a clean dry towel.
Cook ravioli in lightly salted, boiling water until tender but still firm. Drain, rinse with hot water and arrange in shallow 1-1/2-quart baking dish. Dot with pieces of butter, pour over cream and sprinkle with grated Parmesan. Bake in a preheated oven for 20 to 25 minutes or until lightly browned.

Ravioli all'uso di Romagna

Ravioli Romagna style

Serves 4
Difficulty **
Time: 1-1/2 hours, excluding time for drying pasta

1 recipe Basic Pasta

For filling:

**1 lb. ricotta cheese
1/2 cup (2 oz.) grated Parmesan cheese**

**Salt, pepper
1 egg and 1 egg yolk**

For ravioli sauce:

**1 recipe beef sauce Italian style
(See Agnolotti alla ghiotta con ragu, p. 72)**

3/4 cup (3 oz.) grated Parmesan cheese

For filling: Press ricotta through a sieve or food mill into a mixing bowl. Add Parmesan cheese, salt, pepper to taste and eggs (only use 2 yolks if cheese mixture seems too thin).
Prepare and cook ravioli as in Ravioli alla panna gratinati. Place ravioli in a serving dish, adding Italian meat sauce. Sprinkle with grated cheese.

Orecchioni
alla romagnola

Ravioli Romagna style

Serves 4
Difficulty **
Time: 3 hours, excluding time
for drying pasta

1 recipe Basic Pasta

1 lb. ricotta (very fresh)
1 cup (4 oz.) grated Parmesan
cheese
1 egg plus 2 extra yolks
Salt, pepper
1/2 cup (4 oz.) butter

For filling pass ricotta through a
food mill or sieve. In a mixing
bowl, mix with half the Parmesan cheese, eggs and a pinch
of salt.
Prepare and cook as in Ravioli
alla panna gratinati, but cut
dough into 3 inch squares.
Brush with egg, top with 1 teaspoon of filling and fold over to
shape a triangle called an
''orecchioni''. Mix orecchioni
gently with butter, remaining
Parmesan and a good amount
of freshly ground pepper. Serve
immediately.

Orecchioni alla romagnola

Orecchione means "ears" and so, in various parts of Italy, do orec-
chie, orecchiette, recchietelle and ricch'tell. Pasta bearing these names
may be of various sizes and textures, but they are all, as you have certainly suspected, ear-shaped. They are not given this form (with a deft
dig of the pasta maker's thumb) with purely decorative intent, though
the decorative motive is certainly never absent from Italian cooking;
the shape traps whatever sauce is served on orecchione, turning each
piece into a juicy cup of flavor. Many of these ear-shaped pastas are
stuffed.

Agnolotti alla ghiotta con ragú

*Agnolotti
with meat sauce*

Serves 4
Difficulty **
Time: 3 hours

For meat sauce:

2 tbsp. chopped prosciutto fat
2 tbsp. chopped pork fat
1 celery stalk
1/2 clove garlic
1/2 small onion
1/4 lb. ground (minced) rump
of beef
Salt, pepper
1 small bouquet garni made of
thyme, marjoram and bay leaf
1 whole clove
1/2 a 1 oz. package dried
mushrooms, soaked in warm
water
1/4 cup red wine
1 tsp. flour
2 cups chopped tomato pulp
(skin and seeds removed)
2 cups boiling water

For filling:

1/2 small onion
1/4 cup (2 oz.) chopped rather
fat prosciutto crudo
2 tbsp. butter
3 tbsp. olive oil
3/4 lb. minced veal or chicken
1/2 cup dry white wine
Salt, pepper
Nutmeg
1/2 cup beef broth (approx.)
1/4 cup grated Parmesan cheese
1 egg

1 recipe Basic Pasta

To complete dish:

2 tbsp. butter
3/4 cup (3 oz.) grated Parmesan
cheese

Agnolotti alla ghiotta con ragu

For meat sauce put prosciutto fat and pork fat in a casserole. Add all the vegetables, finely chopped, and cook until vegetables soften and begin to change color. Add the meat, season with salt and pepper and brown. Then add bouquet garni, clove and mushrooms well washed and chopped. Cook over low heat, stirring frequently. When meat is well browned, add red wine and cook until liquid is reduced. Add flour, stir and add strained tomato pulp. Add water and continue cooking very slowly, stirring frequently until sauce is thick, about 40 to 45 minutes.

For filling put onion and prosciutto in a frying pan with butter and oil. When transparent, add meat, mix and brown. Add white wine, and, when completely evaporated, season with salt, pepper and a pinch of nutmeg. Add broth and simmer another 5 minutes. Continue cooking until mixture is firm and dry, remove from heat, add Parmesan cheese and, when cool, stir in egg.

Prepare and cook agnolotti as in Ravioli alla panna gratinati, cutting each ravioli with a 2-1/2-inch oval cutter to make agnolotti. Place agnolotti on a heated serving platter. Dot with butter, cover with meat sauce and sprinkle with Parmesan cheese.

Cappelletti alla panna

*Cappelletti
–round ravioli–
with cream*

Serves 6
Difficulty **
Time: 2 hours, excluding time
for drying pasta

For filling:

2 tbsp. butter
1 tbsp. olive oil
9 oz. boneless raw turkey
or chicken meat, diced
1/4 cup (2 oz.) chopped
prosciutto crudo
1 slice mortadella, chopped
Salt, pepper
2 sage leaves
2 chicken livers
2 tbsp. Marsala wine
1/2 cup (4 oz.) ricotta, sieved
2/3 cup grated Parmesan
2 tbsp. dry bread crumbs
1 egg
Nutmeg

1 recipe Basic Pasta

For sauce:

1/4 cup (2 oz.) butter
2 sage leaves
3/4 cup heavy cream
Salt, pepper
1/2 cup grated Parmesan

Cappelletti ("little hats", from their shape) are, like ravioli and tortellini, stuffed. Such picturesquely shaped pastas are not rare; you have also, for instance, sleeves, half-sleeves, bows, tresses, seashells, snail shells, butterflies, tongues, sparrows' tongues, wolf eyes, three fingers, wheels, spirals, stars, spindles, cockscombs, roses, lilies of the valley, wires, strings, hairs, seeds, melon seeds, peppercorns, and Florentine snow. Outsiders from countries where pasta is not so minutely studied may look upon this as mere fantasy. Not so: all these different shapes, with their different textures and their different types of dough, are matched precisely with the many kinds of sauces which can accompany them to arrive in each case at the combination which will produce the tastiest result.

For filling: Melt butter in a saucepan with oil, add poultry meat, prosciutto and mortadella. Salt and pepper meat only slightly. Add sage leaves and chicken livers. Saute until all meats are brown and tender, about 10 minutes. Add Marsala and simmer until it evaporates. Remove pan from heat, remove sage leaves and chop or grind meat mixture until very fine. Transfer chopped meats to a bowl and add ricotta, Parmesan, bread crumbs, egg, a bit of freshly ground nutmeg and mix well. Season to taste with salt.
Prepare pasta and roll out dough thinly on a floured surface. Cut into 2-1/2-inch rounds. Brush rounds with beaten egg and top with 1 teaspoon filling. Pull up edges around filling and pinch together tightly to look like a drawstring bag.

For sauce: Melt the butter in a saucepan with sage leaves. When butter begins to foam, add cream and heat. Season to taste with salt and a little pepper. Cook cappelletti in boiling salted water. Drain al dente and rinse with hot water. Place in serving bowl. Pour over cream sauce. Let dish stand for a few minutes and serve sprinkled with grated Parmesan cheese.

VARIATION:

Cappelletti alla romagnola di magro

*Meatless cappelletti
Romagna style*

For seasoning:

1/2 cup (4 oz.) butter, cooked
until brown
1 cup (4 oz.) grated Parmesan
cheese

For filling:

1 cup (8 oz.) ricotta cheese,
strained
1-1/4 cups (5 oz.) grated
mozzarella cheese

1/2 cup (2 oz.) grated Parmesan
cheese
1 egg and 1 egg yolk
Salt
Nutmeg

1 recipe Basic Pasta

Combine ricotta, mozzarella cheese, Parmesan, 1 whole egg and 1 yolk with a pinch of salt and nutmeg. Prepare and cook cappelletti as in Cappelletti alla panna, using cheese filling. Toss with brown butter and Parmesan cheese.

Pasticcio di maccheroncelli alla toscana

Macaroni pie

Serves 6
Difficulty ***
Time: 2-1/2 hours, excluding time for crust dough to rest
Oven Temp. 350° F.

For filling:

1 small onion, chopped
1 small carrot, chopped
1/2 cup butter
3/4 lb. beef, cut into cubes
1/2 lb. chicken giblets, chopped
7 tbsp. dry white wine
1-1/2 cups chopped tomato pulp (skin and seeds removed)
Salt, freshly ground black pepper
1 pinch thyme and bay leaf, crumbled
1/2 cup chicken broth
1/4 lb. fresh mushrooms, sliced
3/4 cup (3 oz.) grated Parmesan cheese
3/4 lb. maccheroncelli (macaroni)

For butter crust:

1/2 cup butter
2-1/4 cups all-purpose flour
3 egg yolks
1/2 tsp. salt

For crust: Cut butter into flour until particles are very fine. Stir in egg yolks and salt. Knead dough a few times on a floured surface. Wrap in a cloth and chill for about 40 minutes.

For filling: Saute onion and carrot in 1/3 cup of the butter. Add beef cubes and chopped chicken giblets, mix well and continue cooking. Pour in wine and let it evaporate almost entirely, then mix in tomato pulp. Season with salt, pepper, thyme and bay leaf, add broth and mushrooms and cook for about 30 minutes.
Break macaroni into 2-inch pieces. Cook them in lightly salted boiling water, drain while still al dente and rinse with hot water. Mix macceroncelli with half the meat sauce, remaining butter and 2 tablespoons of the grated Parmesan cheese.

Preparation of final dish: Roll out dough on a floured surface into two thin pie crusts, one large enough to line a 9-inch pie pan, the other large enough to cover it. Grease pie pan, line it with larger sheet of dough, fill with macaroni mixture and cover with second sheet of dough. Press two crusts together to seal by crimping edges. Punch a small hole in upper crust and insert a piece of paper tightly rolled to serve as a vent for steam during cooking and bake the "pasticcio" in a preheated oven for 40 to 45 minutes or until crust is brown. Cut into wedges and serve with remaining grated cheese and meat sauce.

Rigatoni ripieni

Stuffed rigatoni

Serves 6
Difficulty *
Time: 1-1/2 hours, excluding time for refrigerating casserole
Oven Temp. 400° F.

1 lb. rigatoni
1 can (7 oz.) tuna, drained and flaked
1 cup (8 oz.) ricotta cheese, sieved
1 cup heavy cream
2 cups (8 oz.) grated Parmesan cheese
Salt, pepper
1 tbsp. butter

Rigatoni is tube-shaped pasta with a ribbed corduroy-like exterior. It comes in fairly short lengths, and may be straight or elbow-shaped. It comes in various sizes, but is necessarily always fairly wide; otherwise there would be no room for the ribbing. It is thus, like cannelloni, ideal for stuffing, boiling and baking.

Cook rigatoni al dente in boiling salted water. Mix tuna and ricotta until a soft paste. Mix cream and Parmesan, salt and pepper to taste. When rigatoni are drained, rinse with hot water. Load a pastry syringe or pastry bag with a large round opening with tuna and ricotta and squeeze a little into each rigatoni. Put rigatoni in a buttered (use 1 tablespoon) pyrex dish side by side. Pour cream and Parmesan mixture over them and refrigerate several hours. When ready to serve, bake in a preheated oven for 25 to 30 minutes or until brown and hot.

Pasta 'ncasciata alla siciliana

Baked pasta Sicilian

Serves 4
Difficulty *
Time: 3 hours, excluding time for drying pasta
Oven Temp. 375° F.

1 recipe Basic Pasta

For meat sauce:

3/4 lb. boneless pork in one piece
7 tbsp. oil
1/3 cup chopped prosciutto fat
1 green onion, chopped
1 small carrot, chopped
1 clove garlic, chopped
1/2 cup chopped celery
4 cups chopped tomato pulp (skin and seeds removed)
Salt, pepper
4 hard cooked eggs
3/4 cup (3 oz.) grated Parmesan cheese

Prepare pasta. Cut dough with a sharp knife into strips 1-inch wide. For sauce: Brown pork in oil and prosciutto fat. Add onion, carrot, garlic, celery and tomato pulp. Season with salt and pepper. Add 1-1/2 cups cold water, bring to a boil, cover and continue cooking for about 2 hours or until meat is tender. Remove meat and chop it coarsely. Return meat to sauce. Simmer, stirring occasionally until sauce is desired consistency.

Cook pasta in boiling salted water. Drain it while al dente and rinse with hot water. Grease a 2-quart baking dish and fill it with a layer of pasta followed by a layer of meat sauce and slices of hard cooked egg and Parmesan cheese, and continue layering, ending with Parmesan cheese. Bake in a preheated oven for 20 to 25 minutes or until piping hot and lightly browned.

Maniche di frate alla caprese

Stuffed giant macaroni Capri style

Serves 4
Difficulty **
Time: 1-1/2 hours
Oven Temp. 400° F.

2 eggplants (aubergines) (small)
Salt, pepper
1 small onion, chopped
5 tbsp. butter
3/4 cup olive oil
1/2 lb. ground (minced) round beef
1/4 lb. sweet Italian sausage removed from casing
1 bay leaf
2 cloves
2 tbsp. dry white wine
1-1/4 lbs. ripe tomatoes, sieved, or 1 can (1 lb.) Italian peeled tomatoes, drained and sieved
1/3 cup flour
2 cups milk
1 lb. giant grooved macaroni
1 egg
Dry bread crumbs, about 3 cups

Cut ends off eggplants, peel, cut into 1/2-inch thick slices lengthwise. Salt slices and let stand in a bowl for 1 hour. Drain slices. Saute onion in 1 tablespoon of the butter and 3 tablespoons of the oil. Add beef and sausage meat. Saute until meat is brown and crumbly. Drain excess fat. Add bay leaf, cloves and wine. Simmer until wine evaporates. Add tomatoes. Cover and cook over low heat, stirring often for 15 minutes. If it becomes too dry, add a little hot water. Before removing from heat thicken with 1 teaspoon of the flour mixed with 1 tablespoon water. Remove cloves and bay leaf. While this sauce is cooking, prepare a bechamel sauce: melt remaining butter and stir in flour. Gradually stir in milk. Stir over low heat until smooth and thick. Season to taste with salt and pepper.

Cook giant macaroni in boiling salted water, draining while still fairly al dente. Dry on a kitchen towel, then using a teaspoon stuff them with meat sauce. Put a layer of bechamel in bottom of a 9x13x2 pyrex baking dish; cover with a layer of stuffed macaroni, then repeat with a layer of bechamel and another of macaroni. Dry eggplant slices, dip in beaten egg and then into crumbs and fry in remaining hot oil until brown on both sides. Drain well. Place eggplant slices in baking dish in an even layer over pasta. Top with remaining bechamel. Brown in preheated hot oven (400° F.) for 20 to 25 minutes or until brown.

Optional: Sprinkle with grated Parmesan before browning.

Basic Potato Gnocchi

Serves 4

2 lbs. potatoes
2-3/4 cups (approx.) all-purpose flour
1 tsp. salt
1 egg
Nutmeg

Cook potatoes in lightly salted boiling water. Drain and peel when tender and put them through a food mill or potato ricer while they are still hot. Place potatoes in a bowl, cool, then stir in flour, salt and egg. Knead dough on a floured surface until smooth and elastic and does not stick to the fingers. If necessary add more flour (the amount of flour varies with the moisture content of the potatoes*). Add nutmeg, if desired. Shape gnocchi into long rolls (3/8 inch diameter). Cut each roll into 1-1/4 inch lengths and with a finger press each gnocchi against a fork or a cheese grater to roughen the surface on one side and to make a dent in the other where the finger presses. Cook gnocchi half the amount at a time in rapidly boiling salted water. As each comes to the surface, remove it with a slotted spoon. Serve as desired.

* In preparing potato gnocchi it is important to realize that potatoes vary in moisture content. This will make it necessary to add flour in varying amounts. The best way to test the gnocchi, to make sure they will not fall apart in the boiling water, is to drop one into the water. If it floats and cooks without becoming mushy prepare the remainning gnocchi. If it falls apart, it is time to knead in more flour. But knead in only a small amount at a time since too much flour can produce gnocchi that are rubbery and tough. Left-over gnocchi can also be sliced and fried until brown in oil and served as a substitute for potatoes.

Gnocchi di patate con pesto

Potato gnocchi with pesto

Serves 4
Difficulty *
Time: 1-1/2 hours

4 sprigs fresh basil
1 clove garlic
1 cup (4 oz.) grated Pecorino or Parmesan cheese

1 cup olive oil
Salt

1 recipe Potato Gnocchi, see basic recipe

Grind basil and garlic using a mortar and pestle or a blender. The garlic may be left out if you don't care for it. Put this pesto in a mixing bowl and beat in half the Pecorino (or Parmesan) cheese and oil. Season to taste with salt if necessary. Leave at room temperature to mellow flavors. Prepare and cook gnocchi as directed in basic recipe. Place gnocchi in a serving bowl, tossing gently with pesto and sprinkling with remaining grated cheese.

Gnocchi alla romagnola

Gnocchi Romagna style

Serves 4
Difficulty **
Time: 2-1/2 hours

1 recipe Potato Gnocchi,
  see basic recipe

1/4 cup bacon fat
1/2 carrot
1/4 of an onion
1/4 cup (2 oz.) butter
9 oz. lean beef (rump) ground
(minced)
1 bay leaf
Nutmeg, salt, pepper
7 tbsp. red wine
1-1/2 cups chopped tomato pulp
(skin and seeds removed)
1/2 cup (4 oz.) tomato paste
1/2 cup beef broth, (approx.)
3/4 cup (3 oz.) grated Parmesan

Pasta is not always pasta—that is to say, its slot in the meal is sometimes filled by another cereal dish which the eater recognizes instinctively as belonging to the same general category. Indeed if one is not attentive one may not always realize that one is not being served pasta proper, expecially if the substitute is the dish which resembles it most closely, gnocchi. (People were not particularly inattentive during the Renaissance, yet they often referred to gnocchi as macaroni). One might think that the Italians consider gnocchi as an insipid dish, for they have borrowed its name to describe a simple-minded person, who is called a *gnocco*—a close parallel to the English puddinghead or the French *tête de lard*. Furthermore, the official translation for gnocchi is "dumplings", a dish which does not suggest much finesse to Anglo-Saxons, Scandinavians or Central Europeans. Nevertheless the Italians make of it a creamy melt-in-your-mouth work of art which far transcends its humble beginnings. The gnocchi family is numerous; one branch uses mashed potatoes as its base, another starts out with polenta, and another with flour.

Prepare, shape and cook gnocchi as described in basic recipe. Chop bacon, carrot and onion and saute in 2 tablespoons of the butter; add meat, bay leaf and season with salt, pepper and nutmeg. Continue cooking until meat is browned. Add red wine, turn up heat to evaporate it, then add tomato pulp chopped fine and tomato paste, diluted in broth. Bring to a boil, lower heat and continue cooking at moderate heat for about 1 hour, adding additional hot broth from time to time. Remove bay leaf.
Drain gnocchi and season with remaining butter, cut into pieces, half the meat sauce and half the Parmesan. Pass remaining meat sauce and remaining Parmesan as you serve the gnocchi.

Gnocchi alla romagnola

79

Gnocchi di patate alla romana

*Potato gnocchi
Roman style*

Serves 4
Difficulty **
Time: 2 hours

---

1 recipe Potato Gnocchi, see basic recipe

1 onion, chopped	**1/4 cup butter**
2 tbsp. olive oil	**Salt**
3 cups chopped tomato pulp	**1 cup (4 oz.) grated Parmesan**
(skin and seeds removed)	**cheese**

Prepare, shape and cook gnocchi as described in basic recipe. Saute onion in oil until transparent. Pass tomato pulp through a food mill, add to onion and cook. Drain gnocchi and toss with butter, tomato sauce, salt and Parmesan.

Polenta sometimes appears where pasta might be expected, especially if it is in its porridge-like form; but it turns up more often later in the meal with various accompaniments—serving, for example, as a sort of raft to carry a miniature flock of tiny birds (*polenta e osei*). It is one of the oldest dishes in the Italian repertory, the *pulmentum* of the ancient Romans, who got it from the Etruscans, who may themselves have borrowed it from the Greeks, where we meet it in the Odyssey when Telemachus comes upon Nestor eating a dish of gruel; it was also the chief food of Spartan boys submitted to the harsh upbringing imposed upon them by Lycurgus. Today it is usually, though not always, made from a flour the ancients never knew—cornmeal. It was probably first made of millet or barley, and later of wheat; it is still occasionally made of wheat or even buckwheat—the latter especially in the Alps. It is in the Alps also that polenta is often served as a sort of mush with the consistency of oatmeal. Elsewhere it is usually thicker, and though it may be porridge-like if eaten hot, is usually allowed to harden, after which it can be sliced and handled like bread or cake. It is eaten in this form in England by persons who would certainly maintain that polenta is unknown there; but what else is Yorkshire pudding? This was a gift to England of the Roman Legions who made their headquarters at Eburacum—York.

Gnocchi alla fiorentina

Gnocchi Florentine

Serves 4
Difficulty *
Time: 1 hour
Oven Temp. 375°F.

**1 lb. spinach, trimmed
6 cups milk
1 cup (5 oz.) semolina
6 tbsp. butter
Salt
1-1/2 cups (6 oz.) grated
Parmesan
1 egg and 2 egg yolks
6 tbsp. flour**

Wash and cook spinach until tender in water left on leaves. Press out all water after cooking and pass spinach through a food mill or sieve. Bring 2 cups of the milk to the boiling point and sprinkle in semolina. Add 2 pinches of salt, 2 tablespoons of the butter and continue cooking for about 6 to 7 minutes, stirring constantly. Remove from heat and mix in spinach, 1/3 of the grated Parmesan cheese, 1 whole egg and 2 additional yolks. Let it cool.

For bechamel sauce: Melt 2 tablespoons of the butter, stir in flour. Gradually stir in remaining milk which has been heated to lukewarm. Stir over low heat until sauce thickens. Stir in 1/2 of the remaining Parmesan. Butter a shallow 1-1/2 quart baking dish and spoon out egg-shaped mounds of spinach mixture, using a moistened spoon to round off spoonfuls. Arrange mounds in a single layer in baking dish. Spoon over the bechamel and sprinkle with remaining Parmesan. Dot with remaining butter and bake in a preheated oven for 20 to 25 minutes or until lightly browned.

Polenta

Polenta

Polenta Basic Recipe

Serves 6
Difficulty *
Time: 1 hour

6 cups water
1 heaping tbsp. coarse salt
2-2/3 cups (1 lb.) yellow
cornmeal

Polenta is best cooked in a copper pot. Bring water to a boil, add salt. Lower heat and sift in cornmeal a little at a time, stirring vigorously at all times to avoid sticking or formation of lumps. Cook polenta for at least 45 minutes, stirring occasionally. The flavor of the polenta can be improved by using half water and half milk instead of only water. When it is cooked, pour it out onto a platter in a mound and cover it with a cloth to keep it hot. Serve as is, or cool and cut into desired shapes.

If you wish, you can first pour the polenta into a moistened 1-1/2 quart dish. Let it stand for 5 minutes then invert dish onto a serving platter. Cut polenta into portion size pieces.

In preparing polenta dishes use yellow cornmeal. The fine grind sold in most supermarkets is adequate but the best texture polenta is made by mixing half and half, the fine and the coarse ground cornmeals. The coarse grind is found in Italian, Spanish or health food stores. The polenta should be stirred and cooked over very low heat for a long time until thick to develop the best flavor. If any polenta is left from the first day pour or spoon it into a pan and chill. It can be then cut into slices, rounds, triangles, cubes and fried in butter and served instead of potatoes. Brown and crusty with a crunchy texture it can be delicious.

Gnocchetti gialli al burro e salvia

Gnocchetti gialli al burro e salvia

Yellow gnocchetti with butter and sage

Serves 4
Difficulty *
Time: 1-1/2 hours
Oven Temp. 350° F.

1 Polenta basic recipe
1/2 cup (4 oz.) butter, heated until golden brown

6 sage leaves
1/2 cup (2 oz.) grated Parmesan

Prepare polenta, remove from heat and, using a wet spoon, scoop out small pieces and slide them into a buttered baking dish. Cover each layer of gnocchetti with butter and sage leaves. Sprinkle with grated Parmesan and bake in a preheated oven for 15 to 20 minutes or until brown.

Polenta mantecata

Boiled polenta with cheese

Serves 6
Difficulty *
Time: 1 hour
Oven Temp. 400° F.

4 oz. thinly sliced Fontina cheese
1 cup milk
1 polenta basic recipe

4 oz. Crescenza (soft Italian cheese) or mozzarella, diced
1/2 cup (4 oz.) Gorgonzola, diced
1/2 cup (4 oz.) butter

Put Fontina slices in a bowl and cover with milk. Prepare basic polenta using water, salt and cornmeal. Remove from heat and add Crescenza, Gorgonzola and butter (reserving a teaspoon of the butter). Stir thoroughly until all ingredients are well blended. Butter a shallow 1-1/2 quart baking dish with reserved butter and fill with polenta, spreading mixture into an even layer. Smooth with a spatula. Cover with slices of Fontina removed from milk. Bake in a preheated oven for 10 minutes and serve.

Polenta con besciamella

Polenta with bechamel cream sauce

Serves 6
Difficulty *
Time: 1 hour, excluding time for making polenta
Oven Temp. 400° F.

1 polenta basic recipe (p. 81)
1/4 cup (2 oz.) butter
6 tbsp. flour
2 cups milk, heated to boiling
1/2 cup (2 oz.) grated Parmesan cheese
1/2 lb. sliced Gruyere (or Swiss) cheese

Prepare polenta. Turn it out onto a platter and let it cool in a mound. If dish is planned for lunch, it is better to cook polenta the day before. If it is to be served at the evening meal, it should be cooked in the morning. Cut cold polenta into 1/2-inch thick slices, using a sharp knife.
Melt 2/3 of the butter in a pan and stir in flour. Let mixture brown slightly, then gradually stir in hot milk. Stir constantly over low heat until sauce thickens. Season with a little salt and pepper and simmer while stirring for 5 minutes. Remove from heat and stir in Parmesan. Spoon a little of this bechamel or cream sauce in the bottom of a greased 1-1/2 quart baking dish. Cover with slices of polenta, add another layer of bechamel, top with a few slices of Gruyere, and continue making layers this way until all ingredients have been used. The final layer should be cream sauce. Dot with remaining butter and bake in a preheated oven for 20 minutes or until lightly browned.

Polenta pasticciata

Polenta pie

Serves 6
Difficulty *
Time: 1-1/2 hours, excluding time
needed to prepare polenta
Oven Temp. 400°F.

Polenta pasticciata

1 polenta basic recipe (p. 81)
1 pkg. (1 oz.) dried mushrooms
1/2 small onion, chopped
1/2 stalk celery, chopped
1 carrot, chopped
1/4 cup (2 oz.) butter
2 tbsp. olive oil
1/2 lb. chopped beef
1/2 lb. (bulk) sausage meat
Salt, pepper
1/3 cup red wine
1 tbsp. tomato paste
1 cup beef broth
1 bay leaf
6 juniper berries
1 tbsp. flour
1/2 cup grated Parmesan cheese

Prepare polenta, cool and then cut into slices 1/4-inch thick. Soak dried mushrooms in water. Drain and chop. Saute onion, celery and carrot in butter and oil. Add beef and brown, then add sausage. Salt lightly and season with pepper and stir in mushrooms. Pour in wine, simmer until it evaporates. Stir in tomato paste mixed with broth, bay leaf and juniper berries. Continue cooking over low heat for 15 minutes. Before removing sauce from heat, thicken it with a little flour if necessary. Remove bay leaf and juniper berries.
Grease a 2-quart shallow baking dish and fill it with alternate layers of sauce, polenta slices and grated Parmesan. The final layer should be sauce. Bake in a preheated oven for 20 to 25 minutes.

Polenta con intingolo di coniglio

Polenta with rabbit sauce

Serves 6
Difficulty *
Time: 2 hours

1 polenta basic recipe
2 tbsp. chopped onion
3 or 4 sage leaves
1/4 cup (2 oz.) butter

2 lbs. boneless rabbit meat, chopped
Salt, pepper
7 tbsp. dry white wine
1 cup sieved tomato pulp

Prepare polenta (see Polenta basic recipe). While polenta is cooking, prepare rabbit sauce. Saute onion and sage in butter; add rabbit meat. Season with salt and pepper and brown, stirring frequently. Add wine and boil until wine evaporates. Add tomato pulp. Bring to a boil, cover and simmer until rabbit meat is well done (add a little hot water if it gets too dry) about 1 hour.
Pour polenta out onto a moistened baking sheet and spread to a thickness of about 1/2 inch. Cut into 6 pieces, put a piece on each plate and cover with rabbit sauce.

In preparing rice dishes use only the converted rice or Italian round grain rice sold in Italian shops. The converted rice stays separate-grained and has the chewy consistency just right for all the rice dishes. It is important to stir rice occasionally during cooking to prevent sticking. Cook only until rice has absorbed all the liquid and also serve immediately, to prevent rice from becoming dry.

Rice is not an Italian grain; it was brought in from the East by the returning Crusaders; but it was developed to such high quality in the valley of the Po that Italian rice has led in Europe ever since. Its superiority was so evident to Thomas Jefferson that he violated Italian law by smuggling some of it out to replant it in the United States. Italy is not only Europe's leading rice producer, she is also the most skilled in cooking it. During Renaissance times, rice was usually sweetened and served as a dessert, perhaps partly because cane sugar had reached Italy at the same time, from the same source. Rice desserts still remain, but they are greatly outnumbered nowadays by the multitude of unsweetened rice dishes, whose varieties are literally uncountable.

Riso e uva alla veneziana

Rice and grapes Venetian style

Serves 4
Difficulty*
Time: 1-1/2 hours

1 cup Malaga grapes
1 clove garlic, chopped
2 tbsp. chopped parsley

2 tbsp. olive oil
2 cups (1 lb.) rice
1/2 cup grated Parmesan

Wash grapes, drain and remove seeds. Saute garlic and parsley in oil, pour in the rice, stir until rice is golden. Add boiling salted water and simmer until rice is tender, about 20 to 25 minutes. Drain. Stir in grapes and Parmesan.

Riso e chnolle

Rice with polenta balls

Serves 4
Difficulty **
Time: 2 hours plus 2 hours chilling time
Oven Temp. 400° F.

Using milk, cornmeal and a pinch of salt prepare polenta (see page 81). Let the polenta cool for 5 minutes, then beat in Parmesan and eggs. Chill for 2 hours. Shape into balls 1 inch in diameter. Cook rice in plenty of salted water for 20 minutes or until firm but tender. Drain and place in a bowl and mix in fontina. Put polenta gnocchetti in a greased 9×13×2 inches baking dish, and spoon over rice mixture. Pour melted butter over top. Place in preheated oven for about 15 minutes. Serve piping hot in the baking dish.

3 cups milk
1-1/2 cups cornmeal
Salt
1/2 cup grated Parmesan
5 eggs

1-1/2 cups natural rice
1/2 lb. Valle d'Aosta fontina cheese, cubed
1/3 cup butter, melted

Riso e chnolle

What is the difference between a rice dish, period, and a risotto? The technical answer is that rice dishes not otherwise identified are usually made from boiled rice; a risotto is steamed. (I cannot guarantee that popular usage does not sometimes ride roughshod over this definition.) There is sometimes a tendency to confuse risotti with pilafs, but they are not the same; a pilaf is cooked in the Oriental fashion, that is to say in a liquid (for instance, bouillon) which is completely absorbed by the rice. Like boiled rice, risotti can assume an uncountable number of forms.

Risotto alla sbirraglia

Rice policeman style

Serves 6
Difficulty **
Time: 1-1/2 hours

1 chicken, fryer (including giblets) about 3 lbs.	Salt, pepper
1/2 lb. beef, cut into 1/2-inch cubes	1/4 cup (2 oz.) chopped bacon
2 stalks celery, chopped	1/4 cup butter
2 small carrots, chopped	1/2 cup dry white wine
1 onion, chopped	3 tomatoes
	1-1/4 lbs. rice
	2/3 cup Parmesan cheese

Skin and bone raw chicken and cut into pieces. Put bones into a pot, together with beef, liver and gizzard of chicken and half of the celery, carrots and onion. Cover with 8 cups water, add salt to taste and simmer covered until beef is tender, about 1 hour. Put bacon and remaining vegetables in a saucepan with half the butter and saute until vegetables are tender. Put vegetables and drippings through a food mill and return to saucepan. Add pieces of chicken; season with salt and pepper to taste and brown them over a rather high heat. Add wine and simmer uncovered until liquid evaporates. Put tomatoes into boiling water for an instant, peel them and cut them into big pieces; add to saucepan and continue cooking for 10 minutes. Drain broth from chicken bones into a large saucepan, bring to a boil and add rice. Cook until liquid is absorbed and rice is tender. Remove from heat and stir in remaining butter and grated Parmesan. Spoon rice onto a platter and top with chicken and tomato sauce.

Risotto alla sbirraglia

Risotto alla maggiorana

Rice with marjoram

Serves 4
Difficulty *
Time: 45 minutes

2 ripe tomatoes
1/2 cup butter
2 cups (1 lb.) rice
1/2 cup dry white wine
4 cups (1 quart) boiling
chicken broth

1 tbsp. chopped fresh thyme
1 tbsp. chopped fresh marjoram
Salt
1/4 cup grated Parmesan cheese

Peel tomatoes, remove seeds and cut pulp into strips. Melt half the butter in a saucepan, add rice and heat for a few minutes, stirring continuously. Add wine and broth gradually while stirring. When rice is about half cooked, add strips of tomato pulp. When rice is three-quarters cooked, add thyme and marjoram. Taste and, if necessary, season with salt. When rice is cooked, remove from heat and stir in remaining butter and Parmesan. If necessary, stir in additional broth to moisten rice and let it stand for a few minutes before serving.

Risotto alla milanese

Risotto Milanese

Serves 4
Difficulty *
Time: 1 hour

1/2 cup (4 oz.) butter
2 tbsp. chopped beef marrow
1/2 small onion, chopped
Salt, pepper
1/2 cup dry white wine

2 cups (1 lb.) rice
1 tsp. crumbled saffron
4 cups (1 quart) chicken broth,
(approx.)
1/2 cup grated Parmesan

Melt half of the butter in a saucepan. Add beef marrow, onion and a pinch each of salt and pepper. When onion is tender but not brown, add wine and let it boil until half its original volume. Stir in rice. Dissolve saffron in broth and add to pan. Stir to keep rice from sticking. When broth is simmering stir occasionally and cook until rice is cooked al dente and liquid is absorbed. Add more broth from time to time, if necessary, to prevent sticking. Stir in remaining butter and grated Parmesan. Let stand over very low heat for a few minutes, then serve.

Risotto alla milanese

Risotto alla paesana

Risotto country style

Serves 4
Difficulty *
Time: 2 hours

1 small onion, chopped
2 tbsp. olive oil
1/2 cup shelled peas
12 raw asparagus tips
2 small zucchini, sliced
Chicken broth (approx. 6 cups)
2-1/4 cups chopped tomato pulp
(skin and seeds removed)

1/2 cup cut green beans
Salt, pepper
2 cups (1 lb.) rice
1/4 cup butter
3/4 cup (3 oz.) grated Parmesan
cheese

Saute onion in oil until transparent. Add peas, asparagus tips and zucchini and continue cooking for 1 minute. Add 1 cup of the broth and continue cooking over moderate heat for 10 minutes. Add tomato pulp and beans and season with salt and pepper. Simmer for another 15 minutes. Stir in rice and add enough broth as may be needed and simmer until rice is cooked and liquid is absorbed. Add butter and half of the Parmesan cheese and mix well. Let dish stand for a minute, then serve with remaining Parmesan cheese.

Risotto con punte di asparagi

Risotto with asparagus tips

Serves 6
Difficulty *
Time: 45 minutes
Oven Temp. 400°F.

1-1/4 lbs. asparagus
2 tbsp. butter
2-1/2 cups (1-1/4 lbs.) rice
6 cups (1-1/2 quarts) boiling chicken broth
1/2 cup (2 oz.) grated Parmesan

Cut off the tough part of the asparagus stalks, leaving only the tender upper stalks and tips. Cut off tips, peel the upper stalks and wash in running cold water. Reserve tips. Cut stalks into thin slices. In a fairly large saucepan melt butter, and as soon as it is melted, add rice, asparagus stalk slices and 1/2 cup of the boiling broth. Stir rice and gradually add remaining broth. After rice has cooked for about 15 minutes, add asparagus tips and simmer for another 7 or 8 minutes or until rice is tender. Remove from heat and stir in grated Parmesan.

A variation: If you wish to serve individual portions, make six portions in custard cups, keeping the asparagus tips aside. Put custard cups in oven for about 5 minutes, loosen edges with a knife and turn out onto plates. Saute asparagus tips in butter until tender. Decorate rice with asparagus tips.

Risotto verde

Green rice

1 small onion, chopped
1/4 cup (2 oz.) butter
1 tbsp. olive oil
1 lb. rice
8 cups (approx.) boiling chicken or beef broth
1 lb. spinach (or greens)
1 cup heavy cream
3/4 cup (3 oz.) Parmesan cheese
Salt

Serves 4   Difficulty *   Time: 1 hour

Saute onion in half the butter and oil. Add rice, stirring with a wooden spoon. Let it brown for a minute or two, then gradually, as rice cooks, add hot broth. While rice is cooking clean spinach, wash well in cold running water and steam it (the water left from the washing phase is enough to steam the spinach). Drain, squeeze excess moisture out and then chop fine. Add chopped spinach to rice while rice is still al dente. At last moment add cream and Parmesan and mix until well blended. Season to taste with salt. Serve in a bowl, garnished with remaining butter cut into pieces. This dish may also be served with small squares of bread fried in olive oil.

Risotto alla paesana

Risotto alla monzese

*Monza rice
—variation of Milanese
risotto*

Serves 6
Difficulty *
Time: 30 minutes

1/2 onion, chopped
1 lb. rice
1 tbsp. olive oil
1 tbsp. butter
1 tsp. crumbled saffron

1/2 cup dry white wine
6 cups (1-1/2 quarts) boiling beef
or chicken broth
1/2 lb. sweet Italian sausage
3 tbsp. grated Parmesan cheese

Saute onion and rice in oil and butter until golden. Add saffron, wine and boiling broth (add broth little by little). Cook until rice is tender but still firm. Meanwhile, cook sausage until brown. Sprinkle grated Parmesan over rice. Toss and spoon into serving dish. Cut sausage into 1/4 inch crosswise slices and sprinkle on top of rice.

Risotto di mare

*Seafood risotto
with crab*

Serves 4
Difficulty *
Time: 1-1/2 hours

2 blue shell crabs
or 1 Dungeness crab
1 lb. shrimp
2 carrots, chopped
2 ribs celery, chopped
1/4 cup parsley

1/2 onion, chopped
2 tbsp. butter
3 tbsp. olive oil
2 cups (1 lb.) rice
1/2 cup dry white wine
Salt, pepper

Wash shellfish and half-cook in a court bouillon consisting of 6 cups salted water flavored with half of the carrots, celery and parsley. Reserve court bouillon. Drain shellfish. Crack crab claws and remove meat. Shell shrimp. Put shells in court bouillon and keep simmering over very low heat for 30 minutes. Cut meat of shellfish into small pieces. Saute remaining vegetables and onion in a saucepan with butter and oil. As soon as they are wilted add rice and season with pepper. Mix well and add wine. Add strained court bouillon. Simmer until rice is tender but still firm, stirring occasionally. Stir in shellfish meat and simmer another 5 minutes. Season to taste with salt and pepper.

Risotto
ai frutti di mare

*Seafood risotto with
clams, shrimp and mussels*

Serves 4
Difficulty *
Time: 1 hour

5 large shrimp
2 lbs. mussels (30 mussels)
2 lbs. small clams (12 clams)
1 carrot, chopped
1 onion, chopped
1 stalk celery, chopped

6 sprigs parsley, chopped
1/2 cup olive oil
1/2 cup dry white wine
2 cups (1 lb.) rice
4 cups (1 quart) boiling beef broth
Salt

Shell and wash shrimp. Clean mussel and clam shells with a stiff brush and wash thoroughly under cold running water. Put mussels and clams in a large frying pan over heat, cover and as shells open, remove clams and mussels and discard shells. Reserve juice released by shellfish and strain through cheesecloth.
Saute carrot, onion, celery and parsley in oil in a large frying pan. Add white wine and simmer until it evaporates. Stir in rice and gradually add the reserved juice and broth. Simmer until rice is tender, about 20 minutes. Stir in shrimp, clams and mussels. Add salt to taste (this will take very little salt). Reheat for 5 minutes or until shrimp are cooked. Parmesan should not be used with this risotto

Risotto con funghi

Rice with mushrooms

Serves 4
Difficulty *
Time: 30 minutes

1/4 cup dried mushrooms
2 tbsp. butter
2 tbsp. oil
1 small onion, chopped

1-1/2 cups rice
1/2 cup dry white wine
3 cups chicken broth
1/4 cup grated Parmesan cheese

Soak dried mushrooms in warm water, wash and chop them. Heat butter and oil in a saucepan. Add onion. Saute until onion is transparent, add rice and mushrooms, stir for a few minutes. Add wine and then, gradually, add boiling broth; take care to continue stirring all this time. Simmer until rice is tender, about 17 minutes. Stir in grated Parmesan cheese and serve.

Risotto con rognone al porto

Risotto with lamb kidneys in port

Serves 4
Difficulty *
Time: 1 hour

2 cups (1 lb.) rice
4 cups (1 quart) chicken broth
2/3 cup (5 oz.) butter
1/2 onion, chopped
2 tbsp. chopped parsley
8 lamb kidneys
1/4 lb. cultivated mushrooms
(caps only)

Salt, pepper
1-1/2 tsp. flour
1/4 cup port wine
1 cup (4 oz.) grated Parmesan
2 packages (3 oz. each) cream cheese, cut into small cubes

Cook rice in boiling chicken broth until tender and liquid is absorbed, about 20 minutes. Melt 1/3 of the butter, add onion and parsley and saute over low heat until wilted. Cut fat tubules away from kidneys and slice them 1/2-inch thick. Remove mushroom stems, slice mushroom caps and add to onions. Saute until wilted. Add kidneys. Raise heat and cook for about 10 minutes, stirring frequently. Sprinkle with salt and pepper. Stir in flour mixed until smooth with port wine. Stir well to blend pan juices thoroughly and keep hot while preparing risotto. Stir Parmesan and cream cheese into rice until mixture is well blended. Season to taste with salt. Serve kidneys over rice.

Risotto con scampi

Risotto with shrimp

Serves 4
Difficulty *
Time: 2 hours
Oven Temp. 400°F.

1/2 carrot, chopped
1/4 small onion, chopped
2 tbsp. chopped celery
6 tbsp. butter
1 tbsp. olive oil
1/4 cup brandy
Pinch of thyme

2/3 cup dry white wine
1 lb. raw shrimp, shelled
and deveined
2 cups (1 lb.) rice
6 cups chicken broth, approx.
Salt

Saute chopped vegetables in half of butter and oil. Add brandy and thyme and saute until onion is transparent. Add wine and simmer until liquid is reduced to about one-half. Cut raw shrimp into bite-size pieces, add them to sauteed vegetables and cook for 15 minutes. Keep this shrimp sauce hot while you prepare rice. Add rice to boiling broth. Season with a pinch of salt, bring to a boil once again, then place pan covered in preheated oven for about 20 minutes. Drain rice. Separate grains with a fork and stir in remaining butter. Serve rice topped with shrimp sauce.

SOUPS

I remarked in the preceding section of this book that the Italian meal almost always included pasta. "Aha!" you might say, "but isn't the pasta course frequently replaced by soup?" Sometimes, yes; but soup may be pasta too.

There are two kinds of pasta in the Italian repertory. Only the first was discussed in the pasta chapter—*pasta asciutta*, dry pasta. There is also *pasta in brodo*, pasta in soup. Its simplest form occurs when a fine variety of pasta—vermicelli, say—goes into consommé. More characteristic is the inclusion of pasta in one of the rich vegetable soups classed under the head of minestrone. That the Italian, consciously or unconsciously, classes together his dry pasta and his pasta in soup, is betrayed by another term occasionally used—*minestra asciutta*. Dry soup. And what is dry soup? Why, pasta, of course.

The affinity sensed in Italy between dry pasta and pasta in soup goes all the way back to the Middle Ages, when soup did not mean a liquid dish, but a piece of bread cooked in the liquid; the bread was eaten and the liquid thrown away. (This original meaning of the word "soup" is retained in the English word "sop".) The words "minestrone" and "minestra" come from the Italian verb *ministrare*, which once signified the act of putting the sop in the soup. Italy is still putting the sop in the soup (but it eats the soup too), in the form of pasta. So soup does not replace the pasta course; it *is* the pasta course.

Minestra di riso e fagioli alla genovese

Zuppa Pavese

Egg soup Pavese

Serves 4
Difficulty *
Time: 20 minutes

2 tbsp. butter
2 tbsp. olive oil
Loaf of long French bread,
cut into 1-inch slices
1 quart beef or chicken broth
(See Brodo pieno alla calabrese
or Brodo di manzo con sorbetto
di pomodoro)
4 eggs
1/4 cup grated Parmesan cheese

Put butter and oil in a frying pan over high heat. Fry sliced bread until golden brown on both sides. Heat the broth in a frying pan until it comes to a boil. Break eggs and slide them carefully into simmering broth. When eggs are poached, place toast in soup bowls. Place eggs on toast. Spoon over broth and sprinkle with grated Parmesan.

Zuppa Pavese

Zuppa pavese is a very simple soup with a very pretty legend. The story goes that when François I of France was taken prisoner at the battle of Pavia, a servant girl was told to take a bowl of consommé to him. She thought this not a very dainty dish to set before a king, so she dropped a raw egg into it. This is what zuppa pavese is basically today—an economical soup which, perhaps for that reason, used to be restricted chiefly to family meals at home; it was apparently considered unworthy to put before guests or to figure on the bills of fare of any but workmen's restaurants. I rejoice to discover it more frequently nowadays on restaurant menus, from which I deduce that (1) middle-class Italian restaurants have become less snobbish; or (2) that Italian eaters are nowadays more appreciative of the virtues of simple rustic dishes; or (3) that eggs are now so expensive that no one any longer is ashamed to serve them.

Brodo pieno alla calabrese

Chicken soup Calabrian style

Serves 4
Difficulty *
Time: 2 hours

For chicken broth:

1 young chicken cut-up, plus necks, wings, heads and skinned feet of 3 additional chickens

1 small carrot, chopped
1 leek, chopped
1 tbsp. coarse salt
2 quarts water

For soup:

6 cups basic chicken broth
3 eggs
1 cup dry bread crumbs

1/4 cup grated Pecorino cheese
6 sprigs parsley, chopped

Combine broth ingredients and simmer covered 1-1/2 hours. Skim foam. Strain broth. Makes 6 cups. Beat eggs, stir in bread crumbs, half the grated Pecorino and parsley. As soon as the broth has reached a boil pour in egg mixture, stirring constantly with a whisk. Simmer for a few minutes and serve immediately. Sprinkle with remaining Pecorino.

Brodo di manzo con sorbetto di pomodoro

Beef broth with jellied tomato

Serves 6
Difficulty *
Time: 2 hours plus refrigeration time

For jellied tomato:

6 cups beef broth
2 envelopes unflavored gelatin
3 cups chopped tomato pulp,
(skin and seeds removed)
Salt
1 black truffle, thinly sliced

For broth:

2-1/4 lbs. beef (rump, short
ribs, sirloin tip, lean meat
of shin and shin-bone,
brisket)
1 young chicken (or neck,
wings, feet and carcass)
about 2 lbs.
1 marrow bone, 4 inches long
2 small carrots, chopped

2 leeks, chopped
1 stalk celery, chopped
1 onion, chopped
1 clove garlic, chopped
"Bouquet garni" of thyme, bay
leaf and parsley
1 tbsp. salt, 2 peppercorns
1/2 veal hock (knuckle)
3 quarts water

For broth: Combine broth ingredients in a large pot and simmer covered 1-1/2 hours. Skim foam. Strain through cheesecloth. Boil until 6 cups. Makes 6 cups.

For jellied broth: Stir gelatin into hot broth until dissolved. Pour into consomme cups and chill until firm.

For tomato: Drain tomato pulp as much as possible (the drier the better) and place into a saucepan. Season with salt and stir over high heat until thick. Line a sieve with cheesecloth, place over a bowl. Pour in tomato pulp and let moisture drip out while standing in refrigerator for several hours. Place puree in a bowl and freeze until just hard.
When ready to serve, use a spoon to cut out shapes like plum tomatoes from sherbet and put one on top of each cup of broth. Garnish with thinly sliced black truffle.

Brodo di manzo con sorbetto di pomodoro

Minestra siciliana di riso e asparagi

Minestra estiva
di asparagi

*Summertime
asparagus soup*

Serves 4
Difficulty *
Time: 1 hour

1 lb. asparagus spears,
tough ends trimmed
1/2 cup butter
2 tbsp. flour
3 chicken bouillon cubes
Salt, coarsely ground
white pepper
1 egg yolk
1/2 cup heavy cream
1/2 cup grated Parmesan cheese
6 sprigs parsley, chopped
6 tbsp. chopped cooked ham
4 slices bread, cut into
1/2-inch cubes

Cook asparagus in 2 quarts of lightly salted boiling water (or steam in asparagus cooker). Drain, reserving 6 cups of the cooking water. Cut asparagus into 1-inch pieces. Melt half of the butter in a saucepan. Stir in flour. Gradually stir in asparagus cooking water. Add bouillon cubes, salt and pepper to taste. Simmer for 5 minutes. Beat yolk with cream, 3 tablespoons of the Parmesan and parsley. Pour soup into tureen, add asparagus pieces and ham. Fry bread cubes until golden brown in remaining butter. Serve soup topped with croutons and remaining Parmesan cheese.

Italian dictionaries (or at least the four I have) define minestra as soup—one of them goes so far as to define it as soup with bread in it, which harks back to medieval times. Italian restaurants blithely disregard this from time to time, and lump together on the bill of fare as minestra everything that might serve as a first course (*primo piatto*)—ignoring antipasti, considered as a prelude, not a full-fledged course on its own. Belluno has a dish called minestra which is far from being a soup—it is a pâté of hare—and Modena has one that is a sort of paste of ground veal steak and beef kidneys; *minestra del Paradiso* is pasta made from bread crumbs; and the Polesina even has two dishes described as minestre which are of duck! Minestra meaning soup, however, goes back at least to the Renaissance, when *minestra di passatelli antica* was a favorite of the Manfredi, the ruling family of Faenza. Duke Cesare d'Este preferred *minestra di lasagnotti e fagioli alla faentina*, which contained, besides the pasta and beans specified in its name, a number of other enlivening ingredients. And Tuscany has its *minestra gialla all'imperiale*, a superb cream soup flavored with saffron and almonds.

Minestra siciliana
di riso e asparagi

*Sicilian rice
and asparagus soup*

Serves 4
Difficulty *
Time: 1-1/2 hours

1 lb. asparagus tips *, tough
stems removed
4 strips bacon, chopped
1/2 onion, chopped
1 clove garlic, chopped
6 sprigs parsley, chopped

2 tbsp. olive oil
1/2 cup rice
1/4 lb. caciocavallo cheese
(available in Italian grocery
stores), diced
Salt

Cook asparagus tips for about 12 minutes in lightly salted boiling water to cover. Drain and reserve cooking water, which will be needed later. Add enough water to make 4 cups. Chop asparagus. Saute bacon, onion, garlic and parsley lightly in oil. Pour in reserved asparagus cooking water and bring to a boil. Pour in rice and cook until tender yet firm. A few minutes before removing from heat, stir in cheese and asparagus. Season to taste with salt and serve immediately.

* Out of season this soup can be prepared with 2 packages (10 oz. each) frozen asparagus.

Minestra di verdure alla primaverile

*Springtime
vegetable soup*

Serves 4
Difficulty *
Time: 2 hours

Minestra di verdure alla primaverile

3/4 cup (5 oz.) dried navy beans
or flageolet
1/3 cup (1/2 oz.) dried mushrooms
1-3/4 cups (7 oz.) green beans, cut
into 1-inch pieces
2 potatoes, diced
2 zucchini, diced
2/3 cup (5 oz.) peas
4 Italian plum tomatoes, chopped
2 tbsp. olive oil
7 oz. large quadrucci (pasta
dough cut into squares, these
are sold commercially)
2 tbsp. pesto (see Pesto
recipe p. 65)
Salt

Boil white beans and drain while they are still al dente. Soak
mushrooms, dry and chop coarsely. Bring about 2 quarts water to a
boil. Add white beans and green beans and cook for about 30
minutes. Add potatoes, zucchini, peas, tomatoes, mushrooms and
oil. Simmer about 30 minutes. Add pasta squares, stir and simmer
until pasta is done, about 20 minutes. Stir in pesto. Season to taste
with salt. Remove from heat and let stand at room temperature for
a few minutes before serving.

Minestra di ceci alla contadina

*Chick pea soup
country style*

Serves 4
Difficulty *
Time: 3 hours, plus time required
to soak chick peas

1 lb. dried chick peas
1/4 cup (2 oz.) chopped prosciutto
1/2 small onion
1 clove garlic
6 sprigs parsley
1 tsp. crumbled marjoram
2 tbsp. olive oil
3/4 cup (6 oz.) chopped tomato
Salt, pepper
1/2 lb. bacon rind, chopped
1 head escarole (endive),
trimmed and shredded
4 slices bread
1/2 cup grated Parmesan cheese

Soak chick peas in warm water for 24 hours. Chop prosciutto,
onion, garlic, parsley and marjoram. Put in a saucepan, add oil,
chick peas, tomato, about 2 quarts water and salt to taste. Bring to
a boil. Add bacon rind and continue simmering, covered, over
moderate heat. After about 1-1/2 hours, stir in shredded escarole
and a pinch of pepper. Toast bread and place in soup bowls. Stir
soup well before pouring over toast. Serve sprinkled with grated
Parmesan cheese.

Minestra di crostacei alla trapanese

*Crawfish bisque
Trapani style*

Serves 4
Difficulty **
Time: 2 hours

2 small lobsters (or crawfish) weighing about 1-1/4 lbs. each
1/4 cup butter
Salt, pepper
2 tbsp. olive oil
2 cloves garlic, chopped

1/2 onion, chopped
1 cup chopped tomato pulp, skin and seeds removed
2/3 cup rice
6 sprigs parsley, chopped

Have tails removed from lobsters. Shell tails and slice raw meat into 1/4-inch slices. Saute lobster for about 10 minutes in hot butter seasoned with salt and pepper. (Pan should be covered, heat should be moderate.) Put top half of lobster and tail shells, crushed with a mallet, in a saucepan. Add about 1 quart water. Season with salt and bring to a boil. Boil 5 minutes. Strain broth through a fine-meshed strainer, pressing to remove all liquid. Heat oil and saute garlic and onion. Add tomato pulp, lobster broth and about 1 quart of hot water. Add lobster meat together with cooking juices and simmer for 5 minutes. Sprinkle in rice, cook for 15 minutes or until rice is tender but firm. Season to taste with salt. Sprinkle with chopped parsley.

Minestra con battuto alla ligure

*Italian noodle soup
Ligurian style*

Serves 4
Difficulty *
Time: 1 hour

1/3 cup (3 oz.) chopped pork fat
3 cloves garlic
2 tbsp. olive oil
1/2 cup (4 oz.) chopped tomato

1 pkg. (8 oz.) linguine
Salt, pepper
3/4 cup grated fresh Parmesan cheese
1 tsp. chopped fresh basil leaves

Saute pork fat and garlic until golden brown in oil in a saucepan. Add tomato and 1-1/2 quarts water. Bring to a boil. Add linguine which have been broken into pieces about 1-1/2 inches long and cook until al dente. Season to taste with salt and pepper. Remove from heat, stir in one-half the grated cheese and basil. Serve soup with sprinkled remaining cheese.

Minestra con battuto alla ligure

Minestra di funghi freschi

Fresh mushroom soup

Serves 4
Difficulty *
Time: 2 hours

3 tbsp. butter
1 tbsp. chopped onion
1 clove garlic, chopped
1-1/2 lbs. fresh mushrooms, trimmed and sliced
1 cup chopped tomato pulp, skin and seeds removed
Salt, pepper

6 cups chicken broth (see Brodo pieno alla calabrese p. 94)
2 egg yolks and 1 whole egg
6 tbsp. grated Parmesan cheese
Nutmeg
2 tbsp. chopped parsley
8 1/2-inch thick slices French bread fried in butter until brown

In a saucepan heat butter and saute onion and garlic for 1 minute. Add mushrooms, stir over high heat for 1 minute. Add tomato pulp, salt and pepper to taste and continue cooking over moderate heat for 5 minutes. Add broth. A few minutes before serving, beat 2 yolks and 1 whole egg with grated Parmesan, a pinch of nutmeg and 2 tablespoons of the broth. Remove soup from heat and beat in egg mixture. Add chopped parsley. Reheat and stir until hot and slightly thickened. Do not boil. Serve soup with fried bread placed on top of each serving.

Minestra di cavolfiore

Cauliflower Soup

Serves 6 to 8
Difficulty *
Time: 30 minutes

1 large head cauliflower
1/2 onion chopped
1/4 cup olive oil
1/4 cup butter

1-1/2 quarts chicken broth
1 cup (8 oz.) rice
1/4 cup grated Parmesan cheese

Remove green leaves from cauliflower and separate into flowerets. In a large saucepan saute onion in oil and half of the butter until brown. Add broth, cauliflowerets and rice. Cook for 20 minutes and, before removing from heat, stir in remaining butter and Parmesan cheese.

Minestra di riso e luganega alla veneta

Rice and pork sausage soup Venetian style

Serves 4
Difficulty *
Time: 1 hour

1/2 lb. pork sausage
1 cup diced turnips
6 tbsp. chopped ham fat
1 small onion, chopped
8 cups beef broth (see Brodo di manzo con sorbetto di pomodoro)

1 cup rice
2 tbsp. butter
6 sprigs parsley, chopped
Salt
1/4 cup grated Parmesan cheese

Cut luganega or other pork sausage into 1-inch pieces and cook for 10 minutes in boiling water. Separately cook the diced turnips for 10 minutes. Saute fat and onion in a saucepan for 1 minute. Drain sausage and turnips and add to pan. Add broth, bring to a boil. Sprinkle in rice and cook for 20 minutes or until rice is tender but firm. Stir in butter and parsley. Season to taste with salt. Sprinkle each serving with grated Parmesan.

Minestra
di pasta e fagioli

Pasta and bean soup

Serves 4
Difficulty *
Time: 2-1/2 hours.
(Soak beans overnight)

3/4 cup (5 oz.) dried white beans
1 stalk celery, chopped
1 onion, chopped
1 carrot, chopped
1 clove garlic chopped
2 tbsp. chopped parsley
1 small ham bone
7 oz. maccheroncini or tubeti
(short lengths of macaroni)
1 tbsp. olive oil
1/2 cup (2 oz.) grated Parmesan
cheese
Salt

The night before put beans to soak in water to cover overnight in a 6 quart saucepan. In the morning drain. Add celery, onion, carrot, garlic, parsley and ham bone. Add water to just cover ingredients. Simmer gently about 2 hours or until beans are tender, adding water from time to time to keep up level of liquid. When beans are cooked strain half of them through a food mill and add to soup. Add maccheroncini and continue cooking until the pasta is done, about 20 minutes. Stir in olive oil and grated Parmesan. Add more water if soup is too thick. Season to taste with salt. Serve pasta and bean soup with a red wine.

A specialty of the Veneto in general and of Padua in particular, pasta and bean soup is a good example of the ubiquity of pasta in Italian vegetable soups. Beans might seem thick enough all by themselves to require no aid from pasta, but pasta goes into this soup all the same. Tuscans, it is true, sometimes make bean soup without pasta, but Tuscans are an exception, being such confirmed bean fanciers that they even make one bean soup composed of beans in beans—a thick gruel of crushed beans with whole beans swimming in it, and nothing else at all, not even pasta, except the seasoning.

Minestra di riso e
fagioli alla genovese

*Genoese rice and
bean soup*

Serves 4
Difficulty *
Time: 2 hours

2 cups (8 oz.) fresh beans or
canned flageolet
1/2 green cabbage, chopped
2-1/2 cups (5 oz.) fresh spinach,
trimmed and coarsely chopped
1 cup (5 oz.) diced, peeled beets
2 potatoes, sliced

2 tbsp. chopped onion
1 leek, only white part, chopped
2 tbsp. olive oil
Salt, pepper
1 cup (8 oz.) rice
1 tbsp. pesto (see Pesto p. 65)

Place beans, cabbage, spinach, beets, potatoes, onion, leeks, oil, salt and pepper to taste in a large pot. Cover with 1-1/2 quarts water. Bring to a boil and simmer for about 1 hour over moderate heat. Add rice and continue cooking for 15 minutes. Add pesto and cook for another 15 minutes or until rice is tender. Remove from the heat and allow to stand 10 minutes at room temperature before serving.

Minestrone siciliano di pasta e carciofi

Minestrone siciliano di pasta e carciofi

Sicilian pasta and artichoke soup

3 strips bacon
1/2 onion, chopped
1 clove garlic, chopped
1/2 celery rib, chopped
6 sprigs of parsley, chopped

2 tbsp. olive oil
1/2 cup sieved tomato pulp
2 artichokes
1-1/2 cups uncooked elbow macaroni
Salt, pepper
1/2 cup grated pecorino cheese

Serves 4
Difficulty *
Time: 2 hours

Saute bacon, onion, garlic, celery and parsley in the oil. Add tomato pulp and simmer to flavor for about 10 minutes. Clean artichokes, removing chokes, and cut into segments. Add to tomato. Pour over 6 cups cold water and simmer over low heat. Add pasta and simmer, about 15-20 minutes, until pasta is tender yet firm. Season to taste with salt and pepper. Pour soup into a tureen and stir in pecorino cheese. Serve very hot.

Tortelloni is bigger than tortelli or tortellini, panettone is richer than pane (bread), so you can divine from these words that minestrone is a "big" soup—"big" in this case meaning "rich", which most minestrones certainly are. They are usually crammed with a variety of vegetables, plus pasta, and are generously sprinkled with grated cheese. A good example of the sumptuousness of minestrone can be found in Genoa, which claims to have invented this dish—most improbably, for peasants all over the world are accustomed to keeping a pot simmering on the stove, into which are put from time to time whatever farm produce is handy. *Minestrone alla genovese* contains cabbage, zucchini, fava beans, red beans, string beans, tomato, eggplant (aubergine), celery, onion, garlic, olive oil, herbs, and any kind of pasta you fancy—especially tagliatelle, though other favorites are ditalini, vermicelli, penne and rigatoni. Another example is the Abruzzi minestrone, which does not tie you down to any particular list of ingredients, so long as you make sure that each of six categories is represented: fresh vegetables, which vary with the season; dried vegetables; aromatic vegetables (celery, fennel, etc.); seasoning vegetables (onions, carrots, herbs); pasta (your choice); and even a little meat, usually pork (ham, pig's feet, pig's ears).

Minestrone alla brianzola

Vegetable soup Brianza

Serves 4
Difficulty *
Time: 1-1/2 hours

1/4 cup (2 oz.) chopped bacon or ham rind
1-1/4 cups (10 oz.) rice or ditali pasta
3 tbsp. olive oil
1-3/4 cups (7 oz.) 1-inch pieces green beans
2 tbsp. chopped onion
3 stalks celery, diced
2 carrots, diced
1 potato, peeled and left whole
2 tomatoes, diced

1/4 head savoy cabbage, chopped
1/4 cup chopped parsley
2 tbsp. butter
2 tbsp. (1 oz.) bacon, diced
1 cup dry white wine
Herbs: 1/4 tsp. *each* oregano, thyme, basil, marjoram
Salt and pepper
Beef broth, about 6 cups
(see Brodo di manzo con sorbetto di pomodoro p. 95)
1/3 cup grated Parmesan cheese

Boil rind in water until tender; drain. In another saucepan cook the rice or pasta in boiling salted water. Drain while still al dente. Stir in 2 tablespoons oil and set to one side. Put vegetables into a pot with butter, bacon rind, bacon and 1 tablespoon of oil. Add wine, herbs and salt to taste. Cover with a good quantity of boiling beef broth. Cover and simmer for about 1 hour. Remove potato, mash, return to broth. Add rice (or pasta) and continue cooking for 5 minutes, taking care to remove from heat while rice or pasta are still al dente. Season to taste with salt and pepper. Sprinkle with Parmesan, pour into a tureen and let stand for a few minutes at room temperature. This soup is good either hot or cold.

Minestrone
alla milanese

Milanese thick soup

Serves 4
Difficulty *
Time: 2-1/2 hours

4 strips bacon
1/4 lb. bacon rind (1/2 cup chopped)
1 bunch parsley, chopped
1 clove garlic, chopped
1 stalk celery, chopped
2 potatoes, chopped
2 carrots, chopped
1 zucchini, chopped
1 cup (1/4 lb.) 1/2-inch pieces, green beans
1 cup (7 oz.) dried borlotti beans or navy beans
3 tomatoes, peeled and diced
Salt
1 cup coarsely grated savoy cabbage
1 cup (8 oz.) natural rice

Chop bacon extremely fine until it is almost a pulp. Place bacon, bacon rind, parsley, garlic, and celery in a soup pot. Saute 5 minutes. Add potatoes, carrots, zucchini, green beans, beans and tomatoes. Cover with water and season to taste with salt. Bring to a boil over high heat, lower heat and simmer covered for at least 2 hours. Add water from time to time to keep up level of liquid. After first hour add cabbage. Thirty minutes before serving add natural rice and simmer, being careful to keep rice al dente. Remove bacon rind and season to taste with salt. Serve with or without a little grated Parmesan cheese.

> The distinguishing mark of Milanese minestrone is that it contains rice, while most other varieties contain pasta. Milan even dares to insinuate that its minority version is the genuine minestrone, taking advantage of the fact that many Italian dictionaries are published in Milan, so that I find this astounding entry in my most imposing lexicon: "Minestrone, a soup quite common among the people of Lombardy, into which enter, along with rice, beans, cabbage and often also celery, carrots and other vegetables." Most Italians would be brought to the simmering point on being told that minestrone is peculiar to Lombardy, and to a violent boil by the assertion that its classic cereal constituent is rice instead of pasta.

Zuppa di fagioli
alla marchigiana

Bean soup Marchigiana

Serves 4
Difficulty *
Time: 3 hours

2/3 cup (5 oz.) diced bacon rind
1-2/3 cups (11 oz.) dried navy beans, soaked
Salt, pepper
1/2 small onion, 1/2 celery stalk and 6 parsley sprigs, chopped together
1/3 cup olive oil
1/4 cup tomato paste
3-1/2 cups (7 oz.) chopped white cabbage leaves
1-1/2 cups (7 oz.) peeled and diced potatoes
1 cup (4 oz.) cauliflowerets
1 bunch beets, peeled and diced
1/2 cup (4 oz.) peas
4 slices bread lightly toasted

Blanch bacon rind in boiling water, drain and cut into small pieces. Put in a saucepan with beans, 2 quarts water and salt to taste. Cook until beans are tender, about 1 hour. Drain beans and reserve liquid. Saute onion, celery and parsley in oil. Stir in tomato paste diluted in 1/4 cup water. Add cabbage, potatoes, cauliflowerets, beets and salt and pepper to taste. Cover with water drained from beans and cook for 30 minutes, adding more water if needed. Pass half the beans through a food mill. Mix bean puree, whole beans, bacon rind, cooked vegetables and their liquid and peas. Adjust seasoning with salt and pepper. Simmer for 5 minutes. Place toasted bread slices in a tureen, pour in soup and let stand for a few minutes before serving.

Brodetto di sogliole all'anconetana

Sole soup
Ancona style

Serves 4
Difficulty *
Time: 2 hours

3/4 cup dry white wine
Juice of 1/2 lemon
1 carrot, chopped
1 onion, chopped
Salt, pepper
8 sole fillets, approx. 2 lbs.
7 tbsp. olive oil
1 clove garlic, chopped
1 rib celery, chopped
1-1/2 cups sieved tomato
pulp (or canned peeled Italian
tomatoes)
1 bouquet garni containing
thyme, bay leaf, parsley
1 pinch saffron
16 slices French bread

Brodetto di sogliole all' anconetana

Put 1 quart water in a saucepan; add wine, lemon juice, carrot and 1/2 of the onion. Season with salt and pepper and add sole fillets which have been rolled into this court bouillon. Simmer for 15 minutes. Drain off pan juices, strain and reserve.
Pour 2 tablespoons of the oil into a frying pan. Add remaining onion, garlic and celery. Saute until wilted, then add tomato pulp, bouquet garni, saffron dissolved in a very little warm water and strained fish broth. Simmer for 15 minutes. Add sole fillets and simmer for 8 to 9 minutes. Meanwhile fry bread slices in remaining oil and put them in the bottom of a large deep platter, tureen or individual soup dishes. Top bread slices with fillets. Pour broth over them, sprinkle with chopped parsley and serve piping hot.

Minestrone con il lardo

Minestrone with bacon

Serves 4
Difficulty *
Time: 2-1/2 hours
plus soaking time overnight

2/3 cup (4 oz.) dried pea beans
1/3 cup (2 1/2 oz.) chopped bacon
6 sprigs parsley, chopped
2 cloves garlic, chopped
2 tbsp. butter
2 tbsp. olive oil
1 green onion chopped
2 ripe tomatoes
4 potatoes, diced
1 small savoy cabbage, chopped

2 carrots, diced
1 rib celery, chopped
Several fresh basil leaves,
chopped
Salt and pepper
Broth (approx. 6 cups)
7 oz. grooved macaroni (usually
sold as mostaccioli rigati or
penne rigate)
1/4 cup grated Parmesan cheese

Soak beans overnight. Saute bacon until lightly browned. Add parsley and garlic and saute lightly for 1 minute. In another pan melt butter, add oil, and when mixture is good and hot add onion and saute until onion is transparent. Cut tomatoes in half and remove seeds. Add tomatoes, drained beans, sauteed bacon mixture and all of the vegetables and basil. Salt and pepper to taste and cover with broth. Continue cooking over moderate heat for at least 2 hours. While the minestrone is cooking taste it from time to time; if liquid does not seem well seasoned, add a little salt or, better yet, a beef bouillon cube. Add pasta and cook for 15 minutes or until tender but firm. Sprinkle with grated Parmesan cheese, mix and serve.

Brodetto del pescatore dell'Alto Adriatico

Adriatic fisherman's chowder

Serves 4
Difficulty *
Time: 2-1/2 hours

1-3/4 lbs. assorted fish (trout, snapper, flounder, bass)
1 lb. squid
7 tbsp. olive oil
1 leek, chopped
1 stalk celery, cut into strips, 1/4" × 2"
2 cloves garlic, mashed
2 tbsp. vinegar
Salt, pepper
1 small onion, sliced
1 bay leaf
1 stick cinnamon
1 sprig parsley, chopped
16 slices stale firm-type bread

Have fish cleaned, (keep heads), wash and drain. Remove bone and ink sac from squid, scrape with a paring knife, wash and cut into pieces. Heat half the oil and saute leek, celery and garlic until wilted. Add heads of fish and squid. Sprinkle with vinegar and cook until vinegar is evaporated. Season with salt and pepper. Add enough water to cover fish heads and continue cooking for 40 minutes. Remove squid and set aside.

Strain sauce, mashing fish heads through sieve, and set liquid aside. Pour remaining oil into a saucepan. Saute onion until soft. Add assorted fish, salt and pepper to taste, bay leaf, cinnamon and parsley. When fish is well flavored, add squid and fish sauce which was set aside. Cook over moderate heat for 15 minutes or until fish flakes. Remove cinnamon stick and bay leaf. Arrange slices of bread in a large, deep platter or tureen, cover with pieces of fish and piping hot broth.

Zuppa di pesce delle osterie romane

*Fish chowder
Roman tavern style*

4 lbs. mixed fish (red mullet, flounder, halibut, eel, squid, sole, etc.)
2 tbsp. chopped onion
1/2 cup chopped parsley
1 tbsp. salt, 6 peppercorns
2-1/2 cups dry white wine
24 mussels
2/3 cup olive oil
2 leeks, chopped
2 heads Boston (cabbage-type) lettuce, shredded
Pinch of thyme and bay leaf
4 fillets of anchovy ground to paste in mortar
2 cloves garlic, chopped
4 slices toasted French bread

Serves 4   Difficulty *   Time: 3 hours

Clean fish removing heads and bones. Wash in cold running water. Prepare a court bouillon using heads, bones, trimmings, onion, 1/4 cup of the parsley, peppercorns, salt, 3 cups water and 2 cups of the wine. Simmer court bouillon for 30 minutes, then strain through a fine sieve.

Wash mussels thoroughly in cold running water, heat in 1/4 cup of the oil until they open, then remove meat from shells and place into their strained pan juices. Heat 1/4 cup of the oil, saute sliced squid. Add leeks, shredded lettuce hearts, thyme, bay leaf, salt and freshly ground pepper. Cook over moderate heat about 30 minutes. When squid are almost cooked, pour in remaining wine. Simmer until wine evaporates. Add anchovies and remaining fish. Simmer for a few minutes, stirring constantly.

Add strained court bouillon and continue cooking for 10 minutes. Finally add mussels and their juice. Separately saute garlic briefly in remaining oil until golden. Remove garlic and discard, then pour oil into chowder. Put bread in soup dishes, pour chowder over it and sprinkle with remaining chopped parsley.

Brodetto alla triestina

Fish soup Trieste style

Serves 4
Difficulty **
Time: 2 hours

2-1/2 lbs. assorted fish
(could include haddock,
flounder, snapper, halibut,
red mullet, sole)
7 tbsp. olive oil
1/2 cup dry white wine

1 onion, chopped
2 cloves garlic, chopped
6 sprigs parsley, chopped
1/4 cup tomato paste
3 tbsp. wine vinegar
Salt

Clean fish and cut larger ones into pieces. Heat oil in frying pan. Add fish pieces, wine and 1 cup water. Simmer over low heat for 20 minutes. When fish is almost completely cooked, remove pieces and reserve. Add onion, garlic and parsley to pan. Add tomato paste mixed with 1 cup hot water. Simmer for 45 minutes, stirring occasionally. Add fish and wine vinegar and simmer for another 10 minutes. Season to taste with salt. Serve piping hot.

Mention Italian soup, and everyone thinks immediately of minestrone, which is not *a* soup, but a whole family of soups. For coastal populations, the equivalent of minestrone (soups richly stocked with a variety of vegetables) is brodetti (soups richly stocked with a variety of fish), another whole family of soups. You might call brodetti the minestrone of the sea. Brodetti are probably older than minestrone: in Homer's Greece and Romulus's Rome the choice of vegetables was limited, but the fish which swam in Mediterranean waters were as varied then as they are now. The various fish chowders covered by the name brodetti are said to have been invented by the Greeks; Brindisi calls its version *zuppa alla greca*. Agamemnon and Achilles are supposed to have eaten it under the walls of Troy, and in comparatively modern times Julius Caesar downed a bowl of it before crossing the Rubicon. Dante ate it in exile at Porto Corsino, Napoleon fortified himself with it before escaping from Elba, and Field Marshal Montgomery celebrated victory with brodetti at almost the same spot where Caesar indulged in it.

Zuppa di pesce al finocchio

Fish soup with fennel

Serves 4
Difficulty *
Time: 1-1/2 hours

4 lbs. assorted fish and
shellfish (grey mullet, red mullet,
shrimp, clams, mussels)
1/4 cup olive oil
1 onion, chopped
2 cloves garlic, chopped
6 sprigs parsley, chopped

4 ripe tomatoes, diced and
seeds removed
1/2 cup chopped fennel tops
1 tsp. crumbled saffron
Salt, pepper
8 slices of French bread fried
in butter and oil until brown

Clean all fish. Place shellfish in a frying pan with 2 tablespoons of the oil. Remove meat from shells as they open. Shell shrimp when they turn pink. Be sure to reserve pan juices after straining. Saute onion, garlic and half the parsley in remaining oil until wilted. Add tomatoes, fennel tops and saffron dissolved in strained shellfish juices. Simmer until sauce thickens. Add all fish and just cover with boiling water. Season to taste with salt and pepper and cook over very high heat for 8 to 10 minutes. Stir in shellfish. Before removing from heat sprinkle in remaining parsley. Serve in hot soup dishes topped with browned bread slices.

Nasello al burro nocciola

FISH

Take one look at the map of Italy, a long thin peninsula thrusting deep into the sea, and you must suspect immediately that this is a country devoted to fish. The ancient Romans blazed the way. Lucullus built elaborate basins at his villa near Naples, fitted out with different types of bottom and of aquatic plants, so that every species could live happily in the sort of surroundings it preferred, on the theory that this would induce it to build up flavor. Gourmets bid the price of mullets up to such extravagant heights that a horrified Emperor Tiberius imposed price ceilings upon them. Trout from the Vosges mountains of Gaul, salmon from the Rhone, were carried to Italy alive in tank carts, and oysters were transported from Britain packed in ice and snow, renewed at intervals along the way at relay stations equipped with ice-houses. Cistern boats ferried live fish from the Indian Ocean to Rome. The most spectacular feature of Trajan's Market (which still stands today) was its top-floor aquarium, where freshwater fish were kept in tanks fed by clear water from the surrounding hills, flowing through one of the great aqueducts, while saltwater fish swam in seawater brought by cart from Ostia. Italians have been important consumers of fish ever since; and it can be argued that nobody in the world cooks them better.

FISH HINTS

When buying fish or shellfish make sure they have a fresh ocean smell, without a hint of ammonia. Shellfish should feel heavy for their size for they shrink inside their shells when they are not fresh. The eyes of the fish should be rounded and smooth and the gills bright red. The fish should feel plump and firm to the touch. To clean fish remove scales with a scaling knife or a dull knife run lengthwise over the fish starting at the tail and running toward the head. Slash fish lengthwise underneath in the belly and remove the entrails. Wash in cold running water. With scissors cut off the tail and fins. Remove head by cutting through the backbone and along the gills. Cut fish crosswise into slices to get fish steaks. To prepare fish fillets, cut fish lengthwise with a thin sharp knife cutting along the backbone on one side. Place fillet skin side down and cut with a thin sharp knife along the skin to remove skin. Repeat on the other side of the fish.

Use the fish bones, head and trimmings to make fish stock. Cover them with water, bring to a boil and simmer 15 minutes. Strain and reserve for use in soups and sauces.

To poach a whole fish, fillets or steaks use a court bouillon to add flavor. Cook water with salt, pepper, carrots, onion and celery. Wine may also be added. Add fish or shellfish to simmering water and cook gently until cooked. The less cooking the better as seafood needs only to be cooked lightly to keep from becoming dry. See *Trota salmonata con agliata alla ligure* on page 123 for the proportions needed for a court bouillon.

If you cannot get fresh fish frozen fish can be used in the same way as fresh. Don't thaw before cooking as usual. Just allow a few extra minutes of cooking time.

Branzino con salsa gustosa

Bass with hot sauce

Serves 4
Difficulty **
Time: 2 hours

Hot sauce:

1-1/2 cups mayonnaise
1/4 cup chopped pickled mushrooms in oil
1/4 cup chopped artichoke hearts in oil
2 tbsp. chopped pickled pearl onions
2 tbsp. chopped pickled gherkins
2 tbsp. chopped red or green pepper in oil

Bass:

1 bass weighing about 2-1/2 lbs.
1 small onion, chopped
1 small carrot, chopped
1/2 rib celery, chopped
6 sprigs parsley, chopped
1 bay leaf
Juice of 1/2 lemon
Salt, peppercorns

Clean bass. Poach bass covering it with cold water to which you have added onion, carrot, celery, parsley, bay leaf, lemon juice, salt and several peppercorns. Simmer over gentle heat for about 15 minutes. Let fish cool in pan juices. Drain carefully and place fish on working surface. Carefully remove skin completely. Cut fish into slices and arrange on a platter.

Sauce: Mix 2/3 of the mayonnaise with remaining ingredients. Pour sauce over fish slices covering them smoothly. Chill until ready to serve. Just before serving garnish with rosettes of remaining mayonnaise squeezed from a pastry bag with a star tip.

> It will come as a revelation to nobody that there is a marked difference between saltwater fish and freshwater fish, which, thought it is hard to define, makes it difficult to mistake one for another (exception made for those fish which spend part of their lives in salt and part in fresh water). It might be hazarded that the qualities of saltwater fish, at their best, are robustness, heartiness, frankness; of freshwater fish at their best, finesse, delicacy, subtlety. If one dared risk a comparison with a category of food so different, one might say that saltwater fish have the virtues of Burgundy wines, freshwater fish those of Bordeaux wines. It is therefore fitting that in Italy, a country of forthright peasant cookery—Burgundian in spirit, if you like—saltwater fish play a more important rôle in the diet than freshwater fish. They seem to appeal more powerfully to the Italian spirit; and, they offer a wider variety.

Branzino con salsa di olive

Bass with olive sauce

Serves 4
Difficulty *
Time: 2 hours

Olive sauce:

1/4 cup olive oil
1 green onion, chopped
1/2 pickled pepper (bell pepper in vinegar) chopped
6 sprigs parsley, chopped
1 tbsp. capers, chopped
1 cup mixed green and ripe olives, pitted and chopped
1/2 cup dry white wine
1-1/2 tsp. tomato paste

Bass:

1 bass weighing about 2-1/2 lbs.
Flour
2 tbsp. butter
3 tbsp. oil
Salt, pepper

Clean fish, remove head and cut into 4 equal slices; wash and dry in a kitchen towel. Coat fish slices with flour and fry slowly in hot butter and oil until brown on both sides, about 15 minutes. Season with salt and pepper.

Olive sauce: Heat oil, add onion, pickled pepper, parsley, capers and olives. Stir until wilted. Add white wine and tomato paste. Simmer for a few minutes until sauce thickens slightly. Add fried fish and simmer 5 minutes.
Put slices of bass on serving platter and cover with pan juices.

Alici agreganate alla napoletana

Baked fresh anchovies with oregano Neapolitan

Serves 4
Difficulty *
Time: 1-1/2 hours
Oven Temp. 350° F.

2 lbs. fresh anchovies ("alici")
2/3 cup olive oil
6 to 8 sprigs parsley, chopped
2 cloves garlic, chopped
A pinch of oregano
Salt, peppercorns
2 tbsp. wine vinegar

Scale anchovies, clean them and slit them down one side along the bone, leaving the other side attached ("butterflying"). Remove bones, heads and tails. Wash and drain. Brush a shallow 1-1/2 quart baking dish with 2 tablespoons of the oil and arrange anchovies in it. In a mixing bowl mix parsley, garlic, oregano, a little salt, freshly ground pepper and vinegar. Cover anchovies with mixture. Pour over remaining oil and bake in a preheated oven for about 20 minutes. Serve hot in baking dish.

Most of us know the anchovy only in the form of tiny salted fillets, which gives a tang and a life to anything with which they are combined, though it would be difficult to determine what proportion of the effect is contributed by the fish and what proportion by the ingredients in which it happens to be preserved. Yet fresh anchovy is of delicate and subtle flavor, a treat for the taste buds—but, unfortunately, a treat not available to everyone. The anchovy is a fragile fish, not easily transportable; if you want to taste it, you had better hie yourself to some spot on a coast where it is caught. If you are not so fortunate as to be able to do this, you are advised to substitute smelts for anchovies in the following recipes.

Alici casalinghe con pomodoro

Fresh anchovies with tomato, home-style

Serves 4
Difficulty *
Time: 1 hour 40 minutes
Oven Temp. 350° F.

Scale fresh anchovies, clean, bone and remove heads and tails. Wash and drain carefully. Brush a shallow 1-1/2 quart baking dish with 2 tablespoons of the oil. Put two layers of anchovies in baking dish, pouring in a very little oil after first layer and sprinkling on half of the garlic and parsley. Sprinkle remaining parsley and garlic over the top of the second layer. Sprinkle with salt and pepper. Spread tomato pulp over surface. Sprinkle with bread crumbs and pour over remaining oil. Bake in a preheated oven for about 20 minutes, that is, until top is lightly browned. Serve in baking dish.

2 lbs. small fresh anchovies
2/3 cup olive oil
3 cloves garlic, chopped
1/2 cup chopped parsley

Salt, pepper
1-1/2 cups sieved tomato pulp
1/4 cup dry bread crumbs

Alici casalinghe con pomodoro

Baccalá alla trasteverina

Fried fillets of salt cod Trastevere style

Serves 4
Difficulty *
Time: 1-1/2 hours
Oven Temp. 375°F.

Baccalá alla trasteverina

Soak raisins in a little warm water. Wash cod thoroughly in several changes of water. Remove skin and bones. Cut into serving-size pieces and dry. Coat pieces with flour lightly and fry in hot oil 1/4-inch deep until brown on both sides. Remove from pan and keep hot. Drain cooking oil from pan and reserve. Pour 7 tablespoons oil into same pan and return to heat. Add onion, potatoes and garlic. Sprinkle with salt and pepper and saute over very low heat until wilted and soft. Mash anchovy fillets to a paste and add to onion and potatoes with capers, raisins (drained) and pine nuts. Pour mixture into a shallow baking pan. Arrange cod pieces over it. Pour over 1/4 cup of the reserved cooking oil and bake in a preheated oven for 15 minutes. Sprinkle with parsley and lemon juice just before serving.

1 tbsp. Sultana raisins
1-3/4 lbs. salt cod
Flour
Olive oil
1-1/4 lbs. onions, sliced
1-1/4 lbs. potatoes, peeled and sliced

1 clove garlic, chopped
Salt, white pepper
4 fillets of anchovy, rinsed with cold water
1 tbsp. capers
1 tbsp. pine nuts
6 sprigs parsley, chopped
Juice of 1/2 lemon

It may seem strange that a country rich in fresh fish should also make extensive use of a preserved fish which, as a rule, has to be imported; but Italy is not alone in liking preserved cod. This taste is shared by all the Mediterranean countries, and may perhaps be ascribed to the Normans who for some centuries were dominant in the region. Preserved cod appears in Italy in two main forms; *stoccafisso*, which is air-dried cod; and *baccalá*, which is salt cod. The most famous of an innumerable list of treatments of *baccalá* is no doubt *baccala mantecato*, which means literally "worked cod"—and worked it is, since the preparation of this dish involves long kneading together of the cod with milk and oil, plus a liberal admixture of garlic. This is a classic salt cod dish all around the Mediterranean, which in France is called *brandade* and in Spain *bacalao al ajo arriero*. Not all salt cod dishes demand so much effort from the cook. Baccala alla trasteverina given here is easier.

Triglie alla livornese

Red mullet Leghorn style

Serves 4
Difficulty *
Time: 1-1/2 hours

2-1/2 lbs. red mullet
2 cloves garlic, chopped
2/3 cup olive oil
1/2 onion, chopped

1 lb. ripe tomatoes (about 3 large)
peeled, seeded and chopped
Salt, pepper
Flour
6 sprigs parsley, chopped

Clean red mullet and wash in cold running water. Drain and dry. Saute garlic in 1/4 cup of the oil in saucepan until garlic begins to brown. Discard garlic and add onion. Saute onion until wilted and add tomatoes. Cook sauce over low heat until it is thick, about 15 minutes. Season to taste with salt and pepper. Ten minutes before serving, coat red mullet with flour and fry in remaining oil, turning to cook on both sides. When well browned and crisp, remove red mullet from heat. Drain off excess fatty drippings. Pour sauce over mullet and heat in sauce for 5 minutes before serving. Sprinkle with parsley and serve.

Muggine all'italiana con tartufi e asparagi

Mullet Italian style with truffles and asparagus

Serves 4
Difficulty *
Time: 1-1/2 hours
Oven Temp. 375°F.

1 mullet weighing
approx. 2-1/2 lbs
Salt, white pepper (freshly ground)
Flour
1/2 cup butter
Juice of 1 lemon
1 lb. asparagus, tips only
6 sprigs parsley, chopped
Grated Parmesan
1 white truffle, grated

Have mullet cleaned and filleted. Season fillets with salt and pepper, coat with flour and fry to a golden brown in half the butter. Drain fillets, reserving pan juices, and arrange them in a buttered oven-proof dish, side by side. Baste with pan juices and lemon juice. Boil asparagus tips until tender. Arrange them around fish fillets, sprinkle parsley and grated Parmesan over them and dot with remaining butter. Bake for 15 minutes. Remove from oven. Sprinkle truffle over dish and serve.

> Mullet is a confusing word in English. It covers two different genera of fish, between which both French and Italian make a distinction, but English does not; it can lead the consumer to believe that gray mullets and red mullets are simply two varieties of the same fish, which they are not; indeed they do not even taste alike. English does have at least the excuse that the scientific names of the two resemble each other. Muglidae are gray mullets, which may turn up in Italian either as *cefali* or *muggine*. Mullidae are red mullets, *triglie* in Italian. Both have been much appreciated in Italy since ancient Roman times.

Muggine all'italiana con tartufi e asparagi

Anguille arrostite al lauro

Roasted eel with bay leaf

Serves 4
Difficulty **
Time: 1-1/4 hours
Oven Temp. 350° F.

2 lbs. eels, medium-sized
Flour
7 tbsp. olive oil

10 bay leaves
1 lemon, sliced
Salt, black pepper

Have eels skinned or clean as stated below. With a sharp, slender knife cut the skin around the head of each eel. Pull skin down below slit. Holding the head of the eel, firmly in one hand, with a cloth around it, pull off the skin in a single movement so skin is pulled inside out. Slit eel down its entire length, clean and remove head and fins. Wash and dry thoroughly. Cut into 2-inch pieces and slash meat at several points on each piece. Dip eel pieces into flour to coat. Heat oil to point of smoking in a frying pan. Brown pieces on all sides. Drain when they are a golden brown and arrange them in a baking dish, putting 1 bay leaf and 1 lemon slice between each slice and the next. Season with salt and pepper, cover and bake in a preheated oven for 30 minutes.

Anguille appetitose coi funghi

Appetizing eels with mushrooms

Serves 4
Difficulty **
Time: 1-1/2 hours,
plus marinating time

2 lbs medium size eels
1/2 cup butter
2 thin slices onion
1 bunch parsley
6 peppercorns
1 cup dry white wine
Salt
Juice of 1 lemon
1/2 lb. fresh mushrooms, sliced
1 tbsp. flour
A pinch of nutmeg
2 anchovy fillets, desalted

Have eels skinned. Remove central spine and reserve with head, fins and skin. Cut eels into pieces, wash and dry thoroughly.

Prepare a *fumet de poisson* as follows: put 1 tbsp. of the butter in a saucepan; add half the reserved trimmings from the eels (chop or pound spiny cartilage in a mortar), onion slices, 1/4 parsley bunch and half of the peppercorns. Simmer for a while, then add half of the wine and 3/4 cup water. Season with a pinch of salt and continue simmering until the liquid is reduced to about 1 cup. Strain through a fine sieve.

Put pieces of eel in a bowl, pour 3/4 of the lemon juice over them, sprinkle on 1/2 cup finely chopped parsley, and marinate 1-1/2 hours turning from time to time.
Melt 3 tbsp. of the butter in a pan; remove eel from marinade and dry carefully. Fry to golden brown in butter, drain, salt lightly and reserve, being careful to keep warm.
In another pan melt 2 tbsp. of the butter and cook mushrooms until tender, about 5 minutes. Season with a pinch of salt. Stir flour into pan juices in which eel was fried, add remaining white wine and *fumet de poisson*. Add nutmeg and simmer sauce over moderate heat for 10 minutes. Put eel slices back in pan, add sauted mushrooms and cook gently to blend flavors. Put remaining butter in a bowl, mash with a wooden spoon until creamy. Grind anchovy fillets and remaining peppercorns in a mortar or chop them fine and add to butter. Remove eels from heat, add anchovy butter to pan with remaining lemon juice. Serve on a hot platter.

Anguille arrostite al lauro

The eel is a favorite fish of Italians, and has been so since ancient times. It is so highly appreciated in Rome and Naples that it is called upon there to lend a festive note to dinner on Christmas Eve; they get most of their eels from the lagoon of Orbetello, which is famous for a fat tasty variety known as *capitone*. In Rome, the sale of eels for the Christmas Eve meal provides the occasion for a holiday known as the Cottio, which begins at 2 A.M. December 24 when the mayor of Rome in person opens the eels market. The most famous eel breeding centre in the world is in Italy, that of Comacchio, which Tasso wrote about. You can buy spit-roasted Comacchio eels almost everywhere in the world, for they are widely exported, packed in wine vinegar, as *anguilla amarinata di Comacchio*; but excellent though they are, there is nothing like the fresh fish. So if you happen to be where fresh eels are available, seize the opportunity to sample them in one or another of the tempting Italian dishes described here.

Sgombri grigliati a scottadito

Barbecued mackerel

Serves 4
Difficulty *
Time: 1 hour

**2 mackerel weighing about
1-1/4 lbs. each
1/2 cup olive oil
3 tbsp. lemon juice
1 tsp. salt
1 clove garlic, chopped
6 sprigs parsley, chopped**

Clean mackerel, wash and place in a shallow pan. Add oil, lemon juice, salt, garlic and parsley and marinate for 1/2 hour, turning frequently to coat all sides. Grill over charcoal, brushing on marinade regularly as mackerel cooks. Cook 7 to 8 minutes on each side. Mackerel can also be broiled.

Sgombri grigliati a scottadito

The mackerel, in Italian terminology, is a "Turkish fish". This is a far from scientific category in which all fatty fishes, whatever their kind, are lumped together. Mackerel seems to be most liked in the upper Adriatic, which it invades in great schools in May, devouring voraciously all the smaller fish that come within reach; the local fishermen avenge the victims with such assiduity that at this season they do not say, "I'm going fishing", but "I'm going mackereling". The ancient Romans were highly conscious of the mackerel, but for a somewhat curious reason. They salted the entrails and left them to decompose in the sun, after which they pressed from them an all-purpose seasoning liquid called *garum*, the ketchup of its day.

Dentice con funghi

Red snapper (or rockfish) with mushrooms

Serves 4
Difficulty *
Time: 1-1/2 hours
Oven Temp. 375° F.

**1 red snapper (or rockfish) weighing about 2-1/2 lbs.
Salt
Flour
7 tbsp. olive oil
1/2 cup dry white wine
1 clove garlic, chopped
1 tbsp. butter
1 lb. small button mushrooms left whole, stems trimmed
2 lemons
Several sprigs parsley**

Have fish scaled and cleaned and head removed. Wash fish under cold running water. Dry in a kitchen towel, salt fish inside and out and roll in flour. Heat 1/4 cup of the oil in a large metal baking pan on top of range. Add fish and brown on both sides, turning carefully so as not to damage the fish. Bake in a preheated oven for 20 to 25 minutes, basting with white wine after 10 to 12 minutes. Also baste with pan juices from time to time.

Saute garlic in butter with remaining oil. When garlic begins to brown, remove it and add mushrooms. Stir, salt and after a few minutes sprinkle juice of 1/2 a lemon over them. Cook for 10 to 15 minutes over high heat without adding water (the moisture contained in the mushrooms is enough.) Sprinkle with chopped parsley. Carefully lift out fish and place on a platter. Spoon over mushrooms and pan juices. Garnish with remaining lemon cut into wedges and parsley sprigs.

Note: Red snapper (or rockfish) are substitutes for the Mediterranean fish called "Dentice"

Sarde in saor

Sweet-and-sour sardines

Serves 4
Difficulty *
Time: Must be made the day ahead:
24 hours to marinate fish

2 tbsp. raisins
2 lbs. fresh sardines
Flour
Deep oil heated to 360° F.
2 onions, chopped

2 tbsp. wine vinegar
1 tbsp. sugar
2 tbsp pine nuts
6 sprigs parsley, chopped

Soak raisins in warm water for 30 minutes. Clean sardines and wash thoroughly in cold running water. Dry on paper towels. Coat sardines with flour, shaking off excess. Deep-fry sardines preferably in a basket in preheated oil for 5 to 6 minutes. When they are crisp and golden, drain on paper toweling. Meanwhile heat 3 tablespoons oil in a pan and saute onions until they are translucent, but not brown. Stir in vinegar, sugar, pine nuts and drained raisins. Simmer for a few minutes over low heat. Put sardines in shallow dish side by side. Pour sauce over them. Sprinkle with parsley. Set dish aside and let sardines marinate for 24 hours before serving cold.

Sarde fritte alla ligure

Fresh sardines Ligurian style

Serves 4
Difficulty *
Time: 1-1/2 hours

Clean sardines, discarding heads and tails. Slit open on one side, but without separating halves. Carefully remove bones, wash and dry in a towel. Saute mushrooms in 2 tablespoons oil. Sprinkle with a little salt and place into a bowl. Soak stale bread in milk, wring it out well, then add it to mushrooms with Parmesan, garlic, marjoram, oregano, 1 of the eggs and a pinch of salt. Mix well. Put a little of the mixture into each sardine, spreading it uniformly with a knife. Close sardines. Coat each sardine with flour. Dip into remaining beaten eggs and then into bread crumbs, pressing crumbs firmly to make them adhere. Fry in hot oil 1/4 inch deep until brown on both sides. Serve piping hot.

Sarde fritte alla ligure

16 sardines
1/2 package (1 oz.) dried
mushrooms, soaked and chopped
Olive oil
Salt, pepper
4 slices stale bread
Milk
1 tbsp. grated Parmesan cheese
1 clove garlic, chopped
Several sprigs chopped fresh
marjoram
Pinch of oregano
3 eggs
Flour
Dry bread crumbs

Sogliole all'erba salvia

Sole with sage

Serves 4
Difficulty *
Time: 1 hour

8 fillets of sole
Flour
2 eggs
Salt, pepper
Dry bread crumbs
1/3 cup olive oil
8 sage leaves or 1/2 tsp.
crumbled sage

Coat the fillets with flour, then dip into beaten eggs seasoned with a pinch of salt and pepper and coat with bread crumbs. Press crumbs firmly onto fillets. Fry in oil together with sage leaves. When fillets are crisp and golden brown drain them on absorbent paper, and sprinkle on salt to taste. Arrange on a serving platter and serve.

Sogliole all' erba salvia

The word "sole" automatically raises in the minds of most gourmets the reponse, "Dover sole", and indeed the English Channel fish is worthy of special attention. But though it is less widely known, there are connoisseurs who know both and believe that the sole of the upper Adriatic are as good as, if not better than, those of the Channel. In any case, the sole is a fish admirably adapted to the Italian culinary genius. It is bland enough to serve as a bearer of other flavors. Like pasta, it cries for adornment, enrichment—sauces, garnishes, extravagance. These are what Italian cooks love to provide. Given a good sole for a starter, they are moved to miracles.

Filetti di sogliola al pomodoro e funghi

Fillets of sole with tomatoes and mushrooms

Serves 4
Difficulty *
Time: 1 hour
Oven Temp. 400° F.

8 sole fillets weighing
4 oz. each
1 small onion, chopped
1/4 cup butter
3/4 lb. mushrooms, stems trimmed and sliced

3/4 cup dry white wine
3/4 lb. fresh tomatoes (about 2 large) peeled and diced
Salt, pepper
6 sprigs parsley, chopped

Wash fillets and dry on paper towels. Saute onion in 2 tablespoons of the butter until golden. Add mushrooms and wine. Raise heat and simmer until wine has boiled off. Add tomatoes. Season sauce with salt and pepper. Simmer 15 minutes. Stir in parsley. Butter shallow baking dish, arrange sole fillets in bottom, sprinkle with salt lightly. Pour mushroom sauce over fillets. Bake in a preheated oven for 15 minutes.

Filetti di sogliola con fettuccine al forno

Fillets of sole baked with noodles

Serves 4
Difficulty **
Time: 2 hours
Oven Temp. 350° F.

2 sole, each weighing
1-1/4 lbs., filleted
9 tbsp. butter
1/4 lb. cultivated mushrooms, sliced
8 raw shrimp, shelled and deveined
8 mussels removed from shell

7 tbsp. dry white wine
7 tbsp. fish stock
Paprika, salt, Cayenne pepper
8 oz. very thin egg noodles (fettuccine all'uovo)
7 tbsp. heavy cream
2 egg yolks
Juice of 1/2 lemon

Chop skin and bones of fish. Add fish heads. Cover with water and 1 teaspoon salt. Simmer for 30 minutes. Strain and then boil hard until you have 7 tablespoons left in pan. Melt 3 tablespoons butter in a pan and saute mushrooms until wilted. Add shrimp and mussels. Saute 1 minute. Set aside and keep hot. Brush a shallow baking pan with 3 tablespoons of the butter. Add fillets of sole. Pour over wine and fish broth. Season with a pinch each of salt and paprika. Bake in a preheated oven for 15 to 20 minutes or until fish is just cooked.

Cook noodles in boiling salted water until al dente. Drain and toss with 2 tablespoons of the butter. Grease a shallow baking pan. Cover bottom with layer of cooked noodles. Place fillets on top. Spoon over mushroom and shellfish mixture. Boil pan juices from cooking fish to 1/2 its original volume. Strain through a cloth into a saucepan. Reheat and stir in cream. Simmer for about 10 minutes. Remove from heat. Stir in egg yolks mixed with lemon juice. Add remaining butter and season to taste with salt and Cayenne. Pour sauce over fillets and bake in a preheated oven for 15 minutes. Serve immediately.

Filetti di sogliola "casa nostra"

Fillets of sole with zucchini in tomato sauce

Serves 4
Difficulty *
Time: 2 hours
Oven Temp. 350° F.

1-1/4 lbs. zucchini (courgettes)
Olive oil
Salt, pepper
1 sprig fresh rosemary
6 fresh basil leaves, chopped

1 cup sieved tomato pulp
1/2 cup butter
8 fillets of sole
Dry breads crumbs
Juice of 1/2 lemon

Slice zucchini 1/2-inch thick and fry in hot oil 1/4-inch deep until brown on all sides. Drain off excess oil. Season with salt and pepper. Add rosemary, half of the basil, tomato pulp and 2 tablespoons of the butter. Saute for 3 to 4 minutes. Remove rosemary and set dish aside, keeping it hot. Melt 1/4 cup of the butter in a frying pan and brown sole fillets on both sides. Butter shallow baking pan and put fillets in it side by side. Cover with zucchini in tomato sauce. Sprinkle bread crumbs over them and dot with remaining butter. Sprinkle remaining basil over pan. Add lemon juice and bake in a preheated oven for 15 minutes.

Naselli alla brace alla sardegnola

Barbecued whiting Sardinian style

Serves 4
Difficulty *
Time: 30 minutes

2 whitings weighing about 2-1/2 lbs.
Bay leaves

Salt, pepper
Olive oil

Clean whiting, discard head, cut each fish into 4 crosswise pieces. Spear pieces on heatproof skewers, alternating whiting with bay leaves. Season with salt, pepper and brush with oil. Cook 6 inches above gray charcoal, basting as needed with oil until fish is cooked, about 10 to 15 minutes.

Tuna has held a most important position in the Italian diet since time immemorial. Off the southern coast of Sicily, the tuna season is the occasion for a lively festival, during which these large fish are entrapped, with appropriate ceremony, in labyrinths of fixed nets; the same system, with less ceremony, is used off southern Sardinia. This is a very old method, inherited by the Italians from the Greeks; it is described by Aristotle. Most persons throughout the world know tuna chiefly in its preserved forms; but it can be delicious as a fresh fish, and it is often so served in Italy.

Tonno alla moda calabrese

Tuna Calabrian style

Serves 4
Difficulty *
Time: 1-1/2 hours

4 rather thick tuna steaks weighing 2 lbs. in all
Salt, black pepper
Flour
1/3 cup olive oil
1/2 cup dry white wine
4 slices bacon, chopped

1 small onion, chopped
1 clove garlic, chopped
6 sprigs parsley, chopped
4 fillets of anchovy in oil, mashed
1 lb. ripe tomatoes (about 3 medium) peeled, seeded and sieved

Wash tuna, drain and dry in a kitchen towel. Sprinkle tuna steaks with salt and pepper. Coat tuna with flour. Heat oil in a frying pan and brown tuna first on one side, then the other for 5 minutes. Add wine and simmer until it evaporates. Place tuna on a platter and keep warm. In same pan saute bacon, onion and garlic until golden. Stir in half the parsley, anchovy fillets and tomatoes. Season with salt and pepper and simmer over moderate heat for 15 minutes, stirring occasionally. Put tuna steaks in sauce and heat for a few minutes to flavor them. Serve steaks with sauce spooned over them. Sprinkle with remaining parsley.

Filetti di pesce persico alla milanese

Fillets of perch Milanese

Serves 4
Difficulty **
Time: 2 hours, plus time for marinating perch

**8 lake perch fillets, about
2 to 2-1/2 lbs.
1/2 cup olive oil
Juice of 1 lemon
1 small onion, chopped
Salt, pepper
Flour
2 eggs
Dry bread crumbs
5 tbsp. butter**

If using whole perch, have them filleted and skinned. Cover fillets with a mixture of oil, lemon juice, onion, salt and pepper to taste. Marinate for 1 hour, turning often. Remove fillets from marinade, drain and dry on paper towels. Coat with flour. Dip in eggs beaten with a pinch of salt. Dip in bread crumbs, pressing firmly to make crumbs adhere. Melt 4 tablespoons of the butter in frying pan. Fry breaded perch fillets gently until golden. Transfer to serving platter. Add remaining butter to pan juices and cook until lightly browned, scraping pan. Pour this browned butter over fillets and serve.

> If Italy is rich in saltwater fish, she is less well provided with those of fresh water—or perhaps Italians are less interested in freshwater fish. The mountainous nature of much of the country means, of course, that there are many swift streams which afford trout of excellent quality. The lakes and rivers harbor shad, perch, salmon trout, pike (there is a town on the Po called Luzzara, believed to be derived from *luccio*, pike) and even, in the Po, sturgeon.

Luccio gustoso con le noci

Savory pike with walnuts

Serves 4
Difficulty *
Time: 1-1/2 hours
Oven Temp. 375° F.

**1 pike weighing about
2-1/2 lbs.
Salt, peppercorns
Flour
5 tbsp. butter
1 whole clove
1/2 bay leaf
1 small onion, chopped
1/2 stalk celery, chopped**

**3 tbsp. chopped parsley
7 tbsp. dry white wine
7 tbsp. chicken broth
1 package (1 oz.) dried
mushrooms, soaked and chopped
1/2 cup coarsely chopped
walnut meats
1/4 cup grated Gruyere
(or Swiss) cheese**

Have pike cleaned and cut into fillets. Cut into serving-size pieces. Wash and dry. Season pieces with salt and peppercorns ground in a mortar, and coat with flour. Using 1/4 cup of the butter brown pike on both sides in a pan. Add clove, bay leaf, onion, celery and parsley. Saute briefly until onions are wilted. Pour in wine and broth and mushrooms. Cover and cook for about 15 minutes. Put pike in shallow baking dish and keep hot. Strain cooking juices and boil until reduced to 1/2 its original volume. Mix in walnut meats and pour over fish. Sprinkle on Gruyere, dot with remaining butter and bake in a preheated oven for 15 minutes.

Trota salmonata con agliata alla ligure

*Poached salmon trout
with garlic sauce
Ligurian style*

Serves 4
Difficulty *
Time: 1-1/2 hours

Court bouillon:
1 cup water
1 cup dry white wine
1 carrot, chopped
1 stalk celery, chopped
1 sprig parsley, chopped
1 small onion, chopped
Salt, 4 peppercorns
Juice of 1/2 lemon

**1 salmon trout weighing
2-1/2 lbs.**
1 lb. potatoes, diced
4 cloves garlic, chopped
1 cup soft bread crumbs
2 tbsp. wine vinegar
Salt, pepper
7 tbsp. olive oil
2 lemons
1/4 cup melted butter

Trota salmonata con agliata alla ligure

Court bouillon: Combine all ingredients, bring to a boil and simmer for 5 minutes.

Clean trout, wash, put in a fish kettle and cover with court bouillon. Bring to a boil over moderate heat, lower heat and simmer for 12 minutes. Boil potatoes in salted water until tender. Grind garlic in a mortar, add bread soaked in vinegar and salt and pepper to taste. Add oil, drop by drop, or in a fine stream and beat until smooth. Drain salmon trout carefully, transfer to a platter and garnish with lemon halves. Surround with boiled potatoes mixed with melted butter. Spoon over garlic sauce.

Trota alle olive

Trout with olives

**4 trout weighing about
10 oz. each, cleaned**
1 small onion, chopped
3/4 cup olive oil
**1 lb. potatoes, peeled and
sliced 1/4-inch thick**
**1 can (1 lb.) peeled Italian
tomatoes, undrained and
chopped**
6 pitted black olives, sliced
2 bay leaves
1/2 tsp. crumbled marjoram
6 sprigs parsley, chopped
Salt, pepper
Flour

Serves 4   Difficulty *   Time: 1 hour

Thaw trout, if frozen. Wash trout thoroughly in cold running water. Saute onion in 5 tablespoons of the oil until transparent. Stir in potatoes and a few minutes later add canned tomatoes, olives, bay leaves and marjoram. If sauce gets too thick before potatoes are completely cooked, you can thin it with a little boiling water. Cook potatoes covered, turning them from time to time. When potatoes are done, in about 30 minutes, sprinkle with chopped parsley and leave over very low heat to keep warm. Season to taste with salt and pepper.
While potatoes are cooking, coat trout with flour. Heat remaining oil in a frying pan. Brown trout on both sides. Fry slowly to cook fish completely, about 20 minutes. Sprinkle with salt and pepper to taste. Place trout on a platter and surround with potatoes.

Arselle al pomodoro e basilico

Clams with tomato and basil

Serves 4
Difficulty *
Time: 2 hours

4-1/2 lbs. small clams
5 tbsp. olive oil
2 cloves garlic, mashed in a mortar

6 fresh basil leaves, mashed in a mortar
4 fully ripe tomatoes, peeled and minced
Salt, coarsely ground pepper

Scrub clams. Cook clams in 2 tablespoons of the oil until shells open. Remove meat from shells. Strain pan juices and reserve. Heat remaining oil in a frying pan, add garlic and basil paste. Saute 1 minute then add tomato pulp. Season with a pinch of salt and a little freshly ground pepper. Pour in about 7 tablespoons of the reserved pan juices and simmer until sauce has thickened a little, approx. 5 minutes. Add clams, simmer for about 10 minutes (cooking too long makes clams tough), then serve.

Arselle alla maremmana

Clams Maremma style

Serves 4
Difficulty *
Time: 2 hours

4-1/2 lbs. small clams
7 tbsp. olive oil, approx.
3 cloves garlic, chopped
6 fresh sage leaves, chopped
Salt, peppercorns
7 tbsp. dry white wine

2 eggs
Juice of 1 lemon
6 sprigs parsley, chopped
16 slices of French bread, (1/2-inch thick)

Clean clams with brush and wash thoroughly in cold running water. Put oil in pan, add 2 cloves of the garlic and sage leaves. Saute briefly, then remove garlic and sage. Put clams in oil, season with a little freshly ground black pepper, add wine and cook covered over very high heat for 5 minutes or until shells open. Remove shells. Remove clams from shells and replace in pan juices. Beat eggs in a bowl, add lemon juice and salt lightly. Pour mixture over clams, mix, remove immediately from heat and add parsley and remaining garlic. Toast bread and arrange on large, heated serving platter, cover with clams and egg mixture and serve immediately.

Arselle alla maniera di Vasto

Clams Vasto style

Serves 4
Difficulty *
Time: 2 hours

4-1/2 lbs. small clams
2/3 cup olive oil
1 medium size onion, chopped
1 clove garlic, chopped
1 tbsp. chopped green chili pepper

7 tbsp. dry white wine
1/4 cup tomato sauce
16 slices French bread, cut 1/2-inch thick
Salt
1/4 cup chopped parsley

Heat clams in 2 tablespoons of the oil until they open.
Reserve pan juices after straining. Pour remaining oil in a frying pan, saute onion, garlic and chili pepper briefly. Add wine and simmer until one-half the original volume. Add tomato sauce diluted in 7 tablespoons water. Season to taste with salt and continue cooking for about 5 minutes. Add clams with their juice and simmer for 10 minutes, adding a litle more water if needed (bear in mind that bread slices will absorb a good amount of liquid). Toast bread slices in oven and put 4 in each plate or soup dish. Cover with clam soup. Sprinkle chopped parsley over surface and serve.

Arselle alla maniera di Vasto

The coasts of Italy are blessed with a rich and diversified bounty of types of shellfish which the average American or Englishman would lump together as "clams" leaving finer distinctions to specialists. Italians are more precise. They have popular names for each separate type of clam; but, confusingly, none of them is likely to designate the same shellfish in two different places. The recipes here call for *arselle*; but what are *arselle*? None of my small Italian dictionaries has ever heard of the animal. Of my two big ones, the first maintains they have been extinct since prehistoric times and the second calls them mussels. Pooh. The fact is that you should get good results from these recipes using English cockles or American little-necks, which are indeed called *arselle* in Genoa and Sardinia, though *calcinelli* or *telline* in Ravenna, *capperozzoli* in Venice, and *vongole* in Rome and Naples. The best way to deal with this problem is to forget about it; an *arsella* by any other name would taste as sweet.

Cozze alla pugliese

Mussels Apulian style

Serves 4
Difficulty **
Time: 2 hours
Oven Temp. 375° F.

3-1/2 lbs. mussels
1/4 cup olive oil
2 cloves garlic, chopped
7 tbsp. dry white wine
2 tbsp. tomato paste
Salt, pepper
2 tbsp. grated Parmesan cheese
1 cup thick white sauce *
3 tbsp. dry bread crumbs, fried
in 1 tbsp. oil

Clean mussels with a stiff brush under cold running water, then place them in a pan with 2 tablespoons of the oil. Cook over high heat covered and when shells open, remove mussels from shell. Strain pan juices through cheesecloth which has been soaked in water and then wrung out hard. Saute garlic in remaining oil. Add wine and strained pan juices. Simmer 10 minutes or until 1/2 cup remains. Add tomato paste diluted in 1/2 cup warm water. Season with salt and pepper to taste and simmer for 5 minutes. Stir grated cheese into white sauce and stir this into mixture in pan. Stir in mussels. Pour into a 1-1/2 quart shallow baking pan. Sprinkle with fried bread crumbs and bake in a preheated oven for 15 minutes or until brown on top.

* White Sauce: Melt 1/4 cup of butter. Stir in 1/4 cup flour. Gradually add 1 cup of milk, stirring constantly over low heat until sauce thickens. Season to taste with salt and pepper.

It may well be that mussels are the most appreciated form of shellfish in Italy, though clams would be very close runners-up. Perhaps it is because the mussel lends itself so accommodatingly to subtleties of cooking, thus allowing the fine Italian hand the joy of demonstrating the full extent of its skill in the kitchen. Italy has many varieties of mussel renowned for their special excellence even before the cook has had at them. There are the *datteri* (dates), so called from their shape, which for some reason attain such particularly high quality at La Spezia that the Emperor Frederick Barbarossa ordered that city to pay him its tribute in mussels; the *peòci* of Venice; the *pidocchio* of Ravenna; and everywhere *mitili* or *cozze*, which are just mussels, humble but good.

Cozze crude al limone

Mussels on the half shell

Serves 4
Difficulty *
Time: 1/2 hour

3-1/2 lbs. mussels
2 lemons
Peppercorns

Clean mussels with a stiff brush, wash thoroughly under cold running water. Open with a clam knife and serve them on the half shell with lemon quarters. Pass peppermill so each person may season to taste with freshly ground black pepper.

Cozze crude al limone

Cozze in tecia alla veneta

*Baked mussels
Veneto style*

Serves 4
Difficulty *
Time: 1-1/2 hours
Oven Temp. 375° F.

3-1/2 lbs. mussels
7 tbsp. olive oil
3 cloves garlic, chopped
6 sprigs parsley, chopped

2 tbsp. dry bread crumbs
2 tbsp. wine vinegar
Salt, pepper

Scrape and wash mussels under cold running water; put them in a pan with 2 tablespoons of the oil, cover and put them over high heat. When shells open, remove mussels from shells and place them in a shallow baking dish. Mix garlic and parsley with bread crumbs. Sprinkle this mixture over mussels. Mix remaining oil and vinegar and pour over mussels. Season with salt and pepper. Bake in a preheated oven for 15 minutes.

Granchio alla gran diavola

Deviled Crab

Serves 4
Difficulty *
Time: 1/2 hour

1-1/2 lbs. shelled freshly
cooked or canned crab meat
5 tbsp. butter
2 tbsp. brandy
3/4 lb. cultivated mushrooms
Juice of 1/2 lemon
1 tbsp. flour
1/4 cup heavy cream
Salt, pepper

Cut crab meat into small pieces. Heat 3 tablespoons of the butter in a pan and saute crab meat briefly, stirring occasionally with a fork. Add brandy and simmer uncovered until it evaporates. Wash and slice mushrooms and saute slowly in remaining butter for 15 minutes. Season with lemon juice and add crab meat. Sprinkle flour over crab and mushrooms, mix carefully and, after a few minutes, stir in cream. Simmer, while stirring, until sauce is thick. Season to taste with salt and pepper.

Ostriche gratinate

Oysters au gratin

Serves 4
Difficulty **
Time: 1-1/2 hours
Oven Temp. 400°F.

3 cloves garlic, chopped
2/3 cup dry bread crumbs
Black peppercorns
24 very fresh oysters
6 tbsp. butter
1/4 cup grated Parmesan cheese

In most countries of shellfish eaters, the king of the category is the oyster; in Italy, I have the impression that it lags behind other shellfish in popular favor. This is certainly not for want of habit—the oldest oyster beds in the world are those of Taranto, established by the Greeks who colonized the foot of Italy before this area had become part of the Roman Empire. Oysters are raised there today in almost exactly the same fashion as in antiquity. If Italians are relatively less enthusiastic about oysters, it may be because oysters are at their best when they come from cold water; Atlantic oysters are tastier that Mediterranean oysters. Italy could, of course, import Atlantic oysters (the ancient Romans did) but perhaps she feels no need of them. Her waters are sufficiently rich in other forms of shellfish.

Mix garlic with half of the bread crumbs and a good pinch of freshly ground black pepper. Open oyster shells and remove oysters. Brush a shallow 1-1/2 quart baking dish with half of the butter. Cover bottom with bread crumbs and garlic mixture. Top with oysters. Sprinkle with grated Parmesan and remaining bread crumbs. Dot with remaining butter. Bake in a preheated oven for 10 to 15 minutes or until brown. Serve immediately.

Aragoste alla diavola all'italiana

Deviled lobster Italian style

Serves 4
Difficulty **
Time: 2 hours
Oven Temp. 375° F.

The Mediterranean lobster, Atlantic Coasters should be warned, is not the animal they know by that name; it is the spiny lobster, which exists in the Caribbean and on the Pacific Coast, but not the Atlantic. Generally speaking, you can apply any recipe meant for one to the other, but it is my feeling that the spiny lobster is more appropriate for elaborate treatment; its flavor is a little less assertive than that of the Atlantic lobster and it therefore carries other tastes cooperatively rather than competitively. The Atlantic lobster is usually best with the simplest preparations. *Aragosta alla partenopea.* described here, is a dish with a name which takes us back to antiquity. Partenope was the ancient name of Naples, which borrowed it from the Queen of the Sirens, who, in despite at the failure of the sirens' song to lure Ulysses to destruction, threw herself into the sea and was washed up drowned on the beach at Naples.

Drop lobsters into boiling salted water. When water reboils, boil for 5 minutes. Drain and drench with cold water.

Cut lobsters in half lengthwise, crack legs and claws. Remove "sand sack" and dark-colored intestine. Reserve coral and tomalley. Mix butter until it is creamy. Stir in mustard and creamy parts of lobsters after pressing them through a sieve. Light brandy in a cup and pour flaming over mixture. When flames die, sprinkle with salt and pepper to taste and mix thoroughly. Brush a baking dish with oil. Add lobster halves, cut side up. Spread some of the mustard sauce over them. Bake in a preheated oven for about 15 minutes, basting from time to time with pan juices.

Meanwhile mix bread crumbs with remaining mustard sauce. Remove pan from oven and spread this mixture over lobster halves. Put pan back in oven and continue baking for 5 minutes, until top is well browned. Put lobster halves on serving platter, pour pan juices over them. Garnish with lemon slices and serve.

2 live lobsters, each weighing about 1-1/2 lbs.
3 tbsp. butter
1 tbsp. brown mustard
1/4 cup brandy

Salt, pepper
2 tbsp. olive oil
3 tbsp. dry bread crumbs
2 lemons, sliced

Aragoste alla diavola all' italiana

Aragosta alla partenopa

Lobster Neapolitan

Serves 4
Difficulty **
Time: 1-1/2 hours

1 live lobster weighing
about 3 lbs. or 2 lobsters
1-1/2 lbs. each
2 hearts lettuce
7 tbsp. olive oil
Juice of 1/2 lemon
Salt
1 tbsp. French mustard (brown)
1/2 cup chopped parsley

Aragosta alla partenopa

Drop lobster into boiling water. Cover, lower heat and simmer for 30 minutes. Let lobster cool in its water.
Remove when good and cold, place on cutting board. Remove tail, cut shell with shears, lengthwise (at the cartilage,) remove meat and dice. Crack head, legs and claws, remove all meat and dice as well. Put all of the lobster meat in a flat salad dish. Cut lettuce hearts in quarters and place around edge of dish. Make a dressing by beating oil with lemon juice and a pinch of salt. Add mustard and parsley and beat with a whisk or fork to blend thoroughly. Pour dressing over lobster and serve.

Scamponi alla sorrentina

Prawns Sorrento style

Serves 6
Difficulty *
Time: 45 minutes
Oven Temp. 350 F.

2-1/2 lbs. large prawns
(about 24 prawns)
1 lb. mozzarella cheese

1 can (1 lb.) peeled Italian
tomatoes, undrained and chopped
1 tsp. crumbled oregano
Salt, pepper

Shell and devein raw prawns, wash and dry on paper towels. Cut mozzarella into 24 1-inch cubes. Chop any remaining pieces of mozzarella. Spear 4 prawns and 4 pieces of mozzarella, alternating on heatproof skewers. Place skewers side by side in an oiled shallow baking dish. Pour over tomatoes. Sprinkle with oregano and sprinkle with remaining mozzarella. Sprinkle with salt and pepper. Bake in a preheated oven for about 20 minutes.

Gamberi alla panna

Creamed prawns

Serves 4
Difficulty *
Time: 1 hour

1-1/2 lbs. large shrimp
Bouquet garni of thyme,
parsley and bay leaf

1 cup heavy cream
1 tbsp. chopped parsley
Salt, peppercorns

Cook prawns in salted water containing the bouquet garni and several peppercorns until cooked. Let them cool in water. Drain, shell and devein. Put them in a 1-quart serving dish. Heat cream until hot. Season with salt and stir in parsley. Pour cream over shrimp.

129

Scampi grigliati

Grilled shrimp

Serves 4
Difficulty *
Time: 1-1/2 hours, plus time required to marinate shrimp

2 lbs. large shrimp
1/2 cup olive oil
Salt, pepper
3 cloves garlic, mashed
1/2 cup butter

Shell and devein raw shrimp, wash and dry and marinate for about 1 hour in a mixture of oil, salt, freshly ground pepper, stirring occasionally to make sure all parts are equally marinated. Remove from marinade and spear them on skewers, two at a time. Brush with a little of the marinade and grill for 10 to 15 minutes, turning just once (the final product should be well seared.) Arrange shrimp on a serving platter. Serve topped with garlic butter.

To prepare garlic butter: Peel garlic, blanch for a moment in boiling water, dry and grind to a paste in a mortar (or else chop very fine.) Cream butter until very soft. Stir in garlic and then press through a fine sieve.

Scampi is a word likely to appear without explanation on menus all over the world, for everywhere the Italian word has been adopted, with a special bow to the *scampi* of Venice. The Venetian *scampi* is a prawn, but the name is employed loosely to cover many other kinds of prawns besides the Venetian type, and shrimps as well; this allows a good deal of latitude, since there are several hundred species, all of them more or less edible. Italians manage to make the distinction between *scampi* and *gamberi*, which are crayfish, of which there are also many varieties. Few persons would argue with the assertion that the Venetian scampi is the monarch of them all. There are innumerable fashions of preparing scampi, but my own preference is for one of the simplest—just grilled, since this lets the natural flavor come out.

Scampi grigliati

Lumache al pomodoro alla romana

Snails
with hot tomato sauce
Roman style

Serves 4
Difficulty *
Time: 1-1/2 hours

1 clove garlic, chopped
4 to 5 tbsp. olive oil
1-1/4 lbs. Italian plum tomatoes, peeled and chopped

1 hot red pepper, chopped
2 tbsp. chopped mint leaves
24 large canned snails, drained
Salt

Saute garlic in oil until golden. Add tomatoes and boil sauce over high heat for several minutes. Add hot red pepper, mint, snails and 2 cups water. Simmer for 1 hour. Season to taste with salt. When completed, the sauce should be red and peppery ("hot").

Scampi con riso

Shrimp with rice

Serves 6   Difficulty *   Time: 1-1/2 hours

18 large shrimp
Juice of 1 lemon
Salt, Cayenne pepper
Flour
3/4 cup (6 oz.) butter
1/4 cup olive oil
1/4 cup cognac
1/2 small onion, chopped
1-1/2 lbs. fresh tomatoes
(or 1 lb. can of peeled
Italian tomatoes) peeled, seeded
and sieved
2 cups rice
1 tsp. curry powder
6 sprigs parsley, chopped

Shell and devein raw shrimp, wash in water mixed with lemon juice, dry. Sprinkle shrimp with salt. Coat with flour and saute over high heat in 2 tablespoons of the butter and 2 tablespoons of the oil. Sprinkle with cognac and set aflame. Salt lightly again and set aside. Saute onion until wilted in 2 tablespoons of the butter and remaining oil, add tomatoes, a pinch of Cayenne pepper and salt and boil down until thick, about 10 minutes. Add shrimp and pan juices to sauce and simmer 15 minutes over low heat. Just before removing from heat stir in 5 tablespoons of the butter. Meanwhile, prepare rice. Cook rice in boiling salted water until firm but tender, about 20 to 25 minutes. Drain well and replace in saucepan. Toss over moderate heat in with remaining butter. Stir in curry powder and salt to taste. Heat 2 to 3 minutes. Turn rice out onto a platter and spoon over shrimp in sauce. Sprinkle with chopped parsley.

Fritti con zucchine

*Fried shrimp
with zucchini (courgettes)*

Serves 4
Difficulty *
Time: 1-1/2 hours

2 lbs. shrimp   Olive oil
Salt   1 lb. medium-sized zucchini
Flour   2 lemons

Shell raw shrimp and devein. Wash and dry. Sprinkle with salt. Coat with flour. Fry in hot oil 1/4-inch deep. When crisp and golden on all sides, put them on paper toweling to drain, salting them lightly once again. While shrimp are frying, wash zucchini, dry them and cut off tips. Cut into shoestrings and fry in a separate pan, making sure the oil is good and hot, and about 1/4-inch deep. Heap shrimp on a serving platter, garnish with zucchini and lemon wedges and serve.

Lumache all'aglio all'Italiana

*Snails in garlic sauce
Italian style*

Serves 4
Difficulty **
Time: 1-1/2 hours
Oven Temp. 400° F.

7 oz. butter   Nutmeg
1/4 cup minced parsley   Canned snails, about 40 plus
2 cloves garlic, minced   snail shells
1 tbsp. minced onion   1/2 cup dry white wine
Salt, white pepper

Cream butter and blend with parsley, garlic and onion, a pinch of salt, pepper and nutmeg. Drain snails and dry. Put a little of the creamed butter and herbs into each snail shell. Press snail into shell and close the shell opening with more butter and herb mixture. Arrange snails in a baking dish, pour over wine. Bake in preheated oven for 10 minutes and serve immediately.

Calamaretti fritti

Fried squid

Serves 4
Difficulty *
Time: 1 hour

2 lbs. small squid
Flour
Deep oil, heated to 360° F.

Salt
2 lemons, cut into halves

Clean squid as in Calamaretti alla barese. Cut into bite-size pieces. Coat with flour lightly and deep-fry in oil until golden brown. Season with salt, arrange on a serving platter and garnish with lemon halves.

A category of fish much eaten in Italy but little liked, to put it mildly, in, for instance, America and England, is the family which includes octopus, cuttlefish, inkfish and their ilk. Perhaps the near horror that the idea of eating such beasts inspires in some Anglo-Saxon breasts is compounded partly of fear of the unknown; these species are comparatively rare in the waters of most English-speaking countries. For the brave, they can be found all over the world in Italian groceries, exported from their home territories, preserved in one fashion or another, and may be used in that form to produce the dishes described here.

Calamaretti alla barese

Baby squid Bari style

Serves 4
Difficulty *
Time: 2 hours

2 lbs. baby squid
2 cloves garlic, chopped
2/3 cup olive oil
2 cups sieved tomato pulp
(or sieved canned Italian
peeled plum tomatoes)
Salt, pepper
6 sprigs parsley, chopped

Clean squid by removing ink sac, mouth, eyes, the inner bone; skin, wash repeatedly in cold running water and separate sac and tentacles.
Saute garlic in 7 tablespoons of the oil, add tomato pulp. Season with salt and pepper and simmer sauce for about 10 minutes. In another pan brown the squid in remaining oil, turning constantly; pour the sauce over the squid and simmer covered 1 hour or until squid are tender. Sprinkle chopped parsley over dish and serve.

Calamaretti alla barese

Rane alla semplice al brandy

Brandied frogs' legs

Serves 4
Difficulty *
Time: 1-1/2 hours

**32 very fresh plump frogs'
legs already cleaned
1 cup brandy
Salt, pepper
2 egg whites
1/2 cup butter
Lemons cut in halves for
garnish**

Wash frogs' legs and marinate
for 1/2 hour in brandy. Sprinkle
with salt and pepper and stir
from time to time to coat legs
with brandy. When ready to
cook, beat egg whites until stiff.
Dip frogs' legs into egg whites.
Heat butter until it foams. Fry
legs until golden brown.
Remove from pan, heap them
on a serving platter and garnish
edges of platter with lemon.

Rane alla semplice al brandy

It is the French who have a reputation for being frog eaters, but
Italians have been consuming them too since very early times without
attracting any particular attention. They have sometimes gained
importance on the menu as the accidental result of other developments,
gastronomic by-products of history. Thus when the Emperor Honorius
moved the imperial court to Ravenna, the consumption of frogs in-
creased because the marshes around Ravenna were full of them. Something like a thousand years later, meadows along the Po in Piedmont
were flooded to grow rice; they grew frogs too, which were eaten,
fittingly, in *risotti*.

Rane all'italiana

Frogs' legs
Italian style

Serves 4
Difficulty *
Time: 1-1/2 hours, plus time required
to clean the frogs' legs

**32 very fresh, cleaned frogs' legs
1/2 cup milk
2 whole eggs
Nutmeg, salt, pepper**

**2 tbsp. heavy cream
Dry bread crumbs
6 tbsp. butter
1 cup tomato sauce**

Soak frogs' legs for about 1 hour in cold water to cover with milk
added. Drain and dry. Beat eggs, season with salt, pepper and a
pinch of nutmeg and beat in cream. Dip frogs' legs in this liquid,
then in bread crumbs, pressing firmly to make crumbs adhere. Fry
in hot butter until brown on all sides. Remove from pan and season
with salt. Heap on a serving platter and pass hot tomato sauce
separately.

The Italian is not a particularly carnivorous animal. This may be the result of climate, of history, of inbred preference, or more probably, of a combination of these and other influences. One other may have been poverty. Meat is the most expensive general category of food; and since Italy as a whole has often been poor, and some regions of Italy have always been poor, Italians may have gotten out of the habit of eating meat. There is also the circumstance that most Italian meals include pasta, and after having downed a heaping plateful of *tagliatelle alla bolognese* (which, come to think of it, has meat, finely chopped, in its sauce), only an ogre would feel in need of a hearty helping of meat.

When Italians do bring themselves to eat meat, they almost seem to be afraid of it. For heavy habitual meat eaters, the archetype of meat is roast beef. Roast beef is not unknown in Italy, but it is my impression that it is not particularly popular there; personally I cannot recall ever having eaten it in Italy except once on the farm of a cattle raiser in Tuscany, which eats more beef than any other region of Italy.

Italians do not eat much beef, foreigners are accustomed to assert, because Italian beef is not good; but this is not true. The Chianini steer of Tuscany is one of the leading beef animals of the world, the Brianza region north of Milan produces excellent beef, and even Lombardy Po Valley cattle, though they are bred to give high quality milk, are not bad meat animals either. If Italy is not roast beef country, it is simply because the Italian prefers white meat to red, young meat (*very* young meat) to adult meat, and meat in small pieces to meat in large chunks. In general, the largest piece of meat any Italian feels like tackling is a steak, and then chiefly in Tuscany.

Elsewhere the Italian ideal seems to be to reduce meat to its smallest dimensions. In the Veneto this is almost an obsession; except for *pasticciata alla veneta*, a sort of pot roast of marinated beef, meat is rarely encountered except cut up for stewing, or threaded in small cubes on spits, or chopped into hash. Veal is tolerated in large pieces more often than beef, but all the same it is likely to be cut up for the myriad varieties of *scaloppine*, while both beef and veal are chopped to produce meat balls (*polpette*) or meat loaves (*polpettone*); in Milan alone, a city which does not boggle at serving meat in generous proportions, I know six varieties of *polpette*, seven of *polpettone* and thirteen of *scaloppine*.

Italy's preference for veal over beef is so marked that the antiquary Varro maintained, ingeniously but erroneously, that the very name of the country comes from the word for veal (*vitello=(v)Italia*). It is not the Number One meat of Italy, however. The country eats more pork, but the casual observer may easily fail to notice that fact for much of it is consumed in the form of sausage, which does not always pop into the mind when meat proper is being considered; indeed even ham, another form of meat much eaten in Italy, except when it is eaten fresh, seems a little apart from the mainstream. There is a limited number of important fresh pork dishes in Italy, the most important being, probably, roast loin of pork (Tuscany) and *porchetta*, roast suckling pig.

Italians show little interest in mutton. By the time it has reached the age when it can no longer be called lamb (a status attained earlier in Italy than in Great Britain or the United States), it is, as far as possible, relegated to the function of producing wool. Once again, the taste is for young animals. Italians are enthusiastic about lamb, and the younger the better.

Petto di vitello al forno alla romana

Arrosto di bue al sangue

Boneless rib roast beef with baked tomatoes

Serves 4
Difficulty **
Time: 2 hours
Oven Temp. 425° F., then lower heat to 350° F. for tomatoes

2-1/2 lbs. boneless prime ribs of beef
Salt
1/4 lb. sliced pork fat
1 tbsp. melted butter
2 tbsp. oil

For garnish:

4 not too ripe tomatoes
2 cloves garlic, chopped
6 sprigs parsley, chopped
2 tbsp. dry bread crumbs
3 tbsp. olive oil
Salt, pepper

For roast: Season beef with salt. Tie slices of pork fat to roast. Brush with butter and oil. Roast in a preheated oven for 30 to 35 minutes. Lower heat and leave roast in oven.

For garnish: Cut tomatoes in half, squeeze out seeds and juice. Mix garlic, parsley and bread crumbs and use this mixture to stuff tomato halves. Place into a shallow baking pan. Drizzle with oil, then season with salt and pepper. Bake in a preheated oven for 15 minutes or until top of tomatoes are brown.
Remove roast from oven. Remove string and discard pork fat. Serve beef garnished with baked tomatoes.

Arrosto di bue al sangue

Bue means "steer", so when you find this word on an Italian bill of fare you are being offered beef, and probably roast beef, for this word is seldom pronounced in restaurants except when it is a question of a roast. Manzo is much preferred to describe beef dishes, for manzo means a *young* steer. To determine the honesty of the billing, have recourse to your teeth.

Filetto al limone

Lemon filet mignon

Serves 8
Difficulty *
Time: 30 minutes, plus refrigeration time

2 lbs. filet mignon
Juice of 2 lemons
1 tsp. coarsely ground pepper (freshly ground)

7 tbsp. oil
1 tsp. salt
1 tbsp. chopped parsley
1 tbsp. minced capers

Have filet sliced raw; the slices should be very thin, like prosciutto, so it may be best to have the butcher slice it on a machine. Put the slices on a serving platter, sprinkle with lemon juice and pepper. Let meat marinate for two hours at room temperature. Beat oil and salt with a fork. Add parsley and capers, then pour mixture over sliced meat. Turn meat slices in mixture. Refrigerate until ready to serve.

Costata
di bue al cartoccio

*Roast beef
in aluminum foil*

Serves 4
Difficulty *
Time: 2-1/2 hours
Oven Temp. 350° F.

2 tbsp. butter
**Prime rib of beef weighing
about 4 lbs.**
**A sheet of heavy duty
aluminum foil**
Salt, pepper

2 very ripe tomatoes, chopped
3 carrots, chopped
1 rib of celery, chopped
1 large onion, chopped
6 sprigs parsley, chopped
1/2 tsp. crumbled oregano

Heat butter in a frying pan and sear beef for a few moments over high heat and on both sides. Transfer meat to a sheet of aluminum foil. Sprinkle with salt and pepper. Add vegetables. Pour pan juices over beef and sprinkle on oregano. Seal aluminum foil tightly by folding over and sealing edges all around. Set roast with aluminum foil in a roasting pan and roast in preheated oven for about 2 hours. Open foil, slice roast and serve.

Bue arrosto con legumi

Roast beef with vegetables

Serves 4
Difficulty *
Time: 2 hours
Oven Temp. 375° F.

Tie roast with string, season with salt and pepper and place in a roasting pan with oil; dot with butter and roast in preheated oven for about 1-1/2 hours, turning occasionally. Add 1/2 cup wine half way through roasting. Complete roasting, occasionally basting with pan juices. Meanwhile boil vegetables, separately. Slice roast and arrange slices, slightly overlapping, in middle of platter. Heat roasting pan with juices on top of range. Add cooked and drained vegetables to pan and saute briefly until very hot. Spoon around meat slices.

2 lbs. fillet of beef
Salt, pepper
2 tbsp. olive oil
1/4 cup butter

1/2 cup rosé wine
1 lb. green beans, frenched
1 cup shelled peas
1 cup sliced carrots

Bue arrosto con legumi

137

Bistecchine
alla partenopea
al pomodoro

Steak with tomatoes
Neapolitan style

Serves 4
Difficulty *
Time: 1-1/2 hours

**8 slices fillet of beef weighing
about 2 lbs.
5 oz. prosciutto, half fat,
half lean, chopped
1/2 small onion, chopped
1/2 carrot, chopped
Salt, pepper
7 tbsp. dry white wine
1 lb. ripe tomatoes, skin and
seeds removed and sieved
1/2 cup beef broth
2 cloves garlic, chopped
10 tbsp. olive oil
3/4 lb. fresh small mushrooms
left whole
A few sprigs parsley, chopped
8 slices bread, cut into 1/2-inch
cubes**

Pound fillets lightly to half
their original thickness. Saute
prosciutto, onion and carrot.
Season fillet slices with salt and
pepper. Add to vegetables and
brown quickly on both sides
over high heat. Add wine and
simmer until it evaporates
about five minutes. Add tomato
pulp, broth and a little salt and
pepper and continue cooking
over low heat for 10 minutes.
Meanwhile, saute garlic in 2
tablespoons of the oil until
golden. Add mushrooms, salt
and pepper and continue cooking, adding a little water if
necessary. Sprinkle with chopped parsley and set aside.
Fry bread cubes in remaining oil
and stir until they are crisp and
golden. Arrange slices of fillet
on a hot serving platter, pour
pan juices over them and garnish platter with croutons.
Spoon mushrooms around fillet
slices.

Bistecchine alla partenopea al pomodoro

Bistecche al piccantino

Bistecche con uova alla contadina

Steak with fried eggs country-style

Serves 4
Difficulty *
Time: 30 minutes

6 tbsp. butter
4 slices fillet of beef,
about 1-1/2 inches thick

Salt, pepper
4 slices prosciutto crudo
4 eggs

Put half the butter in a pan. Sear steaks over very high heat, then reduce heat and continue cooking about 5 minutes on each side. The steaks when done, should be rare. Sprinkle with salt and pepper and keep hot. Melt remaining butter in another pan, and when it has turned brown, add prosciutto slices. Fry briefly, then break 1 egg on each of the prosciutto slices. Spoon the hot butter in the pan over eggs as they fry. Sprinkle with salt and pepper and remove carefully from pan, using spatula, and place 1 prosciutto slice with egg on each steak. Serve very hot.

Bistecche di lombo con acciughe e olive

Sirloin steak with anchovies and olives

Serves 4
Difficulty *
Time: 1 hour

12 desalted anchovy fillets
10 tbsp. butter
1 cup green olives

4 boneless club steaks weighing
about 6 oz. each
Salt, pepper

Pound 4 of the anchovy fillets in a mortar or chop them very fine and blend thoroughly with half of the butter until a soft, creamy mixture. Make a sausage-like roll of this in wax paper and refrigerate. Pit olives and scald for 5 minutes in boiling water. Brown steaks on both sides in 3 tablespoons of remaining butter, remove them while still rare (or cook further if desired over moderate heat) and place on a hot serving platter. Sprinkle with salt and pepper and keep them hot. Melt remaining butter in a saucepan. Add olives and saute gently for 10 minutes, stirring occasionally. Garnish each steak with a slice of chilled anchovy butter and 2 curled anchovy fillets; arrange olives around sides.

Bistecche al piccantino

Filet Mignon piquant

Serves 4
Difficulty *
Time: 1 hour

1/2 cup black olives
3 anchovy fillets, chopped
3/4 cup chopped tomato pulp
(skin and seeds removed and
pulp chopped of fresh tomato)

4 filet mignon steaks
weighing about 6 oz. each
3 tbsp. olive oil
2 tbsp. capers
1/2 cup dry white wine
Salt, pepper

Pit olives and chop coarsely. Mix olives, anchovy fillets and tomato pulp. Brown steaks quickly on both sides in oil and remove to a platter. Add tomato pulp mixture and capers to pan juices. Heat until bubbly. Stir in wine and a pinch of pepper and simmer until sauce is thick. Season to taste with salt. Return steaks to pan and cook to desired degree of doneness, turning several times in sauce and making sure that they are not overcooked. Salt lightly and serve immediately with pan juices spooned over them.

Costata di manzo alla valtellinese

*Braised beef
Valtellina style*

Serves 4
Difficulty *
Time: 2 hours
Oven Temp. 400° F.

4 boneless rib beef steaks weighing about 2 lbs. in all sliced 1/2-inch thick
Salt, pepper
8 fresh, very ripe tomatoes, skin and seeds removed and chopped

3/4 lb. "porcini" (cepes or field mushrooms) sliced
1/2 cup butter
1/3 cup beef broth
1 lb. small white onions, peeled and left whole

Remove bone from rib steaks. Season with salt and pepper. Saute tomato and mushrooms in half of the butter until tender and thick, about, 20 minutes. Place some of the tomato pulp and sliced mushrooms on beef. Roll up and tie with string. Grease a shallow casserole, put in meat rolls. Dot with remaining butter and spoon over pan juices left from tomatoes and mushrooms. Pour over broth. Bake in a preheated oven for 1 hour. Boil onions in salted water for 10 minutes. Drain. Add onions to beef rolls. Bake another 30 minutes or until onions are tender.

Costate alla pizzaiola

*Neapolitan
steak pizzaiola*

Serves 4
Difficulty *
Time: 30 minutes

1/4 cup olive oil
4 shell or strip steaks with bone, each weighing 1/2 lb.
Pepper, salt
3/4 lb. very ripe tomatoes

1 clove garlic, chopped
1 tsp. crumbled oregano
2 anchovy fillets
1/4 cup coarsely chopped basil

Heat oil in a pan and sear steaks on each side over high heat until desired degree of doneness. Remove from heat, sprinkle with salt and pepper and set aside, keeping them warm. Peel and cut up tomatoes; squeeze to eliminate part of juice and put them into drippings in pan. Add garlic, oregano, anchovy fillets (crushed to a paste with fork or in a mortar;) and season to taste with freshly ground pepper. Boil mixture over high heat for 2 to 3 minutes or until thick. Return steaks to pan and simmer in pizzaiola sauce for about 5 minutes. Season to taste with salt, remove from heat and sprinkle with basil. Transfer steaks to serving platter, pour pizzaiola sauce over them and serve.

Scaloppine alla toscana

Beef scallops Tuscan style

1-1/2 lb. boneless beef round, sliced 1/4-inch thick
Salt
Flour
1 egg, beaten
1-1/2 tbsp. butter
2 tbsp. olive oil
1/3 cup Marsala wine
1 tbsp. tomato paste
4 anchovy fillets, chopped
1 tbsp. capers, chopped

Serves 4   Difficulty *   Time: 45 minutes

Pound beef very thin, sprinkle with salt and flour on both sides. Dip in egg beaten with a pinch of salt. Melt butter in a pan and add oil. When butter and oil are hot, brown beef slices on both sides. Add Marsala, raise heat slightly and simmer until wine evaporates. Place beef slices on a platter and keep warm.
Into same pan add tomato paste mixed with 1/2 cup water and simmer for 5 minutes. Add anchovies and capers and simmer 2 minutes more. The sauce needs no salting, since anchovies season it sufficiently. Put beef back in pan with sauce and simmer 2 to 3 minutes over very low heat. The serving plate can be garnished with rolled-up anchovies with a caper in centre of each if you wish.

Scaloppine di bue con capperi

Beef scallops with capers

Serves 4
Difficulty *
Time: 1 hour

8 thin slices of fillet of beef (about 3 oz. each)
Salt, pepper
Nutmeg
Flour
5 tbsp. butter
1 tbsp. olive oil
1/4 cup capers
1 tbsp. chopped parsley
2 to 3 tbsp. wine vinegar

Pound beef slices lightly to 1/2-inch thickness and make them uniform size and shape. Season with salt, pepper and nutmeg. Coat with flour, shake off excess and brown in butter with oil. Add capers and parsley and 2 tablespoons cold water. Continue cooking, turning beef occasionally for 5 minutes. In another pan boil wine vinegar over high heat until only 1 tablespoon remains. Pour this over beef and mix again. Place beef on a platter and pour over pan juices.

Scaloppine di bue con capperi

Hamburgers con uova all'occhio di bue

Hamburgers with eggs "bull's-eye"

Serves 4
Difficulty *
Time: 1 hour

2 lbs. ground (minced) chuck beef
8 eggs
6 tbsp. butter

1/2 cup tomato sauce
2 tbsp. olive oil
Salt, pepper

Season chuck with salt and pepper and shape into 8 hamburgers. Heat oil in a frying pan and cook hamburgers until the desired degree of doneness. Set them aside and keep them hot. Poach eggs in simmering salted water. Put 1 egg on each hamburger. Spoon a little hot tomato sauce over each and serve.

Hamburgers al prosciutto affumicato

Hamburgers with smoked ham

Serves 4
Difficulty *
Time: 1 hour

1-1/2 lbs. ground (minced) round beef
1/4 lb. smoked cooked ham, diced
2 egg yolks

Salt, pepper
Flour
Olive oil

Mix ground round, ham, yolks, salt and pepper to taste. Mix ingredients long enough to blend well. Dust hands with flour and shape mixture into 4 hamburgers. Brush with oil and broil (grill) to desired degree of doneness. Sprinkle with salt and serve very hot.

Polpettoncini alla napoletana con pomodoro

Meatloaf rolls with tomato sauce

Serves 4
Difficulty *
Time: 2 hours

1-1/4 lbs. ground (minced) round beef
4 slices stale bread
1/2 cup chopped parsley
2/3 cup grated Parmesan
2 eggs
Salt, pepper
8 oz. mozzarella or Scamorza, cut into 1/2-inch cubes

Flour
6 tbsp. olive oil
2 tbsp. chopped onion
2-1/2 cups sieved fresh tomato pulp, skin and seeds removed
2 tbsp. chopped fresh basil

Place meat in a bowl with bread (soaked in water, then squeezed dry,) parsley, grated Parmesan, eggs and salt and pepper to taste. Mix well. Divide this mixture into 4 equal portions. Place on a moistened surface or board and flatten them to a rectangular shape with the heel of your hand. On each portion place several pieces of mozzarella or Scamorza and wrap meat around cheese to enclose. Shape into a thick roll. Coat meat with flour, then fry in 1/4 cup of the oil until brown on all sides, about 5 minutes. In a separate pan saute onion in remaining oil until wilted. Add tomato pulp and continue cooking over low heat for about 20 minutes, stirring occasionally. Put meatloaf rolls in tomato sauce and simmer for 5 minutes, spooning sauce over them. Sprinkle basil over rolls before serving.

Costolette di vitello alla ghiottona

Veal cutlets gourmand

Serves 4
Difficulty *
Time: 1-1/2 hours

2 veal leg steaks, each cut
into 2 pieces
1/2 cup butter
1/4 lb. small mushrooms, sliced
1/4 cup (2 oz.) chopped cooked
ham
1 small black truffle (Perigord)
sliced
Salt, pepper
Nutmeg
1/2 cup beef broth
Flour
1 egg, beaten
Dry bread crumbs
3/4 lb. spaghetti

Trim bone from cutlets and remove any gristle or membrane. Pound to flatten slightly. Heat 2 tablespoons of the butter and saute mushrooms, ham and truffle until wilted. Season with a little salt and pepper, a pinch of nutmeg and add beef broth. Simmer over low heat for 10 minutes. Salt, pepper and lightly flour cutlets. Dip them into egg, then into bread crumbs, and brown on both sides in 3 tablespoons of the butter heated to frothing. Lower heat and cook for 15 minutes, turning occasionally.
Cook spaghetti al dente in boiling salted water. Drain and rinse with hot water. Toss with remaining butter. Heap spaghetti in centre of a round platter. Arrange cutlets around edge. Spoon over with mushroom, ham and truffle sauce.

In Italy, provided your restaurant proprietor or your butcher is conscientious about his labelling, you can tell quite a bit about the veal you are ordering before you even see it—where it came from, for instance. Usually veal is vitello, but if you should come across vitella, it was probably raised in the South (or in Sardinia). Vitello is calf, vitella heifer. In the North, the males are slaughtered for meat—except for the minimum of reproducers necessary to service the more valuable cows which produce milk and more vitello; but in the South, where pasturage is poorer and cows give little milk anyway, cattle are raised chiefly as draft animals, so the stronger males are kept and the females are killed for meat—except for the minimum number required to maintain the herds. In Sardinia, female veal country, vitella a s'ispidu gives you a further bit of information; it refers to milk-fed veal. For that matter, vitello also *should* mean milk-fed veal; when a calf begins to graze, it becomes vitellone—a big calf. This word is sometimes deceptive, for the vitellone may have graduated from giving veal to making beef long before it is promoted to the status of *bue*, steer. An animal that has not been worked is still a vitellone to a ripe age (three years, say), but the moment he is put into a yoke he becomes, automatically, a steer.

Costolette di vitello alla ghiottona

Costolette di vitello alla "Beniamino Gigli"

Veal chops "Beniamino Gigli" style

Serves 4
Difficulty *
Time: 1-1/2 hours

4 loin veal chops, bones
removed
4 slices prosciutto crudo
1/4 cup chopped pickled gherkins
8 fillets of desalted anchovies
Salt, pepper
4 slices lean bacon
6 tbsp. butter
2 small onions, sliced
1 rib celery, chopped
2 tbsp. *each* chopped parsley
and basil leaves
1/3 cup chicken broth
1/3 cup dry white wine
7 tbsp. heavy cream
2 egg yolks
4 thin French bread slices

Pound chops lightly with flat side of cleaver until 1/4-inch thick. Cover with prosciutto, gherkins and anchovies. Season with salt and pepper and roll up. Wrap each roll in a slice of bacon and tie with a string.

Heat half of the butter and saute onions, celery, parsley and basil for 2 minutes. Add chops and brown on both sides. Pour in broth and white wine. Season with salt and pepper and continue cooking, uncovered, over moderate heat until tender, about 40 to 45 minutes. Remove from pan, discard string and keep hot on a serving platter. Press pan juices and vegetables through a sieve into a saucepan. Stir in cream. Simmer for 5 minutes. Beat a little of the sauce into egg yolks, then stir mixture into sauce in pan. Mix well and stir in 1 tablespoon of the butter. Stir over low heat until sauce thickens. Do not boil. Spoon sauce over chops. Brown bread slices in remaining butter. Place chops on bread slices. Spoon over sauce.

Costolette di vitello con bacon alla valdostana

Veal cutlets with bacon Valle d'Aosta style

Serves 4
Difficulty *
Time: 1 hour
Oven Temp. 375° F.

4 veal scallopini
Salt
2 eggs
Dry bread crumbs
6 tbsp. butter

1 sprig rosemary, finely
chopped
2 tbsp. cognac
4 slices bacon
4 slices fontina cheese
(same size and shape as meat)

Pound veal until paper thin. Dip into lightly salted beaten egg, then into bread crumbs pressing them firmly to make them adhere. Heat 5 tbsp. of butter over moderate heat and fry veal until brown on both sides. Arrange veal in a shallow baking dish lightly greased with remaining butter. Sprinkle rosemary over meat. Sprinkle with cognac and place a slice of bacon and one slice of the fontina on each cutlet. Bake in oven for about 10 minutes. (They are ready when the fontina is half melted and stringy.)

Costolette di vitello con bacon alla valdostana

Arrosto di vitello farcito con prosciutto

Roast veal with prosciutto stuffing

Serves 4
Difficulty **
Time: 2 hours

1-1/2 lbs. boneless veal steak slice
1/2 lb. prosciutto crudo (both fat and lean) cut into thin slices
2 eggs
Salt, pepper
2 tbsp. olive oil
1/4 cup butter
2 bay leaves, crumbled
Chicken broth

Pound veal to a thickness of 1/2 inch. Put prosciutto slices in an even layer on veal. Beat eggs with a little salt and pepper and pour over two meats. Roll veal carefully to keep egg from leaking out. Sew and tie with a thin string. Heat oil, butter and bay leaves in a frying pan. Brown veal on all sides. Lower heat, cover and cook for 1-1/2 hours, basting from time to time with a little broth to prevent sticking. Remove veal, slice and arrange slices on a serving platter.

Roast veal is already found on the menus of Renaissance times, at least in Tuscany; but it was not brought onto the table in one impressive piece. It was sliced in the kitchen and served in individual portions, with a sauce based on hard-boiled eggs. This was not necessarily because of the aversion for meat in large cuts; it may have been simply an echo of the habits of ancient Rome, when meat was cut up in the kitchen too. Knives were not used by the diners, possibly to discourage hot-headed or inebriated guests from carving each other instead of the meat. The Renaissance had its swashbuckling aspects, and a tradition of feuds (see *Romeo and Juliet*), so the absence of knives, then as in Rome, may have been precautionary. Meat is still brought to the table already sliced in Rome, but it is probably safe to assume that nowadays it is for other reasons.

Arrosto di vitello ripieno alla parmense

Roast stuffed veal Parma style

Serves 4
Difficulty **
Time: 2-1/2 hours

For stuffing:

1 lb. fresh spinach
3 tbsp. butter
Salt, pepper
2 eggs
2 tbsp. grated Parmesan cheese
4 slices (3 oz.) sliced bacon

For roast:

2 lbs. leg of veal (cut in a slice about 1/2-inch thick)
Salt, pepper
1/4 cup (2 oz.) butter
3 tbsp. olive oil
7 tbsp. dry white wine
Chicken broth

For stuffing: Cook spinach in a little water, drain, squeeze dry and chop. Saute briefly in 2 tbsp. of the butter and a little salt. Beat eggs, add Parmesan, salt and pepper to taste. Melt remaining butter in frying pan, pour in egg mixture. Prepare as an omelet and brown on both sides. Cool. Set aside bacon for stuffing.

For roast: Pound veal, flattening to 1/4-inch thickness if possible without breaking, salt lightly and cover with bacon and omelet. Spread spinach evenly over veal and roll carefully, making sure that all stuffing is in place. Sew with white thread and tie with string. Melt butter in frying pan with oil. When butter is frothing, place veal in pan and brown on all sides over high heat. Add wine and 3 tablespoons water, cover and cook over low heat for 1-1/2 hours, basting occasionally with pan juices, adding a little broth if necessary to prevent sticking. Remove roast, untie and let cool for a few minutes. Slice and arrange slices on a serving platter. Skim fat from pan juices and spoon over slices.

Arrosto di vitello alla forestiera

Stuffed veal roast forester style

Serves 4
Difficulty **
Time: 3 hours

For stuffing:

1 crusty hard roll
1 cup milk
1/2 lb. ground (minced) beef
1/2 lb. (bulk) sausage meat
1/2 cup (2 oz.) grated Parmesan cheese

1/4 cup chopped parsley
1 tbsp. chopped pistachio nuts
Salt, pepper
1 egg

For roast:

Boneless leg of veal slice, weighing about 1-1/2 lbs.
2 tbsp. butter
1/2 a small onion, sliced
1/2 cup (4 oz.) diced bacon

2 tbsp. olive oil
3/4 cup dry white wine
Chicken broth
Salt, pepper

For stuffing: Soak roll in milk. In a mixing bowl combine beef, sausage, grated Parmesan, roll (squeezed dry), parsley and pistachio nuts. Season with a pinch of salt and pepper. Add egg and mix well.

For roast: Pound veal to flatten it, like a large veal scallopini. Spread stuffing over it, taking care not to get any stuffing closer than 1 inch from edge of veal (otherwise it will come out during roasting process). Roll veal like a jelly roll and sew or tie roll with string. Put butter, onion, bacon and oil in a Dutch oven or frying pan with a domed lid and saute until onion is transparent. Add rolled roast and brown on all sides over high heat. Add wine, simmer until it evaporates. Continue cooking covered for about 1-1/2 hours, basting often with drippings and adding a little broth if necessary to keep roast from sticking. After first 45 minutes, season lightly with salt and pepper. Remove roast when done and cut into slices. Arrange slices slightly overlapping on a serving platter and pour pan juices (fat skimmed off) over them. Serve immediately.

Rotolo di vitello ripieno

Stuffed veal roll

1 small onion, chopped
1/2 lb. (bulk) sausage meat
5 tbsp. butter
1 cup rice
4 cups (1 quart) chicken broth
1 bunch parsley, chopped
1 cup dry white wine
1/2 cup (2 oz.) grated Parmesan
1 slice veal shoulder (2 lbs.) or leg of veal
1 sprig fresh rosemary, chopped
2 tbsp. olive oil

Serves 6
Difficulty **
Time: 2 1/2 hours
Oven Temp. 375° F.

Brown onion and sausage meat in 2 tablespoons of the butter. Add rice, stir for a moment, add salt and pepper to taste and broth. Simmer until rice is tender but still firm. When rice is nearly cooked, add parsley and half of the wine. Cook risotto over low heat, stirring constantly until wine has evaporated and rice is dry. Sprinkle with grated Parmesan. Pound veal until flat and about 1/4-inch thick. Sprinkle with salt and pepper and spread rice over it. Sprinkle with rosemary and roll up like a jelly roll. Tie roll with string and put it in a large shallow baking pan. Brush with remaining butter melted with 2 tablespoons oil. Transfer to oven and roast in a preheated oven for 30 minutes. Add remaining wine and continue roasting for another hour. Remove from oven when done, slice and serve immediately.

Scaloppe alla romana

Veal scallops Roman

Serves 6
Difficulty *
Time: 30 minutes

1-1/4 lbs. veal scallopini
Salt
Flour
3 tbsp. butter
1/4 cup olive oil
6 slices (6 oz.) cooked ham,
thinly sliced
6 slices (6 oz.) Gruyere cheese,
thinly sliced
Fresh sage leaves
1/2 cup dry white wine
2 cups drained canned peas
(or cooked fresh peas)

Pound scallopini, sprinkle with salt and coat with flour on both sides. Heat butter and oil in a pan and fry veal slices. Cover each slice with a slice of ham, one of Gruyere and a sage leaf, securing them with a toothpick. Use a fork to loosen scallopini from bottom of pan, but do not turn them. After a few minutes pour in wine, a little water (enough to just cover only the veal scallopini) and peas. Cover and cook over very low heat for about 15 minutes. Season to taste with salt. Before serving remove toothpicks when scallopini are on serving platter; pour peas and pan juices over them.

> One of the best known Italian dishes outside of Italy, for almost all Italian restaurants abroad serve it, is scaloppine. Here we meet a whole family of dishes, for scaloppine, which are small slices of, usually, veal, (scaloppe are larger cuts) afford opportunity for an unlimited number of variations, especially in the sauces with which they are cooked. I find that in *The Food of Italy* I listed for Milan alone thirteen versions of scaloppine (including two, which, exceptionally, were of beef).

Vitello alla milanese

Veal Milanese

Serves 4
Difficulty *
Time: 30 minutes

4 veal scallopini
1 egg
Salt and pepper

1 cup dry bread crumbs
1/4 cup olive oil
2 tbsp. butter

Pound veal lightly. In a mixing bowl beat egg, salt and pepper to taste. Put veal slices into egg for 10 minutes then coat them with bread crumbs. Press firmly to make crumbs adhere. In a frying pan brown veal on both sides in hot oil and butter. Serve with risotto Milanese (see page 87).

Vitello alla mozzarella

Veal with mozzarella

Serves 6
Difficulty *
Time: 30 minutes

6 slices boneless veal (or
12 small scallopini)
2 tbsp. butter
2 tbsp. olive oil
Salt, pepper

Juice of 1/2 lemon
6 slices prosciutto crudo (fat
and lean)
6 slices mozzarella or Scamorza

Pound veal slices, trim them so they are about same size and shape, then brown in butter and oil. Sprinkle with salt and pepper. Let meat cook to a golden brown, then sprinkle with lemon juice. A few minutes before serving, place a slice of prosciutto and one of mozzarella or Scamorza on each veal slice. Heat until cheese melts and serve immediately.

Oseleti scampai

Oseleti scampai

Skewered veal birds

Serves 4
Difficulty *
Time: 2 hours

1/2 lb. lean veal steak, cubed
1/2 lb. fresh ham steak cubed
1/4 lb. pork liver, cubed
1/4 lb. bacon, cubed

Fresh sage leaves
3 tbsp. oil
7 tbsp. dry white wine
1/2 cup chicken broth

Put veal, ham, liver and bacon cubes on long skewers, alternating various kinds of meat and occasionally putting a sage leaf between one piece and another. Heat oil in a frying pan, add skewers and cook over high heat, turning occasionally. Add white wine and broth and cook for another 10 minutes, turning occasionally. Serve on a bed of polenta.

149

Saltimbocca alla romana

Saltimbocca: veal, prosciutto and sage

Serves 4
Difficulty *
Time: 45 minutes

8 slices veal scallopini
8 slices prosciutto crudo
8 fresh sage leaves
1 tbsp. butter
1/4 cup olive oil
Salt
1 cup dry white wine

On each slice of veal place a slice of prosciutto crudo and a sage leaf and fasten with a toothpick. Melt butter and oil in a frying pan. Brown veal on both sides. Sprinkle with salt and add wine. Simmer for about 10 minutes. Remove veal and place on a platter. Boil pan juices until reduced to half their original volume. Pour pan juices over veal.

Saltimbocca means "jump into the mouth", implying that it is so delicious that it slides down all by itself, without the exertion of will-power by the eater; you might call it the equivalent of "melt in the mouth" in English, though this dish is a trifle solid for melting. It consists of a thin slice of veal skewered to another of ham—*maritati*, married, the Italians put it, and it is a happy marriage. Rome claims this dish as its own, but the fact is that the veal-ham combination appears also in many other parts of Italy, and seems to be indigenous everywhere. Costolette alla bolognese, for instance, which is more elaborate than the Roman dish, goes far back in local culinary history, and has evolved from a heavier to a lighter version. There is a theory that the place of origin of saltimbocca, and all the other ham-veal dishes, was not Rome, but Brescia, in Lombardy.

Saltimbocca alla romana

Ossibuchi, veal shanks, are cooked in many parts of Italy, but the classic version is Milanese. It is served there with the sharply flavored gremolata sauce whose recipe seems to vary with every cook. In other parts of the country, ossibuchi are often accompanied by pasta, but in Milan it is a social error not to serve it with the saffron-flavored risotto alla milanese.

> Vitello tonnato is a curious dish whose object is to reconcile two apparently incompatible tastes—those of veal and of tuna fish. There are two main variations known to me, but no doubt there are others. For one of the two a sauce based on tuna plus anchovies is used, while the other employs mayonnaise to which crushed tuna has been added.

Vitello tonnato

Veal with tuna

Serves 4
Difficulty *
Time: 2 hours

1-1/4 lbs. boneless breast or shoulder of veal, in one piece
Salt
1 rib celery, chopped
1 carrot, chopped
2 tbsp. chopped parsley
1 tbsp. chopped onion
1/2 cup flaked tuna
1 cup mayonnaise
2 tbsp. capers
2 anchovy fillets in oil
1/2 cup dry white wine
1 lemon, cut into slices
1 carrot, sliced and cooked
2 pickled gherkins

Trim membranes from veal. Put a little water and a few pinches of salt in a saucepan; add celery, carrot, parsley and onion. Heat, and when the water comes to a boil add veal. Simmer 1 to 1-1/2 hours or until veal is tender. Drain and set aside to cool. Put tuna through a food mill and blend it with mayonnaise, half of the capers and anchovy fillets. This is best done in a blender. Beat in wine, which serves not only to smooth the sauce but to whiten it. Slice veal and lay slices, overlapping, on a serving platter. Cover with tuna sauce. Sprinkle with the remaining capers and garnish with half slices of lemon, boiled carrot slices and thin slices of gherkin. This sauce is also excellent on boiled beef.

Ossibuchi alla milanese

Ossibuchi Milanese

Serves 4
Difficulty *
Time: 2 hours

1/4 cup butter
Flour
4 ossibuchi, meaty veal shank bones
1 carrot, chopped
1 stalk celery, chopped
1 small onion, chopped
1 clove garlic, chopped
1 cup dry white wine
Salt, pepper
2 ripe tomatoes pressed through a sieve
1 cup chicken broth, approx.
1 tsp. grated lemon rind
6 sprigs parsley, chopped
1/2 tsp. crumbled marjoram

Melt butter in a frying pan. Flour the ossibuchi, tie with string and brown in the butter. Add carrot, celery, onion and garlic; saute until wilted. Add salt and pepper to taste. Add wine and simmer until wine evaporates. Add tomatoes and broth. Cover and cook for at least 1 hour, adding broth if needed, until meat on bones is tender. Add lemon rind, parsley and marjoram. Cook for another 5 minutes to absorb flavor, then transfer ossibuchi to a serving platter. Juices may be thickened with flour mixed with water and poured over ossibuchi.

Agnello con spaghetti al cuturiello alla foggiana

*Lamb with spaghetti
in lamb sauce
Foggia style*

Serves 4
Difficulty *
Time: 1-1/4 hours

2 cloves garlic, chopped
7 tbsp. olive oil
2-1/2 lbs. boneless lamb
cut into 1-inch cubes
Salt, pepper
6 sprigs parsley, chopped
1 lb. purchased spaghetti

Lamb is a much appreciated meat in Italy, and there it *really* means lamb; much of the meat sold outside of Italy under that name would be dismissed disdainfully by Italians as mutton. Lamb in Italy nevertheless is not necessarily suckling lamb, though that is preferred, but it is usually not very much older. One lamb dish much appreciated in Rome (and also in Naples) has little appeal in other countries—lamb's head. It is a very old favorite in Italy; Horace ate it on his first day in Rome, which would probably have been in 49 B.C.; but there was so much garlic in it that it made him ill, and he detested garlic ever after.

Saute garlic in oil, add lamb and brown over high heat. Cover with water and season with salt and pepper. Add parsley and continue cooking, uncovered, for 45 minutes. Fifteen minutes before cooking is completed, cook spaghetti al dente in lightly salted boiling water. Drain and rinse with hot water. Add to lamb and heat. Serve very hot.

Abbacchio al forno con patate alla Romana

*Roast baby lamb
with potatoes
Roman style*

Serves 4
Difficulty *
Time: 1-1/2 hours
Oven Temp. 375° F.

1-1/4 lbs. potatoes
Baby leg of lamb weighing
about 2-1/2 lbs.
1 large sprig fresh
rosemary, chopped
2 cloves garlic, sliced
Salt, coarsely ground pepper
Olive oil
3/4 cup dry white wine

Peel potatoes, wash them and cut into quarters. Keep covered with water until ready to use. Make small cuts here and there on leg of lamb and insert rosemary and garlic slices. Tie leg of lamb with a thin string to keep its shape during cooking. Grease roasting pan with oil, put in leg of lamb and well-drained potatoes. Sprinkle with salt and pepper and brush heavily with oil. Roast for about 1 hour in a preheated oven basting every 15 minutes and turning occasionally. Remove string and transfer roast and potatoes to a heated serving platter. Keep warm. Skim fat from pan drippings and pour into a saucepan. Add white wine and boil until half its original volume. Use this as gravy for lamb.

Abbacchio, suckling lamb, is one of the dishes most firmly associated with Rome, and no wonder; it is older than Rome itself. The first Latins, living near the mouth of the Tiber, were shepherds; lamb and mutton were about the only meat they had, except for a bit of pork now and then. Rome prefers its baby lamb spit-roasted whole, and uses it as a pretext for excursions into the surrounding countryside for barbecue picnics. Spit roasting is not always practical in town, so abbacchio is often cooked more prosaically in the oven; the touch that makes it authentically Roman is rosemary in its seasoning.

Agnello con spaghetti al cuturiello alla foggiana

Agnello con olive all'abruzzese

Lamb with olives
Abruzzi style

Serves 4
Difficulty *
Time: 1 hour

7 tbsp. olive oil
Flour
1-1/2 lbs. lean, boneless
spring lamb steaks (cut from
leg) about 1/2-inch thick
Salt
1 cup black olives, pitted and
coarsely chopped
Pinch of oregano
2 tbsp. finely chopped green
pepper
Juice of 1/2 lemon

The Abruzzi, good high-altitude grazing country, is noted for the quality of its lamb; if you come upon a particularly choice leg of lamb anywhere in Italy, the chances are good that it came from this region. There are any number of recipes for cooking it but olive oil is virtually always present in the cooking sauces of Abruzzi lamb, whether it is a question of a whole leg of lamb (often served there with fettuccine) or of lamb cut into chunks and braised—agnello con sottaceti.

Heat oil in a frying pan. Flour lamb slices lightly and brown in oil on both sides over high heat for 5 minutes. Sprinkle lamb with salt and drain off some of the fat. Lower heat and add black olives, a pinch of oregano, green pepper and lemon juice. Continue cooking over moderate heat for a few minutes. Arrange slices of meat on a serving platter.

Agnello alla pasqualina

Easter lamb

Serves 6
Difficulty *
Time: 2-1/2 hours
Oven Temp. 375° F.

2 legs of lamb, weighing
about 2-1/2 lbs. each
4 artichokes
2-1/2 lbs. potatoes, peeled and
diced
1 lb. small white onions
1 bunch carrots, julienned
1/4 cup butter
2 tbsp. olive oil
Salt, pepper
2 sprigs rosemary
2 sage leaves

The lamb is a Christian symbol connected with Easter—specifically, a symbol of Christ—so agnello alla pasqualina, Easter lamb, may possibly have had its origin in a festive dish with religious overtones, like hot cross buns; but if so, the connection is unknown to me. Easter is in any case the lamb season, so the name of this dish probably has no meaning more profound than that of "spring lamb"—like the Genoese torta pasqualina, the vegetable "Easter" tart, so called because it is at this season that the tender young vegetables which go into it become available.

Bone legs of lamb and tie each leg with string. Discard hard outer leaves of artichokes, and cut hearts into wedges, discarding fuzzy choke part of heart. Parboil separately potatoes, artichokes, onions and carrots in lightly salted, boiling water for 5 minutes. (Completion of cooking will take place in oven with roasts.) Drain vegetables. Put a roasting pan on top of range and heat butter and oil in it. Add lamb and sprinkle with salt, pepper, rosemary and sage. Roast in a preheated oven for 2 hours. Baste meat occasionally with pan juices. When meat is about half-cooked, add artichokes, carrots, onions and potatoes. Baste the vegetables occasionally with pan juices and if juices dry up, add a little hot broth. When cooking is completed, slice lamb and arrange slices on a serving platter, together with vegetables. Skim excess fat from pan juices. Pour pan juices over meat and vegetables before serving.

Ragù di montone "buona donna"

Mutton stew

Serves 6
Difficulty **
Time: 3 hours
Oven Temp. 375°F.

By the time sheep have reached the age where their meat is called mutton rather than lamb, Italians lose interest in them. When mutton appears at all, it is usually in stews (Florence's cazzuda, Liguria's stufato, Abruzzi's ragu). Outdoor food vendors at local fairs or on market days may offer you, in the Abruzzi, cubes of spitted mutton, but it is often still at an age which would cause it elsewhere to be classed with lamb. That favorite form of this meat for Anglo-Saxons, the mutton chop, is a little too husky for such abstemious meat-eaters as the Italians, with one exception, whose existence is explained by other than purely gastronomic considerations. Ravenna offers costolette di montone alla Byron, but it is a deliberate importation of a foreign dish in honor of the indefatigable Lord Byron who spent a year and a half there pursuing one of his numerous loves, apparently with success.

1/2 lb. small onions, left
whole
1/2 cup (4 oz.) rendered pork fat or
lard
2-1/2 lbs. mutton (breast,
shoulder, neck and lower ribs,
in small pieces)
Salt, pepper
1 tsp. sugar
1 tbsp. flour
1 clove garlic, chopped
1/2 cup tomato paste
Bouquet garni (parsley, thyme,
bay leaf)
3 cups chicken broth
3/4 lb. potatoes, diced
8 slices (6 oz.) bacon, cooked until
crisp and crumbled

Saute 1 of the onions, sliced, in fat until wilted in a Dutch oven. Add mutton pieces, brown lightly on all sides and season with salt and pepper. Pour off half of the fatty drippings. Add sugar and, after a few minutes, stir in flour, garlic, tomato paste diluted with 1/2 cup hot water, bouquet garni, a little more salt and broth. Cover pan and simmer for 1 hour. Remove pieces of meat with a slotted spoon. Skim sauce of all fat and put through a sieve. Remove pieces of skin and bone from mutton. Put mutton and sieved sauce back in pan. Add potatoes, remaining onions and bacon. Cover and bake in a preheated oven for 1 hour or until meat is tender.

Ragù di montone "buona donna"

Costolettine di agnello alla Calabrese

Lamb chops Calabrian

Serves 4
Difficulty *
Time: 30 minutes

8 loin or rib lamb chops
Salt, pepper
Flour
5 tbsp. lard
8 anchovy fillets, drained and
rinsed with cold water

2 tbsp. capers
1/2 cup (4 oz.) *each* canned
mushrooms, drained,
and artichoke
hearts in oil, drained

Pound chops to flatten slightly. Sprinkle with salt and pepper. Dip into flour. Heat lard and brown chops for 2 to 3 minutes on each side over high heat. Drain on paper toweling. Arrange on a serving platter and garnish with anchovy fillets, capers, mushrooms and artichoke hearts.

Agnello in agrodolce alla barese

Lamb in sweet and sour sauce Barese style

Serves 4
Difficulty *
Time: 1-1/4 hours

7 tbsp. oil
1/2 onion, chopped
2-1/2 lbs. boneless lamb,
cut into 1-inch cubes

7 tbsp. tomato paste in 7 tbsp.
hot water
Salt, pepper
7 tbsp. wine vinegar
2 tbsp. sugar

Heat oil in a frying pan. Add onion and lamb and saute until lamb is brown on all sides. Stir in tomato paste diluted in hot water. Add salt and pepper to taste. Simmer 25 minutes, then add wine vinegar. Simmer over high heat until one-half its original volume. Stir in sugar. Cover and cook over low heat for another 30 minutes, adding a little hot water from time to time if it gets too dry. Serve immediately.

Epigrammi di agnello alla fiorentina

Lamb cutlets Florentine

Serves 4
Difficulty *
Time: 2 hours, plus time required to soak beans

**Fagioli all'uccelletto
(beans with sage and garlic):**

1-1/2 cups (9 oz.) dried beans
(haricot beans or navy beans)
1/2 cup olive oil
2 tbsp. chopped fresh sage
2 cloves garlic, chopped
Salt, pepper
1-1/2 cup sieved fresh tomato
pulp (skin and seeds removed)

Lamb:

2 lbs. breast of lamb and
4 lamb chops
Chicken broth
1 small carrot, chopped
1 small onion, chopped
1 whole clove
1/2 stalk celery, chopped

Bouquet garni of thyme, parsley
and bay leaf
Salt, pepper
1 egg, beaten
Dry bread crumbs
1/4 cup (2 oz.) butter

Beans: Soak beans in cold water for at least 12 hours. Drain, put them in saucepan, cover with plenty of cold water and simmer over moderate heat until tender, about 1-1/2 to 2 hours. Heat oil with sage, garlic, salt, and a little freshly ground pepper. Drain cooked beans, add them to oil and mix well. After a few minutes stir in tomato pulp and cook for another 10 minutes.

Preparation of final dish: Simmer breast of lamb and lamb chops in broth to cover with carrot, onion, clove, celery and bouquet garni for 1 to 1-1/2 hours or until lamb is tender. Drain lamb and remove bones and fat. Place a mound of the meat between 2 boards and place a weight on top of boards. Chill. Remove lamb and cut into 4 slices having the same general form as cutlets. Sprinkle with salt and pepper. Dip slices into egg and then into bread crumbs. Heat butter in a frying pan. Brown lamb cutlets on both sides. Place on a platter and surround with beans.

Costolettine di agnello alla Calabrese

When Aeneas, a refugee from Troy, landed in Italy, he prepared to sacrifice a sow to the gods who had conducted him safely to the end of a long and perilous voyage; the animal, justifiably alarmed, proceeded to give birth to thirty piglets. This was interpreted as a good omen, and Italians have been consuming large quantities of pork, in one form or another, ever since. Its name in Italian is maiale, since it was pigs which were sacrificed to the mother of Mercury, the goddess Maia. Pork offers an exception to the rule that meat in large cuts is not particularly appreciated in Italy. Roast pork is liked in many sections of the country; and hams, substantial sections of meat too, are cured almost everywhere.

Fresh ham is not rare in Italy, but the country's preserved hams are the most famous—first of all those of Parma (cured mostly in Langhirano) are the best Italian hams you are likely to encounter. Connoisseurs often maintain that the rustic ham of San Daniele di Friuli is superior, but so little of it is made, and it is all so eagerly snapped up, that your chances of ever tasting it are slight indeed. Many foreigners believe that prosciutto is a specific name for the delicate salmon-colored Parma ham which appears on the plate in paper-thin slices, but actually what the word means is, simply, ham—any kind of ham, fresh or cured. Ham is preserved almost everywhere in Italy, in a variety of fashions—smoked in the Valle d'Aosta, in the Basilicata, or in the Barbagia area of Sardinia; air-cured in the mountains of the Abruzzi or the Ogliastro country of Sardinia; salted with the fine salt of Cagliari, also in Sardinia; or by a combination of different methods—Parma ham, for instance, is air-cured first and then salted lightly. The best region for ham in all Italy may well be Emilia (it includes Parma), where the red pigs the ancient Romans knew still fatten on acorns in the oak forests the ancient Romans knew too. A diet of acorns account also for the quality of Abruzzi ham, like prosciutto aquilano, which tastes like the famous mountain ham of Spain, *jamon serrano*. This is hardly surprising; the region learned its present technique for curing ham from the Spaniards who once occupied this part of the country.

Costolette di maiale alla napoletana

Pork chops Neapolitan style

4 loin pork chops
Salt, pepper
Flour
7 tbsp. olive oil
2 cloves garlic, chopped
2 cups chopped tomato pulp, skin and seeds removed
1 cup chopped mushrooms
3 green peppers

Serves 4   Difficulty **   Time: 1 hour

Flatten chops to 1/4-inch thickness, leaving bones on and removing fat. Sprinkle with salt and pepper. Dip chops into flour to coat. Heat 5 tablespoons oil in a frying pan. Brown garlic in oil. Add chops and brown on both sides slowly until cooked. Remove chops and keep hot. Add tomato pulp to pan juices and season with a pinch of salt and pepper. Simmer 5 minutes. Add mushrooms. Simmer 5 minutes. Replace pork chops in pan and cook over moderate heat for about 15 minutes. Singe peppers over high heat. Rub with a cloth to remove outer skin. Remove seeds and inner membrane, then cut into large strips. Saute until tender in remaining oil. Sprinkle with salt. Keep hot. If meat sauce thickens too much, add a little hot water. Transfer pork chops to a serving platter. Cover with hot peppers and tomato-mushroom sauce.

Arista di maiale

*Saddle of pork
Tuscan style*

Serves 4
Difficulty *
Time: 2 hours
Oven Temp. 425°F., then lower to
350°F.

**2-1/2 lbs. pork roast
2 cloves garlic, cut into
slivers
2 sprigs fresh rosemary
Salt, peppercorns
4 tbsp. olive oil**

Cut small slits in pork and stuff
with slivers of garlic and tufts of
rosemary. Season with salt and
freshly ground pepper. Heat
2 tablespoons of the oil in a
roasting pan. Add pork, pour a
thin stream of remaining oil
over it and roast in preheated
oven for about 20 minutes.
When pork is nicely browned,
lower heat and roast for another
1-1/4 hours, turning meat occasionally. Remove from oven,
slice, arrange slices on a serving
platter and serve. This dish is
good either hot or cold.

Arista di maiale

The word "roast" is arrosto in Italian; why does Florence persist
in calling its roast loin of pork arista? It hardly seems likely that Florentines are bad spellers—after all, they were the ones who gave Italy
its present language. There is another explanation. The story goes that a
Greek archimandrite, visiting Florence in Renaissance times, found the
local fashion of roasting pork so admirable that he called it *aris-
tos*—Greek for "best". The name stuck. Florentines season their roast
pork with rosemary; in Lucca it is served with polenta and in the Alto
Adige with horseradish; and in Palermo it is stuffed richly with raisins, pine nuts, and almond paste.

Bocconcini
alla Giulio Cesare

*Pork loin
tidbits Julius Caesar*

Serves 6
Difficulty *
Time: 1-1/2 hours

**8 slices boneless pork loin,
each 3 oz. (1-1/2 lbs.)
4 slices (1/4 lb.) baked or boiled ham
4 slices bacon
2 tbsp. butter**

**3 tbsp. olive oil
Flour
6 sage leaves
Salt, pepper
1 cup milk**

The meat should be sliced very thin. Pound slices and trim them
even around the edges so they are all about the same size and
shape. Dice ham and bacon. Melt butter with oil. Coat pork slices
with flour and put them in the pan. Add several sage leaves. Brown
meat over moderate heat, turning to cook both sides. Sprinkle with
salt and pepper. When pork is nicely browned, after 5 minutes,
remove sage and add ham and bacon. Saute 2 to 3 minutes. Pour
in milk, lower heat and cover. Cook until sauce is thick, about
15 minutes. Use a fork to shift meat from time to time so it does
not stick. If sauce is too liquid, add about 1-1/2 to 2 tablespoons
butter mixed with a little flour. If too thick, add 2 or 3 tablespoons
milk.

Prosciutto alla ricotta

Prosciutto with ricotta

Serves 4
Difficulty *
Time: 1-1/2 hours

3 fennel
2 tbsp. butter
Salt
4 artichokes
2 tbsp. olive oil

Juice of 1 lemon
1/4 lb. ricotta, sieved
1/4 cup (1 oz.) grated Parmesan
8 slices of baked or boiled ham

Clean fennel and cut fleshy parts into strips. Cover with boiling water to which butter and a pinch of salt have been added. Simmer until tender, about 30 minutes. Discard hard outer leaves of artichokes and cut hearts in half. Cover artichokes with water. Add oil, lemon juice and 1/2 teaspoon salt and boil artichokes until tender, about 20 minutes. Drain vegetables well and strain them through a food mill. Add ricotta and Parmesan and mix well. Spread a little of this mixture evenly on each slice of ham. Roll ham slices up like a jam roll. Place on a platter. Serve cold.

Polpette romane

Roman meatballs

Serves 4
Difficulty **
Time: 2 hours
Oven Temp. 350° F.

1 lb. mozzarella (or scamorza) diced
1-1/2 cups milk
1/2 cup (1/4 lb.) minced baked or boiled ham
Nutmeg

Salt,
2-1/4 cups all-purpose flour
2 eggs
2/3 cup grated Parmesan or other grated cheese
1/2 cup butter

In a pan mix mozzarella, 1/2 cup of the milk, ham and a pinch of nutmeg. Sprinkle with salt and stir constantly over medium heat for about 5 minutes or until cheese is melted. Chill. In another saucepan mix flour, eggs and Parmesan. Gradually stir in remaining milk. Set saucepan over low heat and stir mixture until it becomes very smooth and thick. Remove from heat and beat in half of the butter and a pinch of salt. Cool. Turn dough out on a floured board and knead a few times until it becomes a smooth ball.
To prepare meatballs take 2 tablespoons of ham and mozzarella mixture and, using the palms of your hands, roll it into a ball about as large as a walnut. Pinch off pieces of dough and flatten to 1/4-inch thickness. Wrap ball in dough to cover it completely. Continue until you have used up all the ham and all the dough. Butter a shallow pyrex baking dish, put in meatballs in a single layer. Dot each with a bit of remaining butter. Bake in a preheated oven for about 30 minutes or until brown.

Porcellino allo spiedo

Barbecued pig

Serves 8 to 10
Difficulty ****
Time: 4 hours

1 suckling pig (weighing about 25 lbs.)
1/4 cup rendered pork fat
Salt, pepper

1 cup chopped aromatic herbs to taste (but including garlic and rosemary)
Lard or oil as required

Thaw pig if frozen. Cover head with foil to prevent overbrowning. Tie hind legs under pig. Brush inside with pork fat, salt, pepper and aromatic herbs and brush outside with fat. Tie pig with string, insert spit and cook on an aromatic wood fire (olive, juniper or apple.) During cooking (about 3 hours) brush the pig with lard or oil. Serve it well browned.

Porcellino allo spiedo

The single dish most firmly associated with Rome is no doubt porcellino, spitted suckling pig roasted whole. It is a fixture of the boisterous outdoor Noantri festival of July, held in the Trastevere quarter, where smoking porkers turn slowly and fragrantly over the flames, while beside them those which have finished cooking are being sliced into individual portions for an army of joyous eaters. Yet porcellino is probably not native to Rome; it is probable that the ancient Romans took it over from the Etruscans.

Polletti allo spiedo

Polletti allo spiedo

Barbecued broilers
(i.e. spitted squab chicken)

Serves 4
Difficulty *
Time: 1 hour

2 small broilers, (squab chickens)
approx 2 lbs each
Salt, pepper
1/2 cup olive oil

Season chickens inside and out with salt and pepper. Brush with oil. Spear on a rotisserie rod. Cook 8 inches above grey coals, basting from time to time with oil.

The ancient Romans were a little slow about developing the resources of the poultry run; perhaps ordinary domesticated birds were too tame for banqueters accustomed to the splendor of peacocks and flamingos served in their plumage. Foreign inspiration was required to turn them towards chicken and goose, but they seem to have found out about duck all by themselves. Guinea fowl were imported from Africa but apparently disappeared from the Italian table for several centuries after the collapse of the Roman Empire. The banqueters of the Renaissance showed more interest in barnyard poultry than their early Roman ancestors had done, and even revived roast peacock, but it was soon driven from the table by the advent of a new bird from a New World—the turkey. Modern Italy produces all the presently popular varieties of poultry, of excellent quality.

How to bone and cut up a chicken

To bone: Put chicken on cutting board breast down. With a sharp knife, make a vertical cut on neck down the length of neck and separate skin from bones using a thin, very sharp knifeblade. Then pull skin back, without however detaching it. Cut neck off at base, exactly at the point where chest and back begin. Remove the tips of the wings. In this way you leave the rest of the wing attached to the body, the one that serves as a "handle" to chicken breast. Make an incision along entire center of the back. Using a long, thin, sharp knifeblade, begin by detaching back skin, then go on to cut off meat gradually, first on one side, then the other. Next remove flesh from shoulders. When you reach the wings, make a cut at the ends of the wings to facilitate separation of skin from bone. Next remove the wishbone, cutting breast meat from breastbone. Remove meat from thighs and drumsticks. When you have reached this point, carcass is readily separated from the rest of the body. Using a pair of scissors cut small muscles away from bones holding the skin. Boneless chicken can then be stuffed and reshaped. The bones and other trimmings can be used to make broth.

Cutting up chicken: Depending on size, the chicken may be cut into 6, 8 or 12 pieces. In all cases begin by making a slit with a sharp knife: slash skin between body of chicken and leg. Grasp end of legs firmly and turn them outward with a sudden strong tug so that the thigh bone is decisively separated from the body. Then, using scissors or a sharp knife, cut off leg. At the joint cut leg into thigh and drumstick. Cut wings at juncture of wing and breast, making certain to leave the breast intact. Pull wings sharply away from body and cut away at joint. Split carcass remaining on either side of the backbone. Open out and bend chicken backwards until breastbone snaps. Grasp breastbone and pull out. Cut breast into 2 halves. To remove meat cut along wing and wishbone, detaching meat with small slashing cuts. When detaching from wishbone, grasp with the fingers and pull straight up to remove meat in one piece. Repeat on other breast half.

Pollo al forno ripieno

*Roast chicken
with stuffing*

Serves 4
Difficulty **
Time: 2-1/2 hours
Oven Temp. 350° F.-400° F.

1 chicken weighing about 2-1/2 lbs.	1/4 lb. ground (minced) pork
1/2 onion, chopped	1/4 lb. cooked ham, chopped
3 tbsp. olive oil	1/4 cup chopped black olives
Salt, pepper	1 clove garlic, chopped
6 sprigs parsley, chopped	1/4 cup grated Parmesan cheese
2 stale rolls	1 egg and 1 egg yolk
Milk	2 tbsp. butter, melted
1/4 lb. (bulk) sausage meat	1/2 cup white wine

Chop giblets. Saute onion in 2 tablespoons of the oil until wilted. Add chopped giblets, season with salt and pepper and saute for 5 minutes. Stir in parsley. Soak rolls in milk. In a mixing bowl mix sausage, pork, giblets, giblet pan juices, ham, olives, garlic, grated Parmesan, egg and egg yolk. Mix well to bind ingredients, then stuff chicken with mixture. Sew or skewer opening and truss with string. Put chicken in a roasting pan; brush with butter and remaining oil. Season with a little salt and pepper and roast in a preheated oven for 30 to 35 minutes. Raise temperature and roast another 30 minutes, basting often with white wine.

Pollastra in casseruola alla Sardinia

*Chicken casserole
Sardinian style*

Serves 4
Difficulty **
Time: 2 hours
Oven Temp. 400° F.

1 fryer chicken weighing	1/4 lb. Pecorino cheese, grated
3 lbs.	1/4 cup Sultana raisins
2 tbsp. lard	7 tbsp. milk
1-1/2 cups dry bread crumbs	4 tbsp. cream
1-1/2 cups chopped tomato pulp, skin and seeds removed	Salt, pepper
3 eggs	1/4 cup olive oil
	Juice of 1 lemon

Chop liver and gizzard. Brown giblets in lard, add bread crumbs and saute until lightly browned. Remove from heat and stir in tomatoes, 2 of the eggs, Pecorino cheese, raisins, milk, cream and salt and pepper to taste. Hard cook remaining egg. Stuff chicken with mixture. Put hard cooked egg into center of cavity. Sew or skewer opening and truss chicken. Put chicken in roasting pan, season with salt and pepper and brush with oil. Roast for about 1-1/2 hours, basting frequently with lemon juice.

Cappone con noci alla lombarda

*Capon with walnuts
Lombardy style*

Serves 6
Difficulty **
Time: 3 hours

5 tbsp. butter	7 tbsp. heavy cream
4 cups soft bread crumbs	Salt, white peppercorns
1 cup coarsely chopped walnuts	Pinch of nutmeg, cloves and sugar
1/2 cup grated Parmesan cheese	1 capon weighing about 5 lbs.
3 egg yolks	1 small onion, chopped

Cream butter and fold in bread crumbs, walnuts, Parmesan, yolks and cream. Season with salt, pepper, spices and sugar. Use this mixture to stuff capon. Sew or skewer opening, truss capon with string. Place into a large pot and cover with salted water. Add onion. Bring to a bcil, lower heat and simmer for 1-1/2 hours or until tender. Serve broth first and then chicken with stuffing.

Cappone "sorpresa dell'ortolano"

Capon with garden vegetables

Serves 6
Difficulty *
Time: 3 hours
Oven Temp. 375° F.

1 capon weighing about 5 lbs.
2 slices pork fat
1/2 lb. chicken livers, chopped
1/2 lb. prosciutto crudo, chopped
Salt, pepper
1/4 lb. sliced bacon, chopped
2 carrots sliced
1 onion, sliced
A bouquet garni of parsley, thyme and rosemary
1 cup white wine
1 cup chicken broth
5 tbsp. butter
2 cups diced eggplant (aubergine)
2 zucchini
2 green bell peppers, cut into strips
1 heart of celery, sliced
2 cups sliced mushrooms
2 cups chopped tomato pulp, skin and seeds removed

Cover legs of capon with pork fat. Stuff capon with liver and prosciutto. Sprinkle with salt and pepper and truss. In a greased 3-quart shallow casserole put a layer of bacon, carrots, onion and bouquet garni. Set capon on this layer. Pour over wine and broth and roast in a preheated oven for 2 hours or until tender. Heat butter and saute eggplant, zucchini, peppers and celery. After 15 minutes add mushrooms and tomato pulp. Sprinkle with salt and pepper and continue cooking 5 minutes. Place capon on a platter. Press pan juices through a strainer and thicken if desired. Serve capon surrounded with vegetables. Spoon over pan juices.

Cappone "sorpresa dell'ortolano"

Chickens existed in Italy from very early times, but the first birds of ancient Rome were so scrawny that nobody was tempted to eat them; their function was to provide eggs. The Romans learned eventually how to breed and fatten chickens from the Greeks of the island of Cos, and immediately took to them with such avidity that they became a public nuisance in the streets of Rome. The consul Caius Fanius had to issue a decree forbidding the keeping of hens in Rome; but he forgot to include roosters, so Romans raised male birds instead, castrating them to make the flesh tender: thus the capon was invented—or so the story goes. Is the modern Italian lackadaisical about chicken? In France or in the United States chickens of various ages are often referred to by different names, indicating whether they are birds ready for broiling, frying, roasting or boiling, but on Italian menus chicken, whether pullet or fowl, is almost always referred to invariably as *pollo*. Since there are nevertheless any number of tasty and often ingenious chicken dishes in the Italian repertory, it might be deduced that Italian cooks are less interested in the bird itself than in what they can do with it.

Pollo in salsa tonnata
Chicken in tuna sauce

Serves 4
Difficulty *
Time: 1-1/2 hours

1 carrot, chopped
1 celery stalk, chopped
1 small onion, chopped
Salt, pepper
1 chicken weighing about
2-1/2 lbs.
6 to 8 sprigs parsley, minced
1 can (7 oz.) tuna, drained
3 anchovies
1 cup mayonnaise

Put enough water in a pot with carrot, celery, onion and 1 tablespoon kitchen (kosher) salt, to just cover chicken. When water boils add chicken and simmer until well done, about 1 hour. Drain and let it cool completely. Mix parsley, tuna and anchovies and pound in a mortar or mince with a knife until very fine. Add tuna mixture to mayonnaise, stirring gently. Test the sauce for taste and if it becomes too bland, add a pinch of salt. Cut up chicken, skin and bone. Slice chicken and place on a round serving platter. Pour tuna sauce evenly over entire chicken. Garnish with parsley and green olives, both around edges and in center.

Pollo in salsa tonnata

166

Pollo alla diavola

Chicken Diablo

Serves 4
Difficulty **
Time: 1-1/2 hours

1-3/4 cups sauce diablo
(See Salsa alla diavola)
1 chicken weighing about
2-1/2 lbs.
1/4 cup butter, melted
Salt, pepper

Prepare Salsa alla diavola (see following recipe). Wash chicken and split along the breastbone. Open out chicken and flatten it. Pound slightly with the flat side of a cleaver to get chicken as flat as possible. Remove as many small bones as you can. Fasten wings with metal skewers. Brush entire chicken with melted butter and season with salt and pepper. Put the chicken directly onto a pre-heated frying pan and brown quickly on both sides. Lower heat and continue cooking, turning occasionally and basting for about 45 minutes or until chicken is tender. When chicken is well browned, serve topped with sauce diablo. Cut into serving size pieces with a sharp knife or poultry shears.

> One of the most widely known dishes of Florence is pollo alla diavola—dare we translate it as devilish chicken?—which is split in half, flattened as if a steamroller had been run over it, and grilled. The name is explained by its hot seasoning, ginger sauce. Rome claims pollo alla diavola as a local specialty too, but uses no ginger; the effect which justifies the name is achieved by heavy peppering.

Salsa alla diavola

Sauce diablo

Makes 1-3/4 cups
Difficulty **
Time: 3-1/2 hours

Sauce diablo:

2/3 cup dry white wine
1 tbsp. wine vinegar
1 tbsp. chopped scallion
1 thyme leaf
1/2 a bay leaf
6 crushed peppercorns
Salt
1-3/4 cups above meat sauce
1 tbsp. chopped parsley
Cayenne pepper
2 tbsp. butter

Meat sauce for sauce diablo:

1 celery rib, chopped	A pinch of thyme
1 small carrot, chopped	1 to 2 bay leaves
1 onion, chopped	1 clove
2 tbsp. chopped parsley	4 oz. ground (minced) beef
1 to 2 tbsp. butter	4 oz. veal shank, ground
2 tbsp. olive oil	Salt, pepper
1/2 clove garlic chopped	1 cup beef broth

Meat sauce: Put celery, carrot, onion and parsley in a saucepan, add butter and oil and saute until wilted. Add garlic, a pinch of thyme, bay leaf and clove. After 2 minutes add beef and veal. Brown meats until crumbly. Season to taste with salt and pepper and add broth. Lower heat and simmer for about 3 hours, adding either water or broth to prevent sticking. (The final sauce should be about 1-3/4 cups.) When meat sauce is cooked, press it through a food mill or whirl in a blender.

Sauce diablo: Combine in a saucepan wine, vinegar, scallion, thyme, bay leaf, peppercorns and a pinch of salt. Boil vigorously to reduce liquid to 1/3 of its original volume. Stir in meat sauce. Boil for 1 minute more, then press through a food mill or whirl in a blender. Pour into pan again. Heat until bubbly. Stir in chopped parsley, cayenne pepper to taste and butter.

Pollo al prosciutto

Chicken with prosciutto

Serves 4
Difficulty *
Time: 1-1/4 hours

1 young chicken about
2-1/2 lbs, cut-up
Salt, pepper
Flour
1/4 cup butter
2 tbsp. olive oil
1/2 lb. prosciutto crudo
mixed (fat and lean) sliced

1 bay leaf
1/2 cup dry white wine
1 can (1 lb.) Italian peeled
tomatoes, drained and sieved or
1-1/4 lbs. (4 medium) ripe fresh
tomatoes, skinned and sieved

Wash and dry chicken, sprinkle with salt and pepper. Coat pieces with flour. Melt butter and oil in a frying pan and when they foam put in the pieces of chicken. Brown over high heat on all sides, about 10 minutes. Add prosciutto crudo and bay leaf. After 5 minutes pour in wine and simmer until it evaporates, about 15 minutes. Add tomatoes. Cover and simmer over moderate heat, turning pieces of chicken occasionally to avoid sticking, about 40 to 45 minutes.

Pollo con peperoni

Chicken with peppers

Serves 4
Difficulty *
Time: 2 hours

Cut chicken into serving pieces. Roast peppers over heat until skin blisters. Rub skin off with a kitchen towel. Remove seeds and cut peppers into 1-inch wide strips. Saute onion in butter and oil until wilted. Add chicken pieces and brown, turning often. Season with salt and pepper and when chicken has browned, add wine. Simmer until wine has evaporated, add peppers, tomatoes and another pinch of salt and pepper. Add broth. Cover and simmer over low heat stirring occasionally, about 45 minutes or until chicken is tender. Remove from heat and sprinkle with chopped basil (or parsley if you prefer). Pan juices may be skimmed of fat and boiled until reduced to half their original volume. Pour pan juices over chicken.

> Pollo con peperoni is particularly a Roman dish. The combination of chicken and peppers seems to appeal to the capital, for peppers turn up in several other Roman chicken dishes, even though their presence is not trumpeted in the names of these preparations. *Pollo alla romana*, whose title marks it as typically Roman, for instance, is chicken sauted with tomatoes and green peppers.

1 chicken (weighing about
2-1/2 lbs.)
4 to 5 fleshy green peppers
1 large onion, sliced
2 tbsp. butter
3 tbsp. olive oil

Salt, pepper
1/2 cup dry white wine
4 cups fresh chopped tomato
pulp, skins and seeds removed
1 cup chicken broth
1/4 cup chopped fresh basil

Pollo con peperoni

Pollo alla Marengo

Chicken Marengo

Serves 6
Difficulty **
Time: 1-1/2 hours

1 chicken (weighing approx.
2-1/2 lbs.) cut-up
Salt and pepper
1/4 cup butter
3/4 cup olive oil
4 ripe tomatoes, peeled
and sieved
1 clove garlic, chopped
6 sprigs parsley (chop 5 sprigs)
2 cups dry white wine
1/2 lb. wild "porcini" mushrooms
or 1 oz. dried mushrooms

1 small white truffle or black
truffle, sliced
1 small onion, sliced
1 bay leaf
1 rib celery, chopped
Pinch of thyme
Peppercorns
6 large crayfish or shrimp
6 slices sandwich bread, crusts
trimmed
6 eggs

Wash chicken and pat dry. Sprinkle with salt and pepper. Heat 1 tablespoon of the butter and 6 tablespoons of the oil in a large frying pan and brown pieces of chicken, turning to get all sides browned. Add tomatoes, garlic, half the chopped parsley. Boil half of the wine for 2 minutes, add to pan, cover and cook over moderate heat for 20 minutes. Meanwhile, cut off bottoms of mushroom stems (if you are using fresh wild mushrooms,) clean and slice. If using dried, soak in cold water then drain and chop. Put 2 tablespoons butter in a pan with 2 tablespoons of the oil. Add mushrooms and truffle slices to pan. Sprinkle with salt and pepper and saute until wilted. Before removing from heat, sprinkle with remaining chopped parsley. Add mushrooms to chicken. Cover and simmer another 15 to 20 minutes or until chicken is tender. Heat remaining wine in a saucepan. Add onion, unchopped parsley sprig, bay leaf, celery, a pinch of thyme, several peppercorns and 1/2 teaspoon salt. When wine comes to a boil add shrimp and simmer for 5 minutes; drain and reserve shrimp. Shell and devein shrimp. Heat remaining oil in a frying pan and fry bread slices until brown on both sides. Heat remaining butter in a large frying pan and fry eggs until whites are firm and yolks still soft. Remove from heat and place fried eggs on slices of bread. Place chicken in centre of a large round serving dish. Spoon over pan juices. Place slices of bread with eggs around edges, alternating with shrimp.

Pollo alla Marengo can only be called an Italian dish by courtesy, in deference to the geographic accident that the battle of Marengo, of which it was a by-product, was fought on Italian soil. Though created by French chef Dunand, Napoleon's cook, it is not really a French dish either. It belongs to no school of cooking except that of desperate improvisation. Left in the lurch by the movement of battle, the commissary service had not caught up with Napoleon when he demanded dinner after the victory. Dunand, deprived of his usual supplies, had to make do with whatever foragers could rustle up on short notice. This turned out to be a thin chicken, four tomatoes, three eggs, a few crayfish, a little garlic and some olive oil—plus, fortunately, a frying pan. Some military bread was found in one of the soldier's knapsacks. This was barely enough for a hungry warrior, so Dunand threw everything in, even the crayfish, which he considered a rather horrible accompaniment for chicken. Picturesquely, he cut up the chicken with a sabre (or so the story goes) and enriched the gravy with cognac filched from Napoleon's own canteen. A superstitious man, Napoleon associated this dish with victory and asked for it again on the eve of his next battle. Dunand, better provided, strove to improve it by adding white wine and mushrooms, and, above all, getting rid of the crayfish; but Napoleon did not agree. Though not ordinarily observant about food, he noticed the absence of the crayfish—perhaps he had been impressed by them expressly because they went so badly with the rest—and demanded that they be returned to the dish. "You'll bring me bad luck," he complained to Dunand. Now that Napoleon is no longer around to supervise, French cooks make *poulet Marengo* without crayfish, but in Piedmont, respectful of history, they are usually left in.

Petti di pollo con carciofi e patate

Chicken breasts with artichokes and potatoes

Serves 4
Difficulty *
Time: 1-1/2 hours

4 small artichokes
Juice of 1 lemon
9 tbsp. butter
4 potatoes, cooked, peeled and cut into 1/2-inch slices

4 chicken breasts, skin and bones removed
Salt, pepper
Flour
7 tbsp. dry white wine
1/2 cup condensed beef broth

Remove tough outer leaves of artichokes, cut into segments and wash in water containing lemon juice. Drain, dry and fry to golden brown in 2 tablespoons of the butter. Remove artichokes and keep warm. Add 2 tablespoons butter to pan juices and fry potatoes until golden. While potatoes are frying, flatten chicken breasts slightly. Sprinkle with salt and pepper, coat with flour and brown in remaining butter. Arrange chicken on a serving platter and surround with potatoes and artichokes. Pour wine and beef broth into chicken pan juices. Boil over high heat for 5 minutes. Pour juices over chicken breasts and serve.

Costolette di pollo agli asparagi

Chicken joints with asparagus

Serves 4
Difficulty *
Time: 2 hours

Melt 1/3 cup butter and pour off clear butter leaving milky residue behind. This makes 1/4 cup clear clarified butter. Flatten chicken joints slightly, sprinkle with salt and pepper and dip into flour. Fry in clarified butter until brown on all sides. Fry slowly until completely cooked, about 40 to 45 minutes. While chicken is cooking, cook asparagus in lightly salted boiling water until tender. Drain. Saute asparagus in 2 tablespoons of the butter for 1 minute. Keep hot. In another pan melt remaining butter and saute goose liver over very low heat.

When chicken legs are cooked, place them on a serving platter, put goose liver slices on them. Add beef broth to pan juices and boil hard to scrape all brown particles. Boil until thickened. Garnish chicken with asparagus and spoon over gravy.

1/4 cup clarified butter
4 whole chicken legs
Salt, pepper
3 tbsp. flour

1 lb. asparagus spears, tough ends trimmed
3 tbsp. butter
4 slices canned goose liver
1/2 cup condensed beef broth

Costolette di pollo agli asparagi

Anatra al sale

Roast duck in coarse salt

Serves 4
Difficulty **
Time: 2-1/2 hours
Oven Temp. 425°F.

**1 duckling weighing about 5 lbs.
Coarse salt — sea salt, kosher
salt, rock salt, 4 to 5 lbs.**

Thaw duckling if frozen. Remove giblets and reserve for making gravy. Truss to secure legs and wings to body. Cover bottom of deep roasting pan with salt to a depth of 1/2-inch. Put duckling on salt and then cover completely with more salt. Press salt down on duckling. Bake in a preheated oven for 1-1/2 hours. Remove from oven, scrape salt off surface of duckling with a spoon, then grasp trussing cord to lift duckling from salt bed with a quick, decisive movement. Remove final grains of salt with a pastry brush.

Anatra al sale

One species of poultry which the Romans succeeded in raising without foreign help was the duck. Martial wrote that they ate of it only the fillets and the brain; nevertheless they are credited with having invented the combination of duck and fruit, specifically with oranges, which in their day must have meant the bitter orange, the only type they knew. During the Renaissance, duck was cooked not with the fruit itself, but with sauces made from fruit juice; orange-flavored and lemon-flavored duck were both popular. Nowadays La Spezia stuffs duck with olives; the Veneto prefers a complicated stuffing made of duck's liver, veal, bacon, bread crumbs, egg, thyme, tarragon and grated cheese (and also offers anatra alla salsa piccante, which is marinated in a sharply spiced sauce before being cooked in it); and Vicenza incorporates it into a local form of pasta resembling cannelloni.

Anatra in salsa alla veneta

Duck with Venetian sauce

Serves 4
Difficulty **
Time: 2-1/2 hours
Oven Temp. 375° F.

Duckling:

1 duckling weighing about
4 lbs.
1/4 cup (2 oz.) chopped pork fat
4 small dried sage leaves

1 tsp. crumbled rosemary
Salt, pepper
Olive oil

Venetian sauce:

2 cloves garlic, minced
7 tbsp. olive oil
1/4 cup (2 oz.) chopped cooked
lobster meat

2 tbsp. chopped anchovy fillets
2 tbsp. chopped parsley
1 tbsp. wine vinegar
Salt, pepper

Thaw duckling, if frozen and remove giblets. Place duckling on a rack in a foil-lined shallow pan. Mix pork fat with sage leaves and rosemary. Rub duckling with this seasoning inside and out. Sprinkle salt and pepper and brush lightly with oil. Roast duckling for about 1-1/2 hours, basting from time to time with drippings and turning often to brown it on all sides.

For Venetian sauce: Saute garlic in oil until golden. Add lobster, anchovies, parsley and vinegar. Simmer until reduced to 1/3 its original volume, stirring constantly. Season to taste with salt and pepper. Thirty minutes before duck has finished roasting, brush it with some of the Venetian sauce. Finish roasting, place on a platter and spoon over remaining Venetian sauce.

Arrosto di oca ripieno

Roast stuffed goose

Serves 8
Difficulty **
Time: 4-1/2 hours
Oven Temp. 375° F.

A young goose, about 10 to
12 lbs.

Salt, pepper

For stuffing:

1/2 lb. dried pitted prunes
1/4 cup Sultana raisins
Goose giblets, chopped
1/4 lb. blanched almonds,
ground

8 slices firm-type white bread,
crumbled
Milk
1/4 lb. (bulk) sausage meat
Salt, pepper

Thaw goose, if frozen. Sprinkle goose inside and out with salt and pepper.

For stuffing: Soak dried prunes and raisins in warm water. Drain and chop. Mix giblets, almonds, bread soaked in milk and well wrung out, sausage, prunes and raisins. Mix well and season with a pinch of salt and pepper. Stuff goose with mixture and sew or skewer opening. Place goose in a large roasting pan. Roast in a preheated oven for 3 hours, pricking skin with a fork from time to time to allow fat to drip out. When goose is cooked, transfer to a serving platter. Skim fat from pan juices and pass separately as gravy.

Oca in ragù con luganeghe alla veneta

Goose in meat sauce with luganega sausage

Serves 8
Difficulty *
Time: 3 hours

1 goose weighing approx.
4-1/2 lbs.
1 large onion, chopped
2 carrots, sliced
Salt, pepper
7 tbsp. dry red wine
1/4 cup flour
Chicken broth
1 clove garlic, chopped
1/2 cup tomato sauce
1/4 lb. bacon, diced
2 tbsp. olive oil
16 pieces luganega sausage
(spiced Italian sausage)

Thaw goose if frozen. Clean goose and cut into pieces, reserving fat. Dice fat and heat in a frying pan. Add onion and carrots and after a few minutes pieces of goose. Sprinkle with salt and pepper and brown well on all sides. Add wine; simmer until it evaporates. Sprinkle with flour and mix. Add sufficient broth to cover goose, then add garlic and tomato sauce. Cover and cook over low heat, stirring from time to time until tender, about 1 to 1-1/2 hours. When goose is cooked, remove pieces and arrange on a serving platter. Keep warm.
Strain pan juices through a fine sieve and set aside. Brown bacon in oil. Add sausage and pan juices and cook for 10 to 15 minutes. Arrange bacon and sausage around goose and serve.

The ancient Romans did not eat goose until nearly the beginning of our era; this was not out of gratitude for the geese of the Capitol which once saved it from destruction, nor even because the geese were kept there precisely because they had a sacred character. It was because the species the Romans knew did not make good eating. When they conquered Gaul and became acquainted with the fat geese of Picardy, they took enthusiastically to the bird, and drove great flocks of geese all the way from northern Gaul to Rome overland, foraging for food as they passed, which made them about as popular with farmers as were the Legions, also unscrupulous foragers. Goose is usually poor-country poultry, since it exceeds all others in putting on meat from poor pasturage, so one might expect goose to be most popular in the comparatively poor South. This is not the case; goose is probably too fat and too heavy for the climate and eating habits of the South. But it *is* accounted a treat in one of the poorer regions of the North, Friuli; Treviso, also well to the north, is noted for its goose cooked with celery; the recipe given here comes from the same region.

Oca in ragù con luganeghe alla veneta

Filetti di tacchino dorati su crostoni

Filetti di tacchino dorati su crostoni

Turkey breasts on toasted polenta rounds

Serves 4
Difficulty *
Time: 1-1/2 hours

4 raw turkey breast slices weighing about 4 oz. each
Salt, pepper
2 eggs
2/3 cups grated Parmesan

4 slices bacon
Flour
4 thick slices of polenta of same size as turkey slices (see Polenta p. 81)
5 tbsp. butter

Pound turkey until paper thin. Sprinkle with salt and pepper. Dip turkey breast slices in egg and then in grated Parmesan cheese. Fry bacon and set aside, keeping it hot. Reserve bacon drippings in pan. Brown turkey on both sides in bacon drippings. In another pan brown floured polenta slices in butter on both sides. Arrange polenta slices on a serving platter and top each with a turkey cutlet and a strip of bacon.

It is possible that the most popular form of poultry in Italy today is that comparative newcomer, the turkey. It is true that Alexandre Dumas argued valiantly that not only the Romans, but also the ancient Greeks before them, knew this bird, which he identified with what the ancients called the meleagris; but this was almost certainly the guinea fowl. As the meleagris thereafter disappeared from history, Dumas suggested that the species might have been killed off by an epidemic; but then he proceeded to bring it back again by alleging that it had been reimported into Europe in 1432 from India—where it did not exist. Actually the turkey was first introduced into Europe from America by the Spaniards in 1519; it seems to have reached Italy shortly afterwards. In Milan today, as in the United States, turkey is a Christmas dish, roasted for the holiday with a special stuffing which includes the giblets, sausage, chestnuts, quartered apples, prunes, grated cheese and nutmeg. The region of Vicenza is noted for its turkeys.

Arrosto di tacchino ripieno

Roast stuffed turkey

Serves 8 to 10 persons
Difficulty ***
Time: 5 hours
Oven Temp. 350° F.

A young turkey weighing about 8 lbs.
Salt, pepper
4 slices pork fat
2 tbsp. olive oil
2 tbsp. butter
A sprig of fresh rosemary
Several fresh sage leaves

For stuffing:

1 package (1 oz.) dried mushrooms
1 stale dinner roll
Turkey liver and gizzard, chopped
1/4 lb. calf's liver
1/4 lb. (bulk) sausage meat
2 tbsp. chopped prosciutto crudo
1/4 lb. fresh pork fat
1/2 lb. ground (minced) veal
1/4 lb. ground (minced) lean pork
6 sprigs parsley, chopped
2 tbsp. chopped truffle
Salt, pepper
1 egg and 1 egg yolk

Thaw turkey, if frozen. Using the point of a paring knife inside the body cavity of the turkey, delicately separate breast meat from wishbone. Break off bone with your finger and remove carefully, taking care not to break the skin. Placing fingers of one hand in the neck opening and the fingers of the other hand in the opening under the tail, cut the ligaments and tendons and delicately separate the breast meat from the bone. Insert a knife in the turkey, cut off and remove the breast bone. Cut off any remaining small bones with a pair of scissors and remove from inside of fowl. Draw neck skin over the back and fasten in place by sewing or skewering in place.

For stuffing: Put mushrooms and roll to soak separately in a little water. Mix turkey liver and gizzard, calf's liver, sausage, prosciutto, pork fat, ground veal and pork and mushrooms and bread from which water has been well squeezed. Put entire mixture through a meat grinder and place in mixing bowl. Add parsley, truffles, salt and pepper and 1 egg and 1 egg yolk.

Stuff turkey lightly, sew or skewer openings. Season outside with salt and pepper. Cover breast with strips of pork fat and tie with string. Grease a roasting pan with oil. Place stuffed turkey in it and dot with butter mixed with fresh sage and rosemary and roast in a preheated oven. During cooking time baste frequently with pan drippings. After about 2-1/2 hours remove from oven, discard strips of pork fat and return to oven for about 20 minutes more so that skin is crisp and golden brown.

Lepre alla maniera del ghiottone

Lepre alla maniera del ghiottone

Hare gourmet style

Serves 4
Difficulty *
Time: 3 hours, plus time required to marinate hare
Oven Temp. 375° F.

2-1/2 lb. hare (butt end including the leg)
2 cups red wine
1 bay leaf
A sprig of thyme
Rind of 1/2 orange
Salt, pepper
6 tbsp. lard (or butter)
2 garlic cloves, chopped
A sprig of rosemary

Prick hare with a fork. Marinate hare in a mixture of red wine, bay leaf, thyme, orange rind, salt and pepper. Marinate for 6 hours, turning hare every once in a while. Melt lard (or butter) in a frying pan, add minced garlic and rosemary. Remove hare from marinade. Season with salt and pepper. Put hare in a roasting pan and brush with lard. Bake in a preheated oven for 1 hour. While roasting hare, turn occasionally to ensure even browning overall and baste with pan juices. Remove from oven, pour off pan juices and replace them with marinade. Return to oven and continue roasting for 45 minutes or until hare is tender. Remove from roasting pan, cut into pieces and place on a platter. Strain marinade through a fine strainer and pour over meat.

Game, except for those so fortunately placed that they can go after their own, has become an almost prohibitively rare and expensive luxury in the United States. Europe has held out better, since conservation of public woodlands and protection of game animals is centuries old there; but the sprawling growth of cities, and the rising demand from constantly increasing populations have been making inroads in Western Europe too. Italy, aided by considerable areas of difficult terrain, has held out better than most, and game there is still within reach of non-millionaires. At present, the outstanding game areas in Italy include the Maremma marshes on the Tuscan coast, across from Elba; the less accessible uplands of Umbria; the high Alpine regions of Piedmont, Lombardy and Venezia, where the hunter may occasionally bag such rare prizes as heather hen, chamois, ibex or even the almost extinct wild goat, provided an individual animal strays incautiously beyond the confines of the preserves (but you will find none of these on the market or in restaurants—you have to be, or know, a hunter, or, even better, a poacher); the Polesina region of the Veneto, for water fowl; and Sardinia, probably the leading region of Italy for game, though even there the government was obliged to impose a permanent closed season on moufflon, Sardinian stags and Sardinian deer, all of which were threatened with extinction. Several of these areas still harbor wild boar, an animal increasingly rare everywhere in Western Europe.

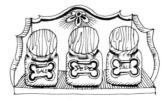

During the Renaissance, hare was a favorite dish in Tuscany, marinated in wine and vinegar, and cooked in the marinating liquid along with onion and spices; today Tuscany cooks it in agrodolce sauce, which is pretty much the same thing. Hare has still not become a rarity in Italy, as it is now in many countries; there are accordingly numerous ways of preparing it, and even a kind of pasta especially conceived to accompany it—pappardelle. Umbria cooks hare as a salmi; Piacenza boils it first and fries it afterwards, with bacon, onion and herbs; and in the Valle d'Aosta it is braised in wine with a dash of cognac and served with truffles and potatoes.

Coniglio
alla valsassinese

Rabbit Val di Sassina style

Serves 6
Difficulty *
Time: Marinate 24 hours
      Cook 1-1/2 hours

**1 rabbit weighing about
3-1/2 lbs.
3 cups dry red wine
3 carrots, chopped
1/2 onion, chopped
1 rib celery, chopped
1/4 cup chopped fresh basil
leaves
6 sage leaves
3 cloves
1 bay leaf
Salt, pepper
Flour
2 tbsp. butter
7 tbsp. olive oil
1 clove garlic, chopped
6 slices (1/4 lb.) smoked bacon
cut into strips
3/4 lb. wild or cultivated
mushrooms, sliced (or 1 oz.
dried mushrooms)
1 cup dry white wine**

Clean rabbit, reserving liver. Cut rabbit into pieces, soak 2 hours in cold water to remove all blood and whiten the flesh. Drain and marinate in red wine containing vegetables and herbs (carrots, onion, celery, basil, sage, cloves, bay leaf and salt.) Marinate for 24 hours. Drain rabbit. Reserve marinade liquid and vegetables for later use. Flour pieces. Heat butter and 5 tablespoons of the oil in a pan. Add rabbit pieces and garlic. Sprinkle with salt and pepper and brown over high heat on all sides. When rabbit is browned, remove garlic pieces, pour in marinade liquid and chopped vegetables. Cover and simmer for 1 hour over low heat. Stir sauce from time to time and shift pieces of rabbit to avoid sticking. Fry bacon in remaining oil until brown. Add chopped rabbit liver and mushrooms. Add wine. Mix 1 tablespoon flour with 1/4 cup water and stir into sauce until it thickens. Pour sauce over rabbit in pan. Stir over heat for a few minutes and serve.

> You may take it pretty much for granted when you find the word "coniglio" on an Italian menu that it refers to domesticated rabbit; if it were wild, it would be described as coniglio selvatico. Venice's way with the rabbit is to cut it up and put it in a stew, or deep-fry marinated chunks of it which have previously been coated with egg and flour. Sicily, where rabbit is more in honor than anywhere else in Italy, handles it in any number of fashions—for instance, cooked in vinegar with fava beans; or stewed with vegetables; or given unwonted character with agrodolce sauce.

Coniglio e peperoni
alla piemontese

*Rabbit and peppers
Piedmont style*

Serves 4
Difficulty *
Time: 2 hours

**1 rabbit weighing about
2-1/2 lbs.
1 sprig fresh rosemary, chopped
1/4 cup (2 oz.) chopped fat of
prosciutto
1/4 cup butter
1 bay leaf
Salt, pepper**

**Chicken broth
2 tbsp. olive oil
4 green peppers, cut up
4 fillets of anchovy, chopped or
ground to paste in mortar
2 cloves garlic, minced
3 tbsp. wine vinegar**

Cut rabbit into serving size pieces. Saute rosemary and prosciutto with half the butter. Add rabbit pieces and bay leaf. Sprinkle with salt and brown at high heat. Continue cooking over moderate heat, basting occasionally with a little broth for 1-1/2 hours. In another pan heat remaining butter and oil and saute peppers with anchovy and garlic. Season with freshly ground pepper and cook slowly, adding vinegar during cooking for 10 minutes. Set aside. When rabbit is tender, add peppers, cook for a few minutes longer and serve.

Coniglio alla ghiotta con madera

Gourmet rabbit with Madeira sauce

Serves 4
Difficulty *
Time: 2 hours, plus time required to marinate the rabbit

1 rabbit weighing about 2-1/2 lbs.
Pinch of cinnamon
1 sprig fresh rosemary, chopped
1 bay leaf
Salt, pepper
2 tbsp. red wine vinegar
1/4 cup olive oil
2 tbsp. butter
1 cup dry Madeira wine
Chicken broth

Coniglio alla ghiotta con madera

Cut rabbit into serving size pieces, wash, dry and put into a large bowl. Marinate in a marinade composed of cinnamon, rosemary, bay leaf, a little freshly ground pepper, a pinch of salt, vinegar and half of the oil. Marinate for 12 to 24 hours, turning pieces occasionally. Heat butter and remaining oil in a frying pan and brown pieces of rabbit after having drained off marinade. Add Madeira wine. Cover and simmer over low heat until tender, about 1-1/2 hours, adding a little hot water or broth as needed. Remove pieces to a platter. Skim fat from pan juices. Simmer pan juices until half their original volume. Spoon juices over rabbit pieces.

Camoscio in salmì

Ragout of venison

Serves 4
Difficulty *
Time: 3 hours, plus time required to marinate meat

2-1/2 lbs. venison (preferably cut from the leg) cut into 1-inch cubes
1-3/4 cups red wine
1 small onion, chopped
2 carrots, sliced
1 rib celery, chopped
1 clove garlic, chopped
Pinch of thyme
1 bay leaf
Salt, peppercorns
6 tbsp. butter
Flour
1/2 lb. fresh mushrooms, sliced
2 tbsp. brandy

Venison is an increasingly rare meat, but there are still huntable deer in Italy—in the Maremma marshes, for instance, and in the Alps —and so it is still offered on the Italian menu. The Veneto serves it as a salmi, while the Alto Adige cuts it into chunks, marinates it in red wine and herbs, envelops the pieces in bread crumbs, and sautes them; it is served with a cream sauce, dumplings, and jelly.

Marinate venison for 48 hours in a marinade composed of the following: Red wine, onion, carrot, celery, garlic, thyme, bay leaf, a pinch of salt and a few peppercorns.
Heat 4 tablespoons of the butter. Drain meat reserving marinade. Dry cubes, coat cubes with flour and brown over high heat. Add marinade, season with salt and pepper and simmer, covered, for at least 2 hours over moderate heat. Meanwhile, saute mushrooms in remaining butter. When meat is tender, pour off sauce and press through a strainer. Pour strained sauce over meat. Add mushrooms and brandy. Reheat until bubbly. Season to taste with salt and pepper.

Pernici "club del buongustaio"

Partridge "Gourmet Club"

Serves 4
Difficulty **
Time: 3 hours

3/4 lb. white beans (or haricot beans)
4 partridges
Salt, pepper
1/4 cup butter
5 tbsp. goose liver, chopped
5 tbsp. chopped truffles

8 pieces pork caul or thin slices of pork fat
1/4 lb. bacon rind
1/4 cup chopped prosciutto crudo
2 tbsp. olive oil
2 cups chopped tomato pulp, skin and seeds removed

Boil beans in unsalted water until tender, about 2 hours. Split partridges into halves. Flatten halves slightly by pounding gently. Remove and discard smallest bones, then season with a pinch of salt and pepper. Heat butter in a large frying pan. Brown halves on both sides. Drain and allow to cool. Stuff halves lightly with chopped goose liver and truffle. Sprinkle with salt and pepper and wrap halves in pieces of pork caul. Put partridges back into pan juices. Set over heat and continue sauteing, turning from time to time. Cook bacon rind in lightly salted boiling water for 1 hour. Remove and dice. Saute prosciutto in oil for 1 minute. Add tomato pulp, season with salt and pepper, and simmer for 10 minutes. Add drained beans, bacon rind and simmer another 10 minutes. Put partridges on platter, pour pan juices over them and serve with beans.

Pernici "club del buongustaio"

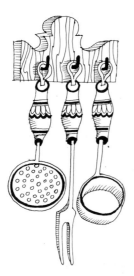

Pheasant is probably the most popular and the easiest to find of all Italian game birds, which is true of many other countries also; but how often is the pheasant served you in a restaurant or sold you in a market a genuine wild pheasant? One reason why pheasant remains relatively plentiful almost everywhere is that it adapts itself readily to being raised artificially; if you have a sensitive palate, you can easily tell the difference. You would be pretty sure of getting the real thing if the name of one of the dishes given here could be taken literally: fagiano alla bracconiera means poacher's pheasant; but I fear that you will have to resign yourself to the fact that this is no more than the name of a recipe.

Fagiano al marsala

*Pheasant
in Marsala sauce
with truffles*

Serves 4
Difficulty *
Time: 1-1/2 hours

**1 pheasant weighing about
3-1/2 lbs.
1/4 cup minced cooked ham
1 black truffle, sliced
6 juniper berries, crushed**

**5 tbsp. olive oil
2 tbsp. butter
Salt, pepper
1/2 cup Marsala wine (dry)**

If freshly caught, hang pheasant in a cool place for 2 or 3 days. Pluck feathers, discard head, feet and neck. Clean thoroughly and then wash in a thin stream of running water, letting water run into cavity as well as outside. If using frozen pheasant, thaw before using. Wash liver and chop. Mix with ham. Add half the truffle slices and juniper berries. Use mixture to stuff pheasant. Sew up cavity to hold stuffing in, truss bird and brown in a Dutch oven in oil and butter. Sprinkle pheasant with salt and pepper. Turn it often while it is browning so that every side is well browned about 10 minutes. Pour in Marsala and cook for 5 minutes over high heat. Sprinkle remaining truffle over pheasant and lower heat. Cover and simmer over low heat. There will be a thick, dark sauce forming in pan. Add a little water from time to time to prevent sticking. It will take from 30 to 45 minutes for the bird to cook through, depending on its age. Prick thigh with a fork to test whether pheasant is done. If juices run clear it is cooked. Transfer to a serving platter; spoon over pan juices.

Fagiano alla bracconiera

Pheasant poacher style

Serves 4
Difficulty *
Time: 2-1/2 hours including
1 hour marinating time
Oven Temp. 400° F.

**1 pheasant weighing about
3-1/2 lbs.
3 slices lean bacon, chopped
1/2 tsp. crumbled sage
1/2 cup cognac
Salt, pepper**

**10 slices prosciutto crudo
2 slices (2 oz.) pork fat
1/2 cup Marsala
2 tbsp. butter
2 tbsp. olive oil**

Clean the pheasant as in recipe for Pheasant in Marsala sauce with truffles. If using frozen pheasant, thaw before using.
Mix bacon, sage and chopped pheasant liver, and use it to stuff cavity. Pour half of the cognac into cavity, then sprinkle with salt and pepper. Sew opening. Truss bird and wrap it in slices of prosciutto and pork fat. Tie slices on with string. Sprinkle with salt and pepper lightly. Put pheasant in a roaster, pour over remaining cognac and Marsala and let it marinate for several hours (minimum 1 hour, if you are pressed for time). Turn pheasant every 15 minutes. Dot with butter, spoon over oil and roast in a preheated oven for at least 1 hour. Baste with pan juices every 15 minutes. When done the pheasant should be very well browned. Prick thigh, juices will run clear when completely cooked.

Piccioni in peperonata

Pigeons and peppers

Serves 4
Difficulty *
Time: 1-1/2 hours

4 pigeons
1/2 cup olive oil
Salt
1 cup dry white wine
1/2 small onion, sliced
2 green bell peppers, with seeds removed, cut into 1/2-inch wide strips
2 red bell peppers, with seeds removed, cut into 1/2-inch wide strips
1-1/4 lbs. ripe tomatoes, peeled seeded and chopped (about 4 medium)

Clean pigeons, singe pigeons to eliminate last remnants of under-feathers, then wash for a long time in cold running water both inside and outside to remove any traces of blood. Drain and brown in half the oil, sprinkle with salt lightly and turn them continually to brown on all sides. Add white wine, raise heat and cook until wine is evaporated and pigeons are golden brown, about 20 minutes. In a separate pan saute onion and peppers in remaining oil until wilted. Add tomatoes to pan. Sprinkle with salt lightly and cook for 10 minutes, stirring from time to time. Add pigeons to pan, cover and cook for 30 minutes or until pigeons are tender. Season to taste with salt.

The pigeon was one bird which interested the ancient Romans, but they preferred it wild. They assured themselves a supply of gamey-tasting pigeons by crossing wild birds with tame ones. Modern Italians have not followed in their footsteps. They take pigeons as they come, either totally wild (like the rock pigeons of Breganze) or utterly tame.

Piccioncelli con piselli freschi

Pigeon with fresh peas

Serves 4
Difficulty *
Time: 1-1/2 hours

4 young pigeons
6 tbsp. butter
2 tbsp. olive oil
2 cups fresh shelled peas
Salt, pepper
Bouquet garni of sage and bay leaf
1 cup chicken broth
6 tbsp. (3 oz.) strips prosciutto crudo, including fat

Clean pigeons and wash under running water. Heat butter with oil in a Dutch oven or frying pan. Brown pigeons on all sides over high heat. Lower heat, put peas in pan around pigeons. Add salt and pepper to taste, bouquet garni and broth. Cover and continue cooking over moderate heat for about 1/2 hour or until pigeons are almost tender. Add prosciutto and simmer another 5 minutes. Transfer pigeons and peas to a serving platter, remove bouquet garni. Boil pan juices, skimming excess fat, until half the original volume. Pour juices over pigeons and peas.

Piccioncelli con piselli freschi

Quaglie in foglia di vite
Quail in vine leaves

Serves 4
Difficulty *
Time: 1-1/2 hours
Oven Temp. 350° F.

Clean quail and remove giblets. Season inside and out with salt and pepper. Wrap each with a slice of bacon. Tie with string and put quail into a roasting pan. Brush with butter. Roast in a preheated oven for 40 minutes. Remove quail from pan and remove bacon slices. Replace bacon with vine leaves, tying leaves with string. Put quail back into roasting pan, baste with brandy and continue roasting another 40 minutes. During cooking add a little broth if needed for moisture. When cooking is completed, arrange quail, still wrapped in vine leaves, on a platter. Remove string and spoon over pan juices.

Quaglie in foglia di vite

8 quail
Salt, pepper
8 slices bacon
1/4 cup butter, melted

8 large vine leaves
1/2 cup brandy
Chicken broth

Sometime during the third century, the city of Syracuse was saved from starvation when, during a famine, Santa Lucia directed a flock of the migrating birds over the city, where they fell exhausted on the beaches to provide much needed food. Under the circumstances, it seems ungrateful of Sicilians to make a joke of the quail—order quail in a *friggitore* (snack bar) and you will get a piece of deep-fried eggplant (aubergine). Quails are treated with greater respect in another region crossed by their migrations, the Marches, where they are cooked in cognac. Piedmont serves them with risotto and the Veneto either with risotto or alla cacciatora, hunter's style.

Quaglie alla pierino
Quail Pierino

Serves 4
Difficulty *
Time: 2 hours
Oven Temp. 350° F.

4 quail
1/2 cup (4 oz.) sausage meat
6 sprigs parsley, chopped
1 fresh sage leaf
1 egg
Salt, pepper

4 slices boneless pork loin (approx. 1 lb.)
4 slices bacon
Olive oil
2 tbsp. butter
7 tbsp. dry white wine

Clean quail, reserving livers. Singe and wash birds. Clean livers and chop fine. Put chopped livers in a bowl. Add sausage, parsley, sage egg, salt and pepper to taste. Mix well and use mixture to stuff quail. Pound pork slices until very thin. Wrap each quail in a slice of meat and wrap a slice of bacon over pork loin. Secure with a metal pin or toothpicks. Arrange quail in shallow baking pan, side by side. Brush with oil and butter. Roast in a preheated oven for 15 minutes. Add wine and roast another 15 minutes. Cover and continue cooking for about 1 hour. The quail are attractive served on slices of toast, or they may be served in the dish in which they were prepared.

Fritto misto all'italiana

Being of canonical age, I can remember when butchers would toss in a large piece of free liver with your order "for the cat." Liver was contemptuously cheap in those days, and many people considered it barely fit for human consumption. Both prices and mental attitudes have evolved since then, and though we still refer gingerly to the internal organs of animals as "variety meats," a euphemism dating from the days when innards were consumed only by foreigners almost everybody nowadays will tackle liver or tongue fearlessly, and many will even stand up to kidneys and sweetbreads. Certain brave pioneers venture as far as brains, but this is about the limit, with the exception of tripe, whose consumption seems to be a regional phenomenon. Fears of such unfamiliar meats are unnecessary, for practically all parts of meat animals are edible; individual tastes are another matter. They seem to cover a wider gamut in Italy, where several organs are eaten which arouse no enthusiasm in us. The heart? Maybe. But spleen? Or lungs? Let us pursue the matter no farther.

Fritto misto all'italiana

Mixed fry, Italian style

Serves 4
Difficulty *
Time: 2 hours

1/4 lb. lamb kidney
1/2 lb. calf's brains
1/2 lb. boneless veal
1/4 lb. calf's liver
Flour
1/2 cup butter

1/4 cup olive oil
Salt
2 medium potatoes, peeled and
cut into 1/4-inch thick slices
2 zucchini, cut into 1/4-inch
thick lengthwise slices

Both vegetables and meat may be varied in this recipe. Suggested vegetables are cabbage, eggplant, carrots etc. Suggested meats are pork, sausage, veal liver, kidneys or lungs, beef, chicken livers, etc.

Remove all fat and tubules from kidneys. Cut them in half lengthwise, and remove spongy inner fiber. Soak them for 30 minutes in cold water mixed with a little vinegar to remove characteristic odor. Drain and wash several times. Soak brains in cold water for 10 minutes. Pull off membrane, being careful not to break brains. Slice kidney, brains, veal and liver. Coat pieces with flour. Fry them in a pan with half of the butter and half of the oil. Brown on all sides with constant turning. (If frying pan is too small, do not crowd it, but make several successive batches.) Drain pieces on absorbent paper. Sprinkle pieces with salt and place on a serving platter. Keep warm. At the same time, in another frying pan heat remaining oil and butter. Brown potato slices slowly on both sides until tender, drain on absorbent paper and sprinkle with salt. Coat zucchini slices with flour and saute in same manner. Arrange potatoes and zucchini around platter of meats and serve very hot.

Fritto di mozzarella, cervella e carciofi

Fried mozzarella, brains and artichokes

Serves 4
Difficulty *
Time: 1 hour, plus time required to soak brains

3/4 lb. calf's brains
1/2 onion, chopped
1 stalk celery, chopped
1 bay leaf
Salt, peppercorns
1 cup olive oil, approx.
Juice of 2 lemons

Sprig of parsley, chopped
4 artichokes
1/2 lb. mozzarella cheese
Flour
3 eggs, well beaten
Additional parsley sprigs and
lemon wedges

Put brains in a saucepan, cover with cold water and add onion, celery, bay leaf, a pinch of salt and a couple of peppercorns. Bring to a boil and simmer for 5 minutes. Drain, cool and peel away membrane. Slice brains and marinate in a mixture of 1/2 cup oil, half the lemon juice and chopped parsley for 1 hour. Remove outer leaves from artichokes, leaving hearts. Remove choke. Cut into wedges and drop each wedge into cold water containing remaining lemon juice (to prevent them from darkening). Cut mozzarella into 1 inch cubes. Flour the cubes and dip them in lightly salted beaten eggs and then brown in plenty of hot olive oil. Do the same for well-drained artichoke wedges and well-drained slices of brains. Drain fried pieces on paper toweling, arrange on a serving platter on a paper doily. Garnish with fresh parsley sprigs and lemon wedges and serve.

185

Fritto misto alla milanese

*Mixed fry
Milanese style*

Serves 6
Difficulty *
Time: 2 hours

2 veal kidneys
1 pair veal sweetbreads
4 artichokes
2 lemons
1 small cauliflower, broken
into flowerets
6 stalks white celery, cut
into 1-inch pieces
1 lb. veal scallopini, cut
into strips

Flour
2/3 cup butter
4 zucchini, cut into 1/2-inch
thick slices
2 cups seasoned mashed potatoes
mixed with 1/2 cup shredded
mozzarella
Deep fat or oil heated to 360° F.
6 sprigs parsley, chopped
Salt

Clean kidneys, wash thoroughly and cook in boiling water with sweetbreads for 2 minutes. Drain. Peel membrane from kidney and sweetbreads, then slice thin. Discard harsh outer leaves of artichokes, cut into wedges, remove choke and soak in cold water with 2 tablespoons lemon juice. Cook cauliflower and celery until tender. Dip all meats into flour and fry in half of the butter until tender and brown on all sides. Dredge vegetables in flour and deep-fry in very hot oil for 2 to 3 minutes. Shape potatoes into balls, roll in flour and fry 3 to 4 minutes. Put meats, potato balls and vegetables together on a hot platter. Brown remaining butter and pour over "fritto misto." Sprinkle with parsley and salt. Squeeze on a little lemon juice and serve.

Fritto misto alla fiorentina

Mixed fry Florentine style

Serves 4
Difficulty *
Time: 2 hours

1-1/4 cups sifted all-purpose
flour
1/2 tsp. crumbled rosemary
Salt, pepper
Fat or oil
2 eggs, separated
Nutmeg
1/2 cup white wine
4 artichokes

1 lemon
1 calf's brain
1 pair calf's sweetbreads
2 slices calf's liver, cut
into 1-inch wide strips
4 rib lamb chops, fat and
bone removed
4 zucchini cut into 1/2-inch
thick slices

Put flour in mixing bowl, season with crumbled rosemary, salt and pepper. Add 3 tablespoons oil, egg yolks, a pinch of nutmeg, wine and enough water to make a batter the consistency of heavy cream. Beat until smooth. Let batter stand for 1 hour. Discard harsh outer artichoke leaves and cook artichokes in salted boiling water with 2 tablespoons lemon juice for 10 minutes. Drain and cut into wedges, removing choke. Cook brains and sweetbreads in boiling water for 5 minutes. Drain, peel off membrane and slice them 1/2-inch thick. Preheat fat to 360° F. in 2 pans. When ready to fry, beat egg whites until stiff and fold into batter. Dip meat and vegetable pieces into batter. Fry meats and vegetables separately in 2 pans until brown and crisp on all sides, 2 to 3 minutes for vegetables and 5 to 6 minutes for meats. Serve with lemon wedges.

Fegato di vitello alla milanese

Calf's liver Milanese

Serves 4
Difficulty *
Time: 1-1/2 hours

1-1/2 lbs. calf's liver
6 sprigs parsley, chopped
plus additional for garnish
Salt, pepper
1/4 cup olive oil

2 eggs
Dry bread crumbs
5 tbsp. butter
1 lemon, cut into wedges

Remove outer membrane and tubules from liver. Cut liver into slices, arranging slices in a deep dish. Sprinkle chopped parsley over them. Sprinkle with salt and pepper and add 2 tablespoons of the oil. Leave liver to marinate at room temperature for about 1 hour. Beat eggs very lightly in a bowl, barely enough to blend yolk and white. Sprinkle with salt lightly. Remove liver from marinade, drain. Dip slices in egg and then coat with bread crumbs. Fry in butter and remaining oil over high heat until golden brown on both sides. Serve with lemon wedges.

Fegato di vitello alla veneziana

Calf's liver Venetian style

Serves 4
Difficulty *
Time: 15 minutes

1/2 lb. onions, sliced
1/3 cup olive oil
1-1/4 lbs. calf's liver
Salt, pepper
2 lemons, cut into wedges
Thick, hot polenta
(see Polenta p. 81)

Fry the onions in the oil golden brown, stirring constantly. Cut liver into thin slices, removing membranes and other tough portions. Season with freshly ground pepper and add to pan. Cook for a few minutes, until brown on both sides. Sprinkle with salt and turn out onto a hot platter. Garnish with lemon wedges. Serve with freshly made polenta as a side dish, or polenta slices browned in oven.

> Venice claims to have invented the combination of liver with onions; there is in any case no place which cooks it better. The Venetian secret is to cook the liver very fast and the onions very slowly. Milan is original in its treatment of liver, which is first marinated, and then, coated with bread crumbs and fried in butter. Genoa uses bread crumbs too, and also grated cheese.

Fegato di vitello alla veneziana

Involtini di fegato con purea di lenticchie

Pork liver rolls with lentil purée

Serves 4
Difficulty *
Time: 3-1/2 hours, allowing overnight soaking time for lentils

For lentil purée:

2 cups (3/4 lb.) lentils (soaked overnight)
Sprig parsley, chopped
1 carrot, chopped
1/4 cup (2 oz.) chopped pork fat
1/2 onion, chopped

1 tbsp. olive oil
1/4 cup dry white wine
1 tbsp. tomato paste
1 cup beef broth
2 tbsp. butter
Salt, pepper

For liver rolls:

1 lb. pork liver
1/2 cup (4 oz.) diced pork fat
Salt, pepper
Nutmeg

8 oz. pork caul or thin slices pork fat
Several bay leaves
3 tbsp. lard (or butter)

For lentil purée: Boil lentils in lightly salted water containing parsley and carrot until tender, about 1 hour. Saute pork fat and onion briefly in oil. As soon as onion has begun to brown, add wine and simmer 5 minutes. Mix tomato paste and broth. Add to onion and cook for about 15 minutes. Drain lentils, add to pan and simmer for a few minutes. Press lentils and sauce through a food mill, then bring to a boil. Simmer while stirring until thick, about 10 minutes. Remove from heat and stir in butter. Season to taste with salt and pepper.

For liver rolls: Dice liver and pork fat until 1/2 inch cubes, season with salt, pepper and nutmeg and let stand for 15 minutes. Soften caul or fat in cold water, and cut into rectangles large enough to wrap walnut-sized mounds of liver and pork fat. Add a piece of bay leaf. Wrap and tie with string. Heat lard in a pan, put liver rolls in and brown slowly for about 40 minutes. Arrange rolls on a platter and serve with lentil purée.

Fegato di vitello alla romana

Calf's liver Roman style

Serves 4
Difficulty *
Time: 30 minutes

1/4 cup lard or other cooking fat
2/3 cup onions, sliced

1-1/2 lbs. calf's liver
1 cup chicken broth
Salt, pepper

Melt the lard or pork fat in a frying pan and saute onions until brown, stirring often. Remove outer membrane and tubules from liver. Slice liver 1/2-inch thick and brown in pan on both sides with onions (about 1 minute over high heat.) Pour in broth and continue cooking over high heat for another 5 minutes, stirring often. Remove liver from heat. Sprinkle with salt and pepper and serve hot with onions and pan juices.

Regaglie di pollo al basilico

Chicken giblets with basil

Serves 4
Difficulty *
Time: 1 hour

1-1/2 lbs. chicken giblets (livers and hearts)
1/4 cup butter
2 tbsp. olive oil
1/2 cup chopped fresh basil leaves
1 cup dry white wine
Salt, pepper

Wash and drain giblets. Cut hearts into thin slices. Heat butter with oil and add basil. When butter and oil are foaming, add giblets and stir. When giblets no longer show any trace of blood, pour in wine and simmer, about 30 minutes, until giblets are cooked. Sprinkle with salt and pepper and stir again before serving.

Fegatini di pollo con piselli

Chicken livers with peas

Serves 4
Difficulty *
Time: 1-1/2 hours

3/4 lb. chicken livers
2 cups shelled fresh green peas
5 tbsp. butter
3 tbsp. chopped parsley
1/2 cup chicken broth
4 slices of toast about 1/2-inch thick
Salt

Clean chicken livers and cut into halves or thirds. Cook peas in lightly salted boiling water until tender but still firm (al dente). Melt 3 tablespoons of the butter in a saucepan, add peas, parsley. Then add chicken livers and broth. Stir frequently and cook for another 5 minutes. Toast bread in remaining butter, put them on a serving platter. Remove chicken livers and peas with a slotted spoon and spoon over toast. Keep warm. Boil pan juices over high heat reducing to half their original volume. Season to taste with salt. Pour over chicken livers and serve.

Fegatini di pollo con piselli

Animella di vitello al burro e salvia

Veal sweetbreads cooked in butter and sage

Serves 4
Difficulty **
Time: 1 hour, plus time for soaking sweetbreads

1 lb. veal sweetbreads
6 tbsp. butter
Several dried sage leaves

Flour
Salt, pepper
1/2 cup beef broth, heated
1 tbsp. lemon juice

Soak sweetbreads for 2 hours in water to cover, changing water from time to time. Drain. Put them in a saucepan, cover with fresh water, salt lightly and bring to a boil covered over moderate heat. Simmer for 6 minutes, drain. Plunge into cold water to firm sweetbreads. Trim them by removing cartilage, tubes, connective tissue and membrane. Wrap sweetbreads in foil tightly and chill for several hours. Cut sweetbreads into 1/2-inch thick slices.
To cook sweetbreads: Heat butter and sage in a pan. Coat sweetbread slices with flour, shaking off excess and brown them in butter. Season with salt and pepper, then add hot broth. Add lemon juice, turn slices, finish cooking them slowly for another 5 minutes.

Lamb Sweetbreads

Note: Lamb sweetbreads should be soaked in warm water for 10 minutes. Drain and place in a saucepan. Cover with cold water, bring to a boil and simmer for 1 minute, then finish preparation as above or use as desired in sweetbread recipes.

Animella di vitello con risotto alla milanese

Veal sweetbreads with Milanese risotto

Serves 4
Difficulty **
Time: 2 hours, plus time required for soaking sweetbreads

For sweetbreads:

1 lb. calf sweetbreads
1/4 cup butter
Salt

For risotto:

1/2 small onion, chopped
1/2 cup butter
2 tbsp. beef marrow
1-1/2 cups (3/4 lb.) rice
1/2 cup dry white wine

6 cups (1-1/2 quarts) chicken broth
1 tsp. crumbled saffron threads
1/2 cup (2 oz.) grated Parmesan cheese
Pepper

Prepare sweetbreads (see Animella di vitello al burro e salvia) then slice and complete cooking in butter. Salt to taste and place on a serving platter, together with Risotto alla milanese (see page 87).

If Europe, including Italy, eats various internal organs of animals usually considered unworthy of attention in America, the United States reverses the roles when it comes to sweetbreads. In Europe the sweetbread is the thymus; but in America the pancreas is sometimes substituted for it, or even the salivary or lymphatic glands. The true sweetbread, European definition, is a delicate dish which deserves more attention than is usually accorded it in the United States.

Animella di vitello con pasta al burro

Veal sweetbreads with fettuccine in butter sauce

Serves 4
Difficulty **
Time: 1-1/2 hours, plus soaking time for sweetbreads

For pasta:
1/2 lb. fettuccine noodles
1/3 cup butter
1/2 cup grated Parmesan

2 sweetbreads
Salt, pepper
Flour

2 eggs, well beaten
Dry bread crumbs
1/3 cup butter

Prepare the sweetbreads as in Animella di vitello al burro e salvia (page 190). Cut away the fat and cartilage. Cut each sweetbread into eight slices of regular shape, and season with salt and pepper. Dip slices lightly into flour, then into lightly salted beaten eggs and finally into bread crumbs.

Heat butter in a pan, put in the slices of sweetbreads and saute until golden brown on both sides, about 5-6 minutes. Drain on absorbent paper, sprinkle lightly with salt. While sweetbreads are browning cook fettuccine separately in boiling salted water. Drain while al dente and rinse with hot water. Toss with butter and grated Parmesan. Spoon fettuccine on a large platter. Surround fettuccine with slices of sweetbreads. Spoon pan juices left from cooking sweetbreads over sweetbread slices.

Animelle di agnello al prosciutto e cipolline

Lamb sweetbreads with prosciutto and onions

Serves 4
Difficulty **
Time: 1-1/2 hours

Prepare sweetbreads for cooking as in recipe Animella di vitello al burro e salvia, page 190. See note on Lamb Sweetbreads. Cut into bite-size pieces. Slice one of the onions, reserving it for later use. Parboil remaining onions whole for 10 minutes. Drain and saute until tender in 2 tablespoons of the butter, about 15 minutes. Add salt to taste and keep warm over very low heat. Saute sliced onion in remaining butter until wilted. Add sweetbreads and prosciutto and continue cooking over moderate heat for about 15 minutes, occasionally adding a spoonful of broth and stirring carefully until liquid evaporates. A few minutes before removing from heat, add hot onions and mix thoroughly. Serve immediately.

1 lb. lamb sweetbreads
3/4 lb. small white onions (about 9)
5 tbsp. butter

Salt, coarsely ground pepper
1/4 cup (2 oz.) diced prosciutto crudo
Beef broth, approx. 1/4 cup

Animelle di agnello al prosciutto e cipolline

Lingua di bue fredda con salsa e uova sode

Cold beef tongue with sauce and hardcooked eggs

Serves 4
Difficulty *
Time: 1 hour

1/2 cup chopped pickled giardinera vegetables (sold in most supermarkets)
1/4 cup capers
6 sprigs of parsley, chopped

4 hardcooked eggs
1/4 cup olive oil
Salt, pepper
2 lbs sliced cooked beef tongue

Mix giardiniera vegetables, capers and parsley. Put chopped ingredients in a bowl. Mash one of the hardcooked egg yolks and add with oil to bowl. Season with salt and pepper to taste, and mix well. Slice tongue; arrange slices on a serving platter and pour sauce over them. Garnish with remaining hardcooked eggs, sliced.

Lingua di bue fredda con salsa e uova sode

Trippa alla genovese

Tripe Genoese

Serves 4
Difficulty *
Time: 1-1/2 hours

2-1/2 lbs. precooked tripe
1 lb. potatoes
1 pkg (1 oz.) dried mushrooms
(or 2 cups chopped fresh mushrooms)
1 small onion, chopped
1 rib celery, chopped
1 carrot, chopped
2 tbsp. olive oil
2 tbsp. butter
Salt, pepper
1-1/4 lbs. fresh tomatoes, peeled
and sieved (about 4 medium)
1 cup condensed beef broth

Scrape tripe, wash it and cut it into strips. Cook in boiling water for 5 minutes, then wash with cold running water. Peel and dice potatoes. Boil in salted water, removing while still firm.
Soak mushrooms in cold water for 30 minutes, and then drain and chop. Saute onion, celery, carrot and mushrooms in oil and butter for 5 minutes. Add tripe. Sprinkle with salt and pepper. Saute 5 minutes. Add tomatoes to tripe. Add beef broth. Cover and simmer over low heat for about 1 hour or until tripe is tender. Add potatoes and simmer uncovered until sauce is thick, stirring occasionally to avoid sticking. Serve hot.

> Tripe has practically no nutritive value; it can therefore be recommended to persons who are watching their weight, but with the warning that it is gelatinous and not always easy to digest. Like several other foods which have little taste of their own, it is well adapted as the solid base to carry flightier taste adventures. It happens that it marries particularly well with ingredients like the tomato, also welcome to weight watchers. However if weight is your preoccupation, avoid the Genoese, Venetian and Piedmont tripe dishes which have potatoes in them—not to mention the *quagghiaridd* of Apulia, which adds lamb's liver, salami, cheese and egg to sheep tripe. Genoa makes a soup from tripe whose name, *sbira*, goes back to medieval times, when policemen (*sbirri*) were popularly supposed to be great fanciers of the dish, which is tripe in beef consommé along with a few bits of braised beef to make it more interesting. In most countries, tripe is tripe, and that is that; but in Italy fine distinctions are made between different kinds of tripe; indeed in Sardinia, several varieties are twisted together into a cord (*corda*, *sa colda*, or *cordula*) so that with each bite the eater gets a taste of every kind.

Trippa alla romana

Tripe Roman style

Serves 6
Difficulty *
Time: 2 hours

2-1/2 lbs. precooked tripe
1 carrot, chopped
1 stalk celery, chopped
2 small onions, chopped
Salt
3 slices bacon, chopped
2 tbsp. olive oil
6 sprigs parsley, chopped
1 clove garlic, chopped
2 slices (4 oz.) baked or boiled
ham, cut into strips 1/2-inch
wide
2 tbsp. tomato paste
2/3 cup grated Parmesan
1 sprig mint, chopped

Scrape tripe, soak for 2 hours in cold water, then cut it into 1-1/2-inch square pieces. Put pieces in a saucepan, cover with cold water, add carrot, celery, half of the onion and a pinch of salt. Boil tripe for about 1 hour or until almost tender. Drain and cut tripe into strips about as wide as your little finger. Saute remaining onion and bacon in a pan containing oil. As soon as onion is wilted, add parsley, garlic clove, ham and tomato paste mixed with 1/2 cup water. Simmer for 5 minutes until it is somewhat thickened. Pour tripe into sauce, cover and simmer for about 1/2 hour over fairly low heat and stir occasionally. If necessary, add a little hot water to prevent sticking. Sprinkle with grated Parmesan and chopped mint leaves. These last two ingredients are characteristic to the Roman style of preparing tripe.

Coda alla vaccinara

*Braised oxtail
cowherd style*

Serves 8
Difficulty **
Time: 6 hours

**1 oxtail weighing about
4-1/2 lbs.
2 bay leaves
2 carrots, chopped
4 cups sliced celery
1/2 lb. lean bacon, chopped
1/4 cup (2 oz.) chopped prosciutto
crudo
1 onion, chopped
1 cup dry white wine
2 cups chopped tomato pulp, skin
and seeds removed and sieved
Beef broth
Pinch of powdered cinnamon
Salt, pepper**

Cut the tail into pieces and soak in cold water for at least 2 hours.
Bring water to a boil with a bouquet garni consisting of bay leaves,
1 of the carrots and 1/2 cup of the celery. Boil oxtail for 1 hour,
skimming occasionally. Drain. Saute bacon, prosciutto crudo,
remaining carrot and onion until golden. Add oxtail and brown
for 10 minutes, then pour in wine and simmer until it evaporates.
Add tomato pulp to pan. Cover and continue cooking for about
3 hours over low heat, adding a little broth as needed. Dice remaining celery and cook for 10 minutes in boiling salted water. Drain
and add to oxtail about 1/2 hour before completion of cooking.
Season with a pinch of cinnamon, salt and a little freshly ground
pepper just before serving.

Coratella di agnello ai funghi alla toscana

*Coratella of lamb with
mushrooms Tuscan style*

Serves 4
Difficulty *
Time: 1-1/2 hours

**3 tbsp. *each* chopped onion,
celery and carrot
3 tbsp. ham fat
5 tbsp. olive oil
1/2 cup chopped mushrooms
1 clove garlic, chopped
4 cups chopped tomato pulp,
skin and seeds removed**

**1 whole clove
Salt, pepper
"Coratella of lamb" (1 heart,
1/2 lb. liver, 1/2 lb. lungs,
1/2 lb. spleen)
2 tbsp. *each* chopped parsley and
marjoram**

In a pan saute vegetables in ham fat and 2 tablespoons of the oil
until wilted. Stir in mushrooms, garlic, tomato pulp, clove, salt and
pepper to taste. Simmer to cook thoroughly, about 10 minutes.
Slice "coratella" into 1/2-inch thick slices. Heat another pan with
remaining oil and add "coratella" ingredients in this order: First
heart, then lung and spleen and, finally, liver. Saute until all slices
are lightly browned. Stir in tomato sauce and continue simmering
for 15 minutes or until meats are cooked. Stir in marjoram, parsley
and salt to taste.

Bolliti misti alla lombarda

Pot-au-feu
(mixed boiled meats)
Lombardy style

Serves 12
Difficulty *
Time: 4 hours

Pot-au-feu:

1 cotechino (spiced pork
sausage – Italian meat market)
1 capon
2 lbs. beef bones and trimmings
3/4 cup (6 oz.) chopped bacon rind
1 cup (8 oz.) pork sausage meat
1 veal knuckle
1 pig's foot
A piece of calf's head
1 onion, left whole
1 whole clove
1 carrot, chopped
1 celery stalk, chopped
Salt

Green sauce:

1/2 cup chopped parsley
2 pickled gherkins
4 anchovy fillets
1 clove garlic
2 slices onion
1/4 cup olive oil
1 to 2 tbsp. red wine vinegar
6 large potatoes, peeled
Salt

If Italians do not usually go in for meat in large segments, there is one conspicuous exception—bollito misto, mixed boiled meat, and when for once they do break their rule against heavy meat consumption, they do not simply break it, but, with characteristic bravura, they shatter it. Bollito misto is Gargantuan; the name refers not to one kind of boiled meat at a time, but to a whole cauldron of boiled meats. Bollito misto country lies well to the north, even north of Tuscany, for though Tuscans are Italy's most enthusiastic meat consumers, they prefer grilling or roasting to boiling. Emilia, Piedmont and Lombardy (the last is prone to call it lessi misti) are the boiled meat areas, plus an island or two in the Alps, a stronghold of heavy eaters. Among the formidable helpings of boiled meats which have been put before me in Italy, let me cite one for each of the three regions named above: in Emilia, I was confronted with a large cut of beef, a whole tongue, a calf's head, a whole ham, and a whole chicken, which had been boiled together, plus a zampone (pig's foot with sausage stuffing) which had been cooked separately, and three sauces to choose from—salsa verda (green sauce), salsa peperata (pepper sauce) and horseradish sauce; in Piedmont the offering was a large piece of beef, a large piece of veal, a whole ham, and a whole chicken, cooked together, with salsa verda and jelly on the side; and in Lombardy, there were two different cuts of beef, a calf's head, and a capon, boiled together, with, again, a zampone which had been cooked separately, and as relishes, salsa verda and the chutney-like Cremona mostarda. In none of these cases was I supposed to down all this by myself; there were two of us.

Prick cotechino here and there at fattest parts. Wrap in cheesecloth and place in a large saucepan. Cover with cold water, bring to a boil and simmer over moderate heat for about 1 hour. Put all the various meats in a large pot or roasting pan. Cover with lots of cold water and bring to a boil. Stud onion with clove. When water boils, skim foam and add onion, carrot and celery. Sprinkle with salt and simmer 1-1/2 to 2 hours, adding more water if necessary. Prepare green sauce. Finely chop parsley, gherkins, anchovy fillets, garlic and onion. Mix chopped ingredients, adding oil and vinegar and a little salt to taste. Boil potatoes. As various meats and cotechino are done, remove from pan and put on a large serving platter. Serve hot, passing boiled potatoes and green sauce separately.

Rognone alla deliziosa

Kidneys deliziosa

Serves 6
Difficulty *
Time: Soak 30 minutes, cook
30 minutes

**2 veal kidneys (weighing
about 1-1/4 lbs.)
2 tbsp. wine vinegar
3 tbsp. olive oil
6 sprigs parsley, chopped**

**6 anchovy fillets in oil,
pounded into a paste
Salt, pepper
Juice of 1/2 a lemon
1 whole lemon, cut into slices**

Remove all fat and tubules from kidneys. Cut them in half lengthwise. Remove spongy inner fiber. Soak for 30 minutes in cold water mixed with a little wine vinegar to remove characteristic odor. Drain and wash several times. Cut them into thin slices. Heat oil in a pan and when it is hot add kidneys. Stir over high heat for 5 to 10 minutes. When they are nearly done, add parsley, anchovy fillets and a little freshly ground pepper. Taste before salting because anchovy fillets may have seasoned dish sufficiently. Sprinkle lemon juice over kidneys and cook for 5 minutes more, then remove from heat. Transfer kidneys to serving platter, garnish with lemon slices and serve.

Rognone di vitello al tegame con funghi

Sliced veal kidneys and mushrooms

Serves 4
Difficulty *
Time: 1 hour

**1 tbsp. chopped onion
1 clove garlic, chopped
7 tbsp. olive oil
1 lb. mushrooms
Salt, pepper
1/4 cup (2 oz.) butter**

**2 veal kidneys (9 oz. each) fat
and tubules removed
2 tbsp. chopped parsley
2 slices bread, cut into 1/2-inch
cubes**

Saute onion and garlic in half of the oil until wilted. Slice mushrooms, add them to pan, sprinkle with salt and pepper to taste and saute until wilted. In another frying pan, heat 2 tablespoons of the butter and remaining oil. Prepare kidney as in Rognone alla deliziosa. Slice kidney and add. Sprinkle with salt and pepper and saute 5 minutes. Add mushrooms and cook together for another 2 to 3 minutes. Place kidneys and mushrooms on a serving platter. Sprinkle with chopped parsley. Heat remaining butter and saute bread cubes until golden brown. Sprinkle over kidneys.

Rognone di vitello al tegame con funghi

Braciole alla pugliese

*Horsemeat cutlets
Apulian style*

Serves 4
Difficulty *
Time: 2-1/2 hours

4 slices horsemeat, each slice
approx 4 oz.
4 slices Pecorino cheese
4 cloves garlic, sliced
4 slices bacon
6 sprigs parsley, chopped
Salt, coarsely ground pepper
7 tbsp. olive oil
1/2 onion, sliced
1 cup dry white wine
1-1/2 lbs. (approx 8) tomatoes,
skin and seeds removed and seived

Note: If horsemeat is not available,
beef round slices may be substituted.

Braciole alla pugliese

Pound meat slightly, then put on each one a slice of Pocorino cheese, sliced garlic clove, a slice of bacon and a little chopped parsley. Season with a pinch of salt. Roll slices and tie with string. Heat oil, and when it is good and hot, add meat rolls to pan and brown over high heat. Lower heat, add onion and cook until onion is wilted. Add wine and simmer until it evaporates. Add tomato pulp. Add salt and pepper to taste, cover and continue cooking over very low heat for at least 1-1/2 hours, stirring occasionally until meat is tender. Add a little hot water from time to time to prevent sticking.

Pignatella fiorentina

Florentine beef pot

Serves 6 to 8
Difficulty **
Time: 3 hours

Salt
1 cup chopped celery
1/4 cup chopped parsley
1 clove garlic, chopped
2 onions, sliced
4 carrots, chopped
2 lbs. oxtail
2 lbs. beef short ribs
2 lbs. beef rump
1 pig's foot or calf's foot
1 cotechino (Italian spiced
sausage) or 1 lb. sweet Italian
sausage
1/2 a capon, cut-up
4 potatoes, peeled and quartered
2 zucchini, diced
1 calf's head

For sauce:

1/2 cup chopped mixed sweet pickles	2 cloves garlic, left whole
1/3 cup chopped parsley	1/2 cup olive oil
4 eggs, hard cooked and chopped	1/4 cup wine vinegar
	Salt, pepper

(The "pignatella" is a kind of terracotta pot with two handles and a cover which is used in Tuscan country cooking for making a mixed boiled dinner made up of the ingredients listed at the left. The meats are served in "pignatelle" (one to a customer) with a plate which the diner is supposed to keep filling from the pot and the vegetable platter.)

Heat a large 12-quart pot half filled with salted water and add celery, parsley, garlic, onions and carrots. When water is boiling, add oxtail, short ribs, beef rump, calf's foot, cotechino and capon (or chicken if capon is not available). Add potatoes and zucchini. Let water get back to a boil, then lower heat, cover and simmer for about 1 hour, removing cotechino and vegetables as soon as they are cooked. Set them aside.
Add calf's head. Simmer 1 to 1-1/2 hours. When meats are all tender, remove meat and all edible portions from bones. Shortly before serving replace whatever ingredients you have removed (potatoes, cotechino, etc.) and meat and reheat. Skim fat from broth. Serve broth separately. Serve meats with a sauce made of mixed pickles, parsley and hard-cooked eggs. Put these ingredients into a bowl, add whole garlic cloves. Beat oil with wine vinegar, adding salt and pepper to taste. Stir into bowl. Mix well and serve.

VEGETABLES

Italian cooks deal with vegetables better than anyone else in the Western world, perhaps because Italian farmers give them better vegetables than anyone else in the Western world. They have been at it longer; and from the beginning they gave loving care to the art of market gardening.

The only Europeans who might have had a head start on the Italians were the Greeks, but the ancient Greeks never worked up much interest in vegetables. They confined themselves chiefly to broad beans, chick peas, lentils, onion, garlic and cabbage (which they did not like). The Romans, on the contrary, were avid producers and devourers of vegetables. They had thirty-seven varieties of peas; shallots as well as onions; cucumbers (which the Emperor Tiberius ate, in season, at every meal); leeks (which Nero consumed in quantity to improve his singinng voice); European squash; radishes, horseradishes, salsify, beets, parsnips, turnips and carrots (they preferred the turnips to the carrots); and a tremendous variety of greens—besides cabbage and lettuce, parsley, fennel, sorrel, mustard, dill, basil, rue, mint, thyme, sage, marjoram, rosemary, laurel, and some still eaten in Italy today but almost nowhere else, like rockets and rasparella (a favorite of Rome).

As for agricultural know-how, it antedates the Romans and even the Latins. It was inherited from the Etruscans, who were so devoted to farming that their very religion was based on the ownership of land. They understood the arts of drainage, irrigation, fertilization, pruning and alternation of crops. Following in their footsteps, the Romans persuaded lettuce to head; developed new varieties of cabbage, including chard, cauliflower, probably broccoli and possibly kohlrabi; and grew the best asparagus in the ancient world in Ravenna, which today grows the best asparagus in the modern world. Somehow or other, vegetables in Italy look more colorful and appetizing than anywhere else, whether in the market or on the plate.

Is it because the Italian eats so many invigorating stimulating vitamin-packed vegetables that he throws himself with operatic passion into whatever he does, whether it is driving a taxi, trading on the Bourse or hawking fresh fish? An Italian housewife choosing a chicken in the market puts on a performance worthy of a coloratura soprano delivering her major aria. Is the South more extrovert, more emotional, more explosive because it eats proportionally more vegetables than the North? This may be because the South is poorer than the North and vegetables are cheap, especially if you grow them yourself, as, in the rustic South, most persons do; but if so poverty is in this case a blessing vegetable, pays off in dynamism.

Rustisana alla piacentina

Carciofi alla Giudea

Artichokes Judean style

Serves 4
Difficulty *
Time: 1-1/2 hours

8 small artichokes
1 cup olive oil
Salt, pepper

Discard harsh outer leaves of the artichokes and the end of the stems (stalks). Hold by remaining stem and beat them several times against the table to open leaves slightly. Put oil in a pan and heat. Fry artichokes, turning to brown on all sides. Drain when they are crisp and golden brown on a piece of paper toweling. Sprinkle with salt and pepper and serve hot.

I discover with surprise that several highly reputable encyclopedias and dictionaries state that the artichoke was introduced into Italy in the fifteenth century by the Saracens. The fact is that the artichoke is in all probability a native of Sicily, which was known to Mediterranean Europe long before the Saracens were. It was eaten by the ancient Greeks and was on the Roman menu at least as early as 500 B.C. Pliny wrote that he did not like artichokes, an opinion which, several centuries later, was emphatically not shared by Catherine dei Medici, who doted on them, especially in the form of artichoke-heart fritters; on one occasion she ate so many at a single sitting that a contemporary chronicler recorded inelegantly that "she nearly burst". She is credited with having brought the first artichokes to France. Following Catherine's example, Italians consume great quantities of artichokes, in innumerable forms: raw or cooked, as hors d'œuvre; rolled in batter and deep fried, in *fritti misti*; whole, raw or cooked, during the season of a certain type of tiny artichokes which are 100% edible; baked, with more or less rich sauces; stuffed (in the Abruzzi, with tuna!); fried, combined with other vegetables; large artichoke hearts sliced, breaded and fried in olive oil; in omelets; and, on Lazio's Bay of Gaeta, with inkfish!

Rome alone has two very famous artichoke dishes. *Carciofi alla romana* are made from the young artichokes which can be eaten whole, and *carciofi alla giudea*, artichokes Jewish style—accurately named, since this is a dish of the medieval ghetto of Rome. The ghetto is no more, but *carciofi alla giudea*, is still a specialty of restaurants located in the area it once covered.

Carciofi alla romana

Artichokes Roman style

Serves 4
Difficulty *
Time: 1-1/2 hours
Oven Temp. 350° F.

4 small artichokes
Juice of 1 lemon
2 cups soft bread crumbs
4 anchovies, chopped

6 sprigs parsley, chopped
1/2 tsp. crumbled marjoram
Salt, pepper
1/4 cup olive oil

Discard the stem and hard outer leaves of the artichokes. Cut points off remaining leaves and place artichokes in cold water to cover with lemon juice. Put bread crumbs in a bowl and mix with anchovy, parsley, marjoram and salt and pepper to taste. Drain artichokes, press them against the table to separate the leaves. Scoop out the hairy choke and stuff with the filling. Arrange artichokes side by side in a baking dish. Pour oil over them, then add 1/2 cup water to the pan. Cover and bake in a preheated oven for 30 to 35 minutes.

Fondi di carciofo trifolati

Sauteed sliced artichoke bottoms with parsley and garlic

Serves 4
Difficulty *
Time: 1 hour

8 large artichokes
2 cloves garlic, chopped
7 tbsp. olive oil
Salt, pepper
6 sprigs parsley, chopped

Remove all the artichoke leaves and trim off choke, leaving only the fleshy bottom of the artichoke. Slice artichoke bottoms into strips. Saute garlic in oil briefly, then add artichoke bottoms and season with salt and pepper. Cook for several minutes over high heat, then lower heat and continue cooking until artichokes are tender, about 30 minutes. Sprinkle finely chopped parsley over dish just before serving.

Fondi di carciofo trifolati

Carciofi di magro alla napoletana

Lenten artichokes Neapolitan

Serves 4
Difficulty *
Time: 1-1/2 hours
Oven Temp. 350° F.

1-1/4 cups (5 oz.) diced mozzarella or Scamorza
1/2 cup (2 oz.) grated Parmesan
1 tbsp. dry bread crumbs
6 sprigs parsley, chopped
1 egg
Salt, pepper
4 small artichokes, tips trimmed and center and choke removed
4 anchovy fillets
1/4 cup olive oil

Mix mozzarella with Parmesan, bread crumbs, parsley, egg and a pinch of salt and pepper. Stuff the artichokes with this mixture, put a strip of anchovy on each and cook as follows: Put artichokes in a baking dish with half of the oil in the bottom..Fill with enough water to cover bottom half of artichokes. Sprinkle remaining oil over artichokes and cook covered over moderate heat until liquid is almost evaporated. Then put in the oven and bake uncovered for 30 minutes or until artichokes are easily pierced.

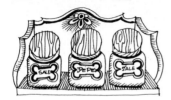

Asparagi in forno all'italiana

Baked asparagus Italian style

Serves 4
Difficulty *
Time: 1-1/2 hours
Oven Temp. 400° F.

24 asparagus
4 thick slices prosciutto
crudo, fat and lean, or ham
6 tbsp. butter
3/4 cup (3 oz.) grated Parmesan
4 slices toast (made by frying
bread in butter)
Salt

Clean asparagus and trim tough ends. Remove scales. Tie asparagus in a bundle. Cook asparagus standing upright with tips above boiling water. Use your coffee pot for this. Drain while still al dente, untie the bundle and let asparagus cool completely. Wrap 6 asparagus tips in each slice of ham and arrange the rolls in a lightly buttered shallow baking dish. Pour about 2 tablespoons of melted butter over them, sprinkle with grated Parmesan, then pour 1 tablespoon more melted butter over the Parmesan. Put the dish in a preheated oven and bake until surface is well browned, about 15 minutes. Meanwhile brown bread slices in remaining butter and transfer them to a serving dish; put a ham-asparagus roll on each slice of toast and serve.

When it comes to asparagus, Ravenna is Italy's oldest city and Milan its fussiest. Martial wrote in the first century A.D. that Ravenna grew the best asparagus in the country; Florence imported it from the same city in the fifteenth and made from it a soup very much in the Renaissance tradition, flavored with saffron, pine nuts and pistachio; Italy in the twentieth still buys Ravenna asparagus by preference—when it is lacking, the country has recourse to an area a little north of Ravenna, Bassano del Grappa, in the northern Veneto. It was in Milan that Julius Caesar praised the city's asparagus with butter, the way it is still presented there today (Ravenna dissolves it in a cream sauce into which all of the asparagus disappears except the taste). Milan has made a cult of asparagus. A special pan has been invented in which to boil it, with the stalks submerged but the tips above the surface, to be cooked by the steam; and a special dish devised in which to serve it, with hollow sides which are filled with boiling water to keep it warm. Sardinia and Trieste prefer wild asparagus to the cultivated variety. So did Juvenal.

Asparagi in forno all'italiana

203

Asparagi alla milanese

Asparagus Milanese style

Serves 4
Difficulty *
Time: 1-1/2 hours

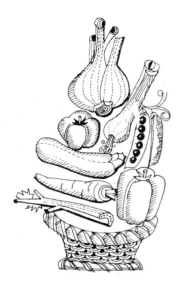

2 lbs. large asparagus	Salt
1 cup (8 oz.) butter	Coarsely ground black pepper
8 eggs	1/2 cup grated Parmesan cheese

Clean and peel asparagus, cut to equal lengths, tie in bundles and cook in lightly salted water (asparagus should be standing, water should not reach higher than tips) until tips begin to be movable, about 20 to 25 minutes. Drain, untie and arrange on a round serving platter in groups of 3 or 4 separated like the figures 12 - 2 - 4 - 6 - 8 - 10 on a clockface; the tips should point toward the center of the platter. Melt 1-1/2 tablespoons of the butter in a pan. Fry an egg, sprinkle with salt and freshly ground pepper. Do the same for the remaining 7 eggs, cooking each so that the white is firm while the yolk remains soft. As each egg is cooked, transfer it to the platter, setting 1 egg between each 2 piles of asparagus (that is, with eggs at positions of 1 - 3 - 5 - 7 - 9 - 11 on the clockface.) Melt the remaining butter in a pan, heat it until foaming, then pour over the asparagus. Sprinkle with grated Parmesan and serve hot.

> *Fagioli di fiasco* is a Tuscan refinement; when beans are cooked in a bottle the vapor which escapes from them is condensed on the sides of the bottle and falls back again into the beans. Thus none of the flavor escapes.

Fagioli cotti nel fiasco alla toscana

Beans in flask Tuscan style

Serves 4
Difficulty *
Time: 3 hours, plus time required to soak beans

3/4 lb. dried toscanelli beans (white haricot beans)	2 cloves garlic, minced
1/2 cup olive oil	4 leaves fresh sage
	Salt, peppercorns

Soak beans overnight in cold water. Drain and transfer to an Italian wine flask (2-quart capacity) from which straw has been removed. Add oil, garlic and sage leaves. Cover beans with water and set flask upright in coals from a damped charcoal fire. Seal mouth of flask loosely with cotton batting (this will hold in flavor yet permit steam to escape.) Cook in coals for about 3 hours, at which point water should be almost wholly evaporated and beans should have absorbed practically all the oil. Pour out onto a serving platter, season with salt and freshly ground pepper and serve.
This is a traditional recipe that can be adapted to modern living. Place beans into a 2 quart bean pot. Add oil, garlic, sage and water to cover. Cover pot with its lid and bake in a preheated slow oven (300°F.) for 3 to 4 hours.

Fagioli all'uccelletto

White beans
"small bird" style *

Serves 4
Difficulty *
Time: 2 hours, plus time required
to soak beans

3/4 lb. dried cannellini or
toscanelli beans (haricot)
1/2 cup olive oil
10 fresh sage leaves
2 cloves garlic, minced
1-1/2 cups sieved fresh tomato
pulp, skin and seeds removed
Salt, pepper

* Italians cook small birds with garlic and sage.

Soak beans overnight, drain and place them in saucepan. Cover with cold water and simmer over moderate heat until tender, about 1-1/2 to 2 hours. Heat oil with sage leaves, garlic and a little freshly ground pepper. Add beans and tomato pulp and mix. Simmer for about 10 minutes. Season to taste with salt and pepper. Serve with roasted or broiled meat or poultry.

Mangiafagioli, bean eaters, is what other Italians call Tuscans. It must be a comparatively new epithet, as Italian history goes, for *fagioli* are haricot beans, natives of America. The *fagiolo* was unknown to Italy before the Renaissance, but perhaps Italians were the first Europeans to eat it, since Pope Clement VII received some of the first beans brought from the New World and had them grown in Tuscany. When Catherine dei Medici left for France to marry Henri II, she carried some of the new beans with her. Before that time Italy knew only the broad bean, or fava, still much eaten in Italy despite the strong competition of the haricot.

Fagiolini verdi all'aglio e pomodoro

Green beans with
garlic and tomato

Serves 4
Difficulty *
Time: 1 hour

1-1/2 lbs. green beans
5 tbsp. olive oil
1 clove garlic, chopped
2 tbsp. chopped onion

Several small leaves fresh
sage, chopped
2 cups chopped tomato pulp,
skin and seeds removed
Salt, coarsely ground pepper

Cut tips off green beans and then cut beans into 1-inch pieces. In a pan heat oil and saute garlic, onion and sage until wilted. Add tomato pulp and green beans. Season with salt and a little pepper, and just barely cover with cold water. As soon as the water comes to a boil, cover and simmer over low heat, stirring occasionally, for 20 to 25 minutes or until beans are tender.

Fagiolini verdi dorati alla milanese

Deep-fried green beans
Milanese style

Serves 4
Difficulty *
Time: 1-1/2 hours

1-1/2 lbs. green beans
2 eggs
Salt

Flour
Deep fat or oil, heated
to 360° F.

Cut tips off green beans. Leave whole. Cook in lightly salted boiling water, draining when slightly underdone, about 20 minutes. Let beans cool completely, then tie them into bunches of 6 or 7 beans each, using white string. Dip bunches into lightly salted beaten egg and then into flour. Fry in preheated oil for 5 or 6 minutes or until golden brown. Drain on absorbent paper, remove string and salt lightly before serving.

Fagiolini verdi al pomodoro al forno

Baked green beans with tomato

Serves 4
Difficulty *
Time: 1-1/2 hours
Oven Temp. 400° F.

1-1/2 lbs. green beans
6 sprigs parsley, chopped
2 cloves garlic, chopped
2 tbsp. chopped pine nuts
1/4 cup olive oil
3 fillets desalted anchovies

1-1/2 cups chopped tomato pulp, skin and seeds removed
Salt
1 cup flaked cooked fish (sole, flounder, halibut, any white fish)
4 slices bread cut into cubes and browned in butter

Cut tips off green beans and cut into 1-inch pieces. Boil in plenty of lightly salted water until tender, about 20 to 25 minutes. Drain. In a large saucepan saute chopped parsley, garlic and pine nuts in oil until wilted. Add anchovies and chopped tomato pulp. Simmer for about 10 minutes, then add green beans. Simmer 5 minutes and add salt to taste. Grease a 1-1/2 quart casserole and put in half of the green beans. Add a layer of fish and one of bread croutons. Top with remaining green beans and bake in a preheated oven for 10 minutes. Turn out onto a platter and serve immediately.

Fagiolini verdi con prosciutto e crostini

Green beans with prosciutto and croutons

Serves 4
Difficulty *
Time: 1 hour

1-1/2 lbs. green beans
1/2 cup butter
Salt, pepper
1/2 cup (4 oz.) strips prosciutto crudo, both fat and lean
8 slices fried bread

Trim ends from beans, wash and cook in lightly salted boiling water for about 20 minutes or until tender. Drain. Melt half of the butter in a pan, add beans, salt and pepper to taste. Saute for a few minutes. Add prosciutto and heat for another 5 minutes. Toast bread by frying in remaining butter on both sides. Serve toast on the side with beans.

Fagiolini verdi con prosciutto e crostini

Fave al guanciale alla romana

Fava beans (broad beans) and bacon Roman style

Serves 4
Difficulty *
Time: 1 hour

1 small onion, chopped
1/4 cup lard or olive oil
1/2 lb. bacon, diced
2 cups fresh shelled fava beans
Salt, pepper

Saute onion in lard or oil until golden. Add bacon and saute until brown. Add fava beans and season with a pinch of salt and a little pepper. Add water to just cover beans. Simmer for 20 minutes or until beans are tender. Serve very hot.

Fave al guanciale alla romana

Barbabietole alla Parmigiana

Beets with Parmesan cheese

Serves 4
Difficulty *
Time: 2 hours
Oven Temp. 375° F.

Final preparation of dish:

8 cooked beets
Meat sauce
1/2 cup (2 oz.) grated Parmesan cheese
2 tbsp. butter

Meat sauce:

1 rib celery, chopped
1 small carrot, chopped
3 tbsp. chopped onion
1/4 cup chopped parsley
2 tbsp. olive oil
1-1/2 tbsp. butter
1/2 clove garlic, chopped
Pinch of thyme

1 bay leaf
1 whole clove
1/4 lb. ground (minced) beef
1/4 lb. ground (minced) veal
Salt, pepper
Beef broth, approx. 2 cups (See Brodo di manzo con sorbetto di pomodoro)

For meat sauce: Put celery, carrot, onion, parsley and oil and butter in a pan, saute briefly and add garlic, thyme, bay leaf, clove and, after a few minutes, beef and veal. Brown meats, season with salt and pepper, adding a little water or broth and stirring often. Lower heat and cook for at least 1 hour over low heat, adding even more water or broth to yield about 1 cup finished sauce.

Final preparation of dish: Peel and slice beets. Butter a 1 quart baking dish, put in a layer of beet slices, cover with a layer of meat sauce, and continue in this way alternating beets with sauce. The top layer should be a good layer of meat sauce and Parmesan. Pour remaining butter, melted, over dish and bake in a preheated oven until surface is well browned, about 15 to 20 minutes. This dish goes very well with grilled meats or roast chicken. It can be served in the baking dish.

Bagna cauda

Serves 4
Difficulty *
Time: 20 minutes

3 cloves garlic
1 cup olive oil
3 oz. anchovies in oil,
chopped

Cut garlic cloves into very thin strips and saute them in oil until soft. Keep garlic from browning and consequently losing its flavor. Remove pan from heat and add anchovies. Crush anchovies with a wooden spoon. Replace on heat and keep hot.

This "bagna cauda", as it is known in Piedmontese dialect, is served in the pan in which it is made, which should ideally be a glazed earthenware bowl, called a "fojot," which should be kept hot either with coals or over a very low chafing-dish flame. The bagna cauda is placed in the center of the table and each person dips strips of raw or very slightly cooked vegetables into it. The classic vegetable used by the Piedmontese is the cardoon, but you may use any of the following: green peppers, raw, slightly parboiled or in oil; or, (again, raw or slightly cooked) celery, cabbage, Jerusalem artichoke, potatoes, etc.

A refinement of bagna cauda calls for adding, just before using, a few tablespoons of heavy cream and a thinly sliced white truffle. A good wine to drink with it is Barbera.

Bagna cauda is a thoroughly local dish, a specialty of Piedmont (which calls it bagna caôda). Either way it means "hot bath," and that is just what it is is—a hot liquid dip for cold raw vegetables. In Piedmont they prefer to dunk cardoons in bagna cauda, but unless you live in France or Italy, you aren't likely to be able to find any. Celery is an excellent substitute, though—and so are fennel or carrots or artichokes or peppers or cauliflower. The best system is to provide a variety of dunkable vegetables, and let each diner select his favorites. Bagna cauda is also sometimes used as a sauce for cooked vegetables.

Cavolo rosso di Agrigento

Agrigento red cabbage

Serves 4
Difficulty *
Time: 1-1/2 hours

1 large red cabbage
1/4 cup olive oil
Salt, pepper
1/3 cup red wine vinegar
Chicken broth
1/2 cup sliced pitted black
olives
3 tbsp. capers, pounded in
a mortar

Remove core. Shred red cabbage. Heat oil in a pan. Add red cabbage, salt, pepper; mix well. Add wine vinegar and continue cooking over moderate heat for 15 minutes, moistening occasionally with a little broth to prevent sticking. Add black olives and capers. Cover and simmer another 30 minutes or until cabbage is tender.

Cabbage is a venerable vegetable in Italy. It was the favorite of the ancient Romans, who developed cabbages weighing as much as 20 pounds a head. They considered that the cabbage possessed important medical virtues; Cato thought of it as a sort of panacea. The ancients had already developed cauliflower from the original form of cabbage, probably broccoli, and possibly kohlrabi as well. France had cabbage before the Medicis arrived, but Catherine and Maria dei Medici brought in new and tastier types developed by Italian gardeners. Cabbage was probably relatively more important in ancient Italy than it is today; after all, it is a comparatively coarse vegetable, and the Italian gift is for finesse.

Carote al marsala

Carrots with Marsala

Serves 4
Difficulty *
Time: 1 hour

1 bunch carrots, sliced	Chicken broth (see Brodo pieno
1/4 cup olive oil	alla calabrese, Soup section)
Salt, pepper	1 tbsp. sugar
	1/4 cup Marsala wine

Put carrot slices in a saucepan with oil. Saute briefly over high heat. Sprinkle with salt and pepper and add a little broth (2 to 3 tablespoons). Cover and simmer over low heat until carrots are tender. Add broth from time to time to prevent sticking. Turn up heat, sprinkle carrots with sugar and stir until sugar is slightly caramelized and carrots are lightly browned. Add Marsala. Simmer until Marsala has evaporated.

Purea di carote

Carrot puree

Serves 4
Difficulty *
Time: 2 hours

8 young carrots	1/2 cup milk
Chicken broth (See Brodo pieno	2 tbsp. butter
alla Calabrese, Soup section)	1/4 cup grated Parmesan
Salt	

Scrape carrots, dry and slice. Put slices in a saucepan, cover with broth, salt lightly and simmer over low heat until carrots are tender but still hold their shape. If broth evaporates, add more boiling broth, stirring constantly as you add new broth. When carrots are cooked the broth should have been absorbed completely. Puree carrots in a food mill or a blender. Put puree in a bowl. Stir in hot milk, butter and grated Parmesan. Mix thoroughly for a couple of minutes and serve.

Carote in fricassea

Fricasseed carrots

Serves 4
Difficulty *
Time: 1 hour

5 tbsp. butter	A pinch of sugar
1 bunch young carrots, scraped	2 egg yolks
and sliced	1/3 cup heavy cream
Salt	

Melt butter in a pan. Add carrots, seasoning to taste with salt and sugar. Cook over moderate heat, about 30 minutes, basting with a little water or broth if they seem too dry. When carrots are cooked, remove from heat. Beat yolks with cream. Pour over carrots and put the pan back onto a moderate heat. Stir until sauce coats a spoon. Remove from heat and serve immediately.

Carote in fricassea

Cavolfiore
alla casalinga

Home-style cauliflower

Serves 4
Difficulty *
Time: 1 hour

**1 cauliflower, weighing
approx. 2-1/2 lbs.
Salt
Juice of 1 lemon
3 eggs
1/2 cup chopped parsley
6 tbsp. butter, browned
1 cup dry bread crumbs**

Cavolfiore alla casalinga

Clean cauliflower, divide into flowerets and soak briefly in water containing lemon juice. Drain, cook in lightly salted boiling water until tender but still firm, about 15 minutes. Hardcook eggs, chop them and mix with chopped•parsley. Drain cauliflower flowerets and arrange them in a hot vegetable dish. Sprinkle with egg and parsley mixture. Pour over them the browned butter mixed with the bread crumbs.

Cavolfiore
alla siracusana

Cauliflower Siracusa style

Serves 4
Difficulty *
Time: 1-1/2 hours

**1 cauliflower, weighing
about 2-1/4 lbs.
6 tbsp. olive oil
1 small onion, chopped
3 leeks, white part only,
chopped
1/4 cup sliced pitted green
olives**

**1/2 cup (2 oz.) grated
Caciocavallo cheese
6 anchovy fillets, chopped
Salt
3 cups red wine
1/4 cup chopped parsley
4 slices of French bread fried
in 1/3 cup olive oil**

Clean cauliflower (keeping the tenderest leaves,) wash and divide into flowerets. Put 3 tablespoons oil in a 2 quart ceramic fireproof casserole. Put a layer in bottom consisting of onion, leeks, olives, cheese and anchovy. Cover with a layer of cauliflower flowerets; season with salt and sprinkle with remaining olive oil. Pour over wine. Cover the casserole and cook over moderate heat *without stirring* for 35 to 40 minutes. Serve sprinkled with parsley and on top of fried bread.

211

Melanzane all'italiana

Eggplant Italian style

Serves 4
Difficulty **
Time: 2 hours
Oven Temp. 400° F.

2 large eggplants (aubergines)
Salt
1 lb. mozzarella cheese,
sliced
1/4 lb. ground (minced) veal
1/4 lb. (bulk) sausage meat
1/2 cup (2 oz.) grated Parmesan
cheese
2 tbsp. chopped fresh basil
leaves
3 eggs
Nutmeg
Flour
Dry bread crumbs
Oil
1-1/2 tbsp. butter
1 leek, chopped
1 can (1 lb.) peeled Italian
tomatoes sieved, or 1-1/4 lbs.
(4 medium) fresh tomatoes,
peeled, seeded and sieved

Cut off ends of eggplant, peel them, cut into 1/2-inch thick slices lengthwise, put them on a rack set above a pan, salt them and leave for at least 30 minutes to allow the bitter juice to run off. Trim mozzarella slices so they are the same size as eggplant slices (save trimmings to use in stuffing). Mix ground veal, sausage meat, grated Parmesan, basil, 1 of the eggs, a little nutmeg, salt and enough bread crumbs to give a good consistency to the filling. Add mozzarella trimmings, chopped. Dry eggplant slices in a kitchen towel. Use 2 slices to enclose 1 slice of mozzarella. Spread a bit of meat filling on mozzarella then close "sandwich" and press with hands. Coat each sandwich with flour, dip it into remaining eggs, beaten, then in dry bread crumbs. Heat a heavy frying pan holding oil 1/2-inch deep. When oil is hot, add eggplant sandwiches, taking care not to pile them up, but to keep each one flat in the pan. Fry as many as can be accommodated in this way, then set them aside while you fry another batch. Brown eggplant sandwiches on both sides. Drain on paper towels or greaseproof paper. Melt butter and saute leek until golden. Stir in tomatoes, adding salt to taste and cook over low heat about 10 minutes, until sauce is thick. When sauce is ready, put one-third in a shallow baking dish; add an overlapping row of eggplant sandwiches. Cover with remaining sauce. Bake in a preheated oven for 10 to 15 minutes.

The southern character, formed by the southern climate, whether in France's Midi or Italy's Mezzogiorno, seems to be in harmony with pulpy vegetables—the tomato, the summer squash (or courgettes), and, more characteristic specifically of the South than the other two, the eggplant (aubergine). The eggplant country may be said to begin, unassertively, at Naples; the farther south you go, the more important the eggplant becomes. It is, after all, a warm weather vegetable which, even when it is started not from seed but from plants already well developed when they are set out in the open, requires 120 days between the last frost of spring and the first of fall to ripen. The number of eggplant dishes is uncountable. One that is a little peculiar in its name is *melanzane al funghetto*, which sounds as though it should mean "eggplant with mushrooms". Actually it is eggplant treated as though it was mushrooms—cut into small pieces and seasoned with garlic, oil, tomato and much pepper. Eggplant lends itself to extravagance too... for instance, *melanzane all'agrodolce*, which is cooked with a sauce of vinegar, sweet wine, sugar, pine nuts, walnuts, raisons, chopped candied cedrat, cinnamon—and chocolate! Eggplant is even pickled—*melanzane sott'olio.*

Melanzane al funghetto

Eggplant with tomato and garlic sauce

Serves 4
Difficulty *
Time: 1-1/2 hours

1 large eggplant (aubergine)
2 cloves garlic, chopped
3/4 cup olive oil
Salt, pepper
1-1/2 cups tomato pulp, cut into
thin strips

Cut end off eggplant, wash and, without peeling, cut into 1/2-inch cubes. Heat garlic briefly in oil, add the eggplant and season with salt and pepper to taste. Cover and simmer 30 minutes, stirring occasionally. Add strips of tomato pulp and simmer another 10 minutes. Serve hot.

Melanzane al funghetto

Caponata alla siciliana

Sweet-and-sour eggplant, Sicilian style

Serves 6
Difficulty *
Time: 1 hour

2 large eggplants (aubergines), diced
1 cup olive oil, approx.
4 bell peppers, chopped
1 large onion, chopped
6 ripe tomatoes, peeled and chopped
1/2 cup whole pitted green olives
3 hearts of celery, chopped
1/4 cup capers
1/2 cup wine vinegar
1/2 cup water
1 tsp. sugar
Salt, pepper

In a pan or Dutch oven brown eggplants in half of the oil for 10 minutes. Remove with a slotted spoon. Add more oil to cooking oil and as soon as oil is hot, add peppers. Cook until wilted and remove with a slotted spoon. Put onion into same oil, saute briefly until wilted. Add tomatoes; simmer until tomatoes are reduced to sauce. Add olives, celery, capers; simmer for another few minutes, then add wine vinegar, water, sugar, bell peppers and eggplants. Season to taste with salt and pepper. Cook over a low heat until vegetables are well cooked and sauce is thick, about 30 minutes.

Finocchi al burro con prosciutto

Finocchi al burro con prosciutto

Buttered fennel with ham

Serves 4
Difficulty *
Time: 1 hour

4 fennel roots ("finocchi")
1/4 cup (2 oz.) butter
1 small onion, chopped fine
3/4 cup chopped baked or boiled ham
2 cups chicken broth
Salt
1/2 cup (2 oz.) grated Parmesan

Discard harsh outer layers of fennel. Remove stems of fennel and cut them into wedges. Heat butter and saute onion. Add ham with fennel and cook over low heat for about 10 minutes. Add broth and cook at a boil until broth is evaporated. Season to taste with salt. Sprinkle grated Parmesan over fennel, remove from heat and serve.

Fennel, a vegetable of respectable antiquity, may be eaten raw with antipasti or cooked in various fashions for its own sake, but it appears most often as a seasoner for other foods. It is a favorite of Umbria, where it gives flavor to roast pork; and in Prato, near Florence, it is fennel which perfumes the local version of mortadella sausage. Be prepared for pleasantries if you chance to buy fennel in Rome's colorful Campo dei Fiori market; in the local slang it means "pederast", I have no idea why.

Finocchi gratinati

Fennel au gratin

Serves 6
Difficulty *
Time: 1-1/2 hours
Oven Temp. 425° F.

6 medium-sized fennel
Juice of 1 lemon
5 tbsp. butter
2 tbsp. flour
2 cups milk

Salt
Nutmeg
1/2 cup (2 oz.) grated Parmesan cheese
1/4 cup chopped smoked tongue

Clean fennel by removing outer layers; wash under cold running water. Add lemon juice to a pot of boiling water (this keeps the fennel white); add fennel and boil until almost done, about 30 to 40 minutes (test with a fork). Cut each fennel from top to bottom into thirds (each slice will be quite thick). Dry in a kitchen towel. Melt 1/4 cup of the butter. Stir in flour. Gradually stir in milk. Stir over low heat until thick. Season to taste with salt and nutmeg. Put a little of the sauce into the bottom of a buttered 2-quart shallow baking dish. Put fennel slices next to each other in a single layer and cover with remaining sauce. Sprinkle grated Parmesan and tongue on top. Dot with remaining butter. Bake in a preheated oven for 10 to 15 minutes or until surface is nicely browned.

Finocchi alla valdostana

Fennel Valle d'Aosta style

Serves 4
Difficulty *
Time: 1-1/2 hours
Oven Temp. 350° F.

4 fennel
4 slices Fontina cheese
1/4 cup butter

Salt
Nutmeg

Remove outer leaves and stalks of fennel. Quarter each fennel and boil for 15 minutes in lightly salted water. Butter a 1-1/2-quart baking dish and put in a layer of fennel; cover with a layer of Fontina and pieces of butter. Season with salt and very little nutmeg. Bake in a preheated oven for 15 minutes until the top is nicely browned. Serve hot.

Cavoli rapa alla chietina

Kohlrabi Chieti style

Serves 4
Difficulty *
Time: 1-1/2 hours

2 bunches kohlrabi, peeled
1/2 cup olive oil
Juice of 2 lemons

6 sprigs parsley, chopped
Salt

For batter:

1 egg
2 tbsp. butter, melted

1 cup all-purpose flour, approx.
Salt
Deep fat or oil heated to 380° F.

Clean kohlrabi, wash and cut into slices 1/2 inch thick. Boil in lightly salted water for about 1/2 hour or until tender but still firm. Prepare a marinade of oil, lemon juice, chopped parsley and salt to taste. Marinate kohlrabi slices for about 1/2 hour. Beat egg with butter. Stir in enough flour to make a batter the consistency of heavy cream. Season to taste with salt. Drain kohlrabi and dip slices into batter. Fry in hot deep fat or oil for 2 to 3 minutes. Drain when they are brown and crisp on paper toweling. Serve with wedges of lemon.

215

Porri con besciamella

Creamed leeks

Serves 4
Difficulty *
Time: 1 hour

**8 leeks (white part only)
1/4 cup butter
1 cup white sauce using 2 tbsp.
butter, 2 tbsp. flour, 1 cup
light cream, salt and pepper
to taste**

The leek is a humble vegetable, but it has an imperial past: Nero used to eat leeks daily to improve his singing voice. Whether or not it was effective, the anecdote testifies to the antiquity of leeks in Italy.

Scrub leeks well to remove all sand. Cook leeks in boiling salted water until almost tender, about 20 minutes. Drain. Saute leeks in butter until lightly browned, about 10 minutes. Drain leeks, arrange on a platter and cover with hot white sauce.

Funghi trifolati

Thin-sliced mushrooms

Serves 6
Difficulty *
Time: 30 minutes

**2 lbs. cultivated mushrooms
1 clove garlic, chopped
2 tbsp. butter
3 to 4 tbsp. olive oil
Salt
Juice of 1/2 lemon
6 sprigs parsley, chopped**

Italians are great mushroom fanciers (Treviso has a market which sells nothing else), and they have numerous varieties to choose from: the milky orange agarics (*ovoli*); the "pig mushrooms" (*porcini*), which means the esteemed boletus; honey mushrooms; red ones therefore called "bloody" (*sanguinaccia*), and cantharellus (*prataioli*) among others. They are served in many fashions—by themselves as hors d'œuvre; in risotti or sauces for pasta (like Liguria's *tocco de fungi*, also good on polenta, or the mushroom sauce of Verona); in soup (the Alto Adige's *Schwammerlsuppe* is cream of mushroom); or large ones of which one makes a separate course, filled with snail butter or with stuffing, or, in Sardinia, served with green sauce.

Clean mushrooms, wash and slice thin. Saute garlic in butter and oil until wilted. Add mushrooms (no water is needed since the mushrooms contain enough moisture). Sprinkle with salt, add lemon juice (which keeps mushrooms from turning black). Watch carefully, for just a few minutes is enough to complete cooking. Sprinkle with chopped parsley. Serve in preheated serving dish to keep mushrooms good and hot.

Funghi trifolati

Funghi alla crema e tartufi

Mushrooms with cream and truffles

Serves 4
Difficulty *
Time: 1-1/2 hours

2 lbs. small wild, or cultivated, mushrooms
1/4 cup (2 oz.) butter
1/2 cup sliced black truffles
Salt, pepper
1/2 cup heavy cream

Clean mushrooms and trim stems. Rub gently with a damp cloth and slice rather thick. Heat butter in a pan, put in both mushrooms and truffles, season with salt and pepper and cook briefly at high heat. Lower the heat and continue cooking for 10 minutes. Pour in 6 tablespoons of the cream, heated to boiling point, and continue cooking. Simmer 5 minutes. Remove from heat. Pour in remaining cream, mix well and serve.

Funghi alla crema e tartufi

Funghi all'italiana panati

Breaded mushrooms Italian style

Serves 4
Difficulty *
Time: 1-1/2 hours

1 lb. mushrooms
2 eggs
Salt

6 sprigs parsley, chopped
Dry bread crumbs
1/2 cup (4 oz.) butter

Trim stems and cut mushrooms into halves. Beat eggs with a pinch of salt, add chopped parsley and dip mushrooms into batter, then one at a time into bread crumbs. Heat butter in a large pan and when it is good and hot, put breaded mushrooms carefully into pan. Fry on both sides until golden. Serve with your favorite tomato sauce.

217

Cipolline in agrodolce

Sweet-and-sour onions

Serves 4
Difficulty *
Time: 1 hour, 40 minutes

1 lb. very small white onions
1 tbsp. sugar
1/2 cup white vinegar and
1/2 cup water
1 tsp. salt

Leave onions whole. Soak in cold water 1 hour. In a saucepan, combine onions, sugar, vinegar, water and salt. Cover and cook for 40 minutes over low heat. Drain and serve hot.

Cipolline in agrodolce

Italians have been eating onions as far back as recorded history goes; the Greeks, of whom it was the favorite vegetable, ate it before the Romans; the Hebrews, before the Greeks; and before everybody, prehistoric man, presumably already a cultivator of onions. In any case, this vegetable has been a cultivated plant for so long that it is unknown as a wild plant anywhere in the world. Onion soup—*carabaccia*—was much appreciated in Florence in Renaissance times. A favorite way of serving onions today is in a sweet-and-sour sauce: the young spring onions which grow along the shores of Lake Como are pickled in vinegar exotically flavored with half a dozen spices; and in Piedmont onions are stuffed with a mixture of ingredients—including macaroons!

Cipolle farcite alla grossetana

Stuffed onions Grosseto style

Serves 4
Difficulty **
Time: 1-1/2 hours

8 medium-sized onions
2 tbsp. olive oil
1/4 lb. fresh mushrooms, sliced
1 cup finely chopped cooked loin of pork or veal
Salt, pepper
Nutmeg
1 egg white
1/4 cup butter
Chicken broth (see Brodo pieno alla calabrese, Soup section)

Clean onions and cook in boiling water for 15 minutes. Drain onions, let cold water run over them and cool. Slice off top of each, reserving these slices to be used later as covers for stuffed onions. Use a sharp knife to dig out the center of each onion, leaving a shell 1/2-inch thick. Chop onion removed and saute in oil with mushrooms until wilted. Add meat to mushrooms, season with salt, pepper and nutmeg and bind the whole with egg white. Use this mixture to stuff onions. Replace tops. Melt butter in a pan. When butter foams, put stuffed onion carefully into pan. Saute 1 minute without stirring. Pour in enough broth to cover onions half way. Cover pan and simmer, basting onions from time to time with pan juices for 20 to 25 minutes or until onions are easily pierced but still hold their shape.

Piselli alla casalinga

Peas home-style

Serves 4
Difficulty *
Time: 1 hour

6 strips lean bacon
1/2 cup chopped small onions
1/4 cup (2 oz.) butter
1 tsp. flour
1 cup chicken broth
1-1/2 lbs. peas, shelled
Small bunch aromatic herbs
(basil, marjoram and rosemary)
Salt, pepper

Saute bacon and onions in butter for 10 minutes over low heat. Remove. Mix flour with pan juices. Stir in broth. Stir constantly and bring to a boil. Add peas and aromatic herbs. Season with salt and pepper, cover and cook over low heat for 10 minutes. When peas are half cooked, add bacon and onion and cook another 10 minutes. Discard aromatic herbs and serve.

Piselli, or if you prefer, *piselli novelli*, are known all over the world—but as *petits pois*. For some reason the French have been granted the credit for developing these tiny tender spring peas, although they had them from the Italians—possibly through Catherine dei Medici, who introduced so many new foods into France, possibly somewhat later than her time.

Risi e bisi

Peas and rice

Serves 4
Difficulty *
Time: 30 minutes

1/3 cup (2-1/2 oz.) bacon or
prosciutto, as fat as possible,
chopped
1/2 onion, chopped
1/4 cup butter
1 tbsp. olive oil
1 lb. fresh peas, shelled
Salt
1-1/2 quarts chicken broth
1 cup (8 oz.) rice
1/4 cup grated Parmesan cheese
6 sprigs parsley, chopped

If an Italian were asked to name the most typical dish of Venice, the chances are good that he would vote for risi e bisi, rice and peas. It does not sound like a particularly exciting combination, and often it is not, outside of Venice. In other parts of Italy, uninspired restaurants are apt to inflict a soggy tasteless mush upon you when you order it. You have to go to Venice to taste the real thing—unless you can reproduce it in your own kitchen. This involves a willingness to take as much pains over this dish as the Venetians do—and above all, to start with tender young spring peas, which makes this pretty much a seasonal dish. Risi e bisi is often listed on menus among the soups, and some gastronomic writers dare call it one. Nonsense! It is served with a fork. Who ever heard of eating soup with a fork?

Risi e bisi is a famous dish from the Veneto region of Italy, and its title indicates that the proportion of peas and rice should be approximately equal, with perhaps even a little more peas than rice. Saute bacon and onion in half of the butter and oil. When onion is transparent, add peas; salt lightly, stir and add broth. Cover and cook over moderate heat until the peas are half cooked. Add rice and stir with a wooden spoon, taking care not to crush the peas, and complete cooking. (The final product should be of a consistency to be eaten with a fork rather than a spoon.) The rice will take about 17 minutes to cook. Before removing from heat, stir in remaining butter, Parmesan and parsley. Stir again, let stand for a few minutes and serve.

Peperoni alla meridionale

Baked peppers with anchovies

Serves 4
Difficulty *
Time: 1-1/2 hours
Oven Temp. 350° F.

8 large green peppers
Salt
2 cans (2 oz. each) flat anchovies, drained and chopped
1 clove garlic, chopped
1/4 cup capers, chopped
6 tbsp. olive oil
2 tbsp. dry bread crumbs

Wash peppers, dry, hold over high heat until skin blisters. As each pepper is roasted, remove outer membrane, which should be charred; wash again and dry. Cut in half lengthwise, discard inner membrane and seeds, then cut into strips 3/4-inch wide. Oil a 1-1/2 quart baking dish or other heatproof casserole. Add a layer of peppers. Sprinkle lightly with salt, anchovies, garlic and capers. Pour 2 tablespoons of the oil over top. Continue to put in layers in the same order until all ingredients have been used. Sprinkle bread crumbs over top layer, pour on remaining oil and bake in a preheated oven for 35 minutes or until peppers are soft and lightly browned. Test doneness with a fork. Serve with a main course of boiled meats or fish.

Peperoni alla meridionale

Peperoni della massaia

Peppers home-style

Serves 4
Difficulty *
Time: 1-1/2 hours
Oven Temp. 350° F.

4 small green peppers
1 cup chopped parsley
Small handful fresh basil
leaves, chopped
1 clove garlic, chopped
2 cups dry bread crumbs
Salt, pepper
8 anchovy fillets, finely chopped
1/2 cup olive oil

Wash peppers, dry and cut in half lengthwise. Discard seeds and white membrane but leave the half stems attached. Cook in boiling water 5 minutes and then drain. Mix parsley, basil, garlic, bread crumbs and salt and pepper to taste. Stuff the pepper halves with this mixture. Sprinkle anchovies over peppers. Pour 1 tablespoon oil on each. Bake in a preheated oven for 35 to 40 minutes until peppers are easily pierced. This dish is excellent with mixed boiled meats.

Peppers are a favorite vegetable in Italy. They appeal to the Italian character in two aspects—they add zest to other foods by their piquant flavor and gaiety by their color—whether it is red, green or yellow. The importance of color is implicit in the name given by the rest of the country to *saltato alla romana*; outside of Rome it is called *saltato alla bandiera*. *Bandiera* means flag, and this dish combines the colors of the Italian flag—it is made of green peppers, red tomatoes and white onions. Peppers are often cut into strips and stewed almost always with tomatoes, whatever else may go into the dish. Yellow peppers are preferred for this purpose in the Veneto, but Calabria combines red, yellow and green peppers. They are also frequently baked after having been stuffed in one or another of a multitude of fashions—with tomato and anchovy in Piedmont; with tomato, anchovy and mozzarella in the Campania (or alternatively with olives and capers); and most economically in Calabria, where bread crumbs and grated cheese, seasoned with garlic and vinegar, suffice.

Peperoni ripieni di riso

Stuffed peppers

Serves 8
Difficulty **
Time: 1 hour and 45 minutes
Oven Temp. 350° F.

9 medium-sized green peppers,
equal in size if possible
11 oz. rice
1/4 cup olive oil
1/2 cup (4 oz.) chopped cooked
ham
1/2 cup (2 oz.) grated Parmesan
cheese
2 tbsp. chopped parsley
2 tbsp. fresh basil leaves,
finely chopped
1 anchovy in oil, chopped
1/4 tsp. nutmeg
2-1/2 cups (1 lb.) diced ripe
tomatoes
Salt

Wash peppers and set one aside for later use. Cut around stems with a sharp-pointed knife and remove stems. Turn upside down and cut a slice from bottom of pepper. Empty peppers by spooning out seeds and fibrous membrane. These peppers will be stuffed upside down. From pepper which you have reserved, cut out 8 little circles large enough to place over holes left by stems and thus keep filling from spilling out. Put rice into boiling water and cook it for 10 minutes, draining it before it is fully cooked. Put rice in bowl. Stir in oil, ham, parmesan, parsley and basil. Stir in anchovy, nutmeg and about half of the tomatoes. Stuff peppers with rice mixture. Arrange them side by side in a baking dish. Spoon remaining tomato on top of the filling. Sprinkle with salt, a little olive oil and replace pepper slices removed. Bake them for 45 minutes in a preheated oven (350° F.). These peppers are also very good cold. The filling can also be used to stuff tomatoes.

Patate alla pizzaiola

*Potatoes pizzaiola
or with tomato sauce*

Serves 4
Difficulty *
Time: 1 hour

**1-1/2 lbs. (4 large) potatoes
3 cloves garlic, crushed
7 tbsp. oil
3 cups sieved tomato pulp
Salt, pepper
A pinch of oregano**

Boil potatoes in lightly salted water until tender but still firm. Drain, peel and slice. Saute garlic in oil until lightly browned. Add tomato pulp and salt, pepper and oregano to taste. Simmer for about 8 minutes over low heat. Add potato slices, simmer 5 minutes to blend flavors and serve in a preheated dish.

The potato was slow to gain favor in Italy—and everywhere else in Europe too, for that matter. When it was first imported from America around 1580, it was initially grown as an ornamental plant in Italy. But how much time elapsed before it escaped from the flower garden into the vegetable garden does not seem to be on record; in France it was some 200 years later. What may seem surprising is that the potato, in itself a rather uninspiring vegetable lacking the subtlety Italians appreciate, gained favor at all; yet there are innumerable potato recipes, in addition to such classics as potato gnocchi. In the Alps, where the climate demands filling foods, the potato is a staple. It is combined with cabbage, another fairly coarse vegetable, in the Belluno area, and in the Valle d'Aosta it is popular not only because it is attuned to the local climate, but also because it grows so well there at high altitudes. Potato soups in Friuli and Trieste seem normal enough, but more surprising is tripe and potatoes in Liguria; mussels and potatoes in Apulia (which also has Taranto tart, with mozzarella); and the enriched mashed potatoes Lord Byron discovered with delight in Ravenna. One of the most ingenious ways of cooking potatoes is the specialty of a very small place, San Rio di Fontecchio, whose only other claim to fame is that Pontius Pilate is supposed to have been born there: this is *patate sotto il coppo*, for which a farmstead hearthstone is swept clean, sliced potatoes are spread out on it, an iron cover is laid over them, and live coals are then shoveled onto this *coppo* to cook them.

Patate e peperoni in tegame

Potatoes and peppers

Serves 4
Difficulty *
Time: 1-1/2 hours

Roast peppers over high heat. Remove skin by rubbing with a towel. Remove seeds and chop peppers coarsely. Cover them with half of the oil. Add a pinch of salt and reserve. Put remaining oil in a frying pan and saute potatoes over low heat until lightly browned. When potatoes are tender, add peppers with oil. Mix well and saute 5 minutes longer. Serve in a preheated dish.

**4 red peppers
7 tbsp. olive oil
Salt**

4 medium potatoes, peeled and cut into 1/4-inch thick slices

Patate e peperoni in tegame

Patate ripiene alla ghiotta

Stuffed potatoes gourmand

Serves 8
Difficulty **
Time: 2 hours
Oven Temp. 400° F.

8 large baking potatoes
1 clove garlic, chopped coarsely
5 tbsp. butter
1/2 lb. (bulk) pork sausage
1/4 cup chopped parsley
1/2 lb. mushrooms, sliced
2 tbsp. olive oil
1/4 cup sliced black truffle
Salt, pepper
Nutmeg
1/3 cup dry bread crumbs

Patate ripiene alla ghiotta

Cover unpeeled potatoes with lightly salted cold water. Bring to a boil and simmer for exactly 5 minutes. Drain, put onto a baking sheet and complete cooking by baking in preheated oven for 1 hour or until easily pierced. Let them cool, cut in half lengthwise without peeling and remove insides, leaving a layer about 1/2-inch thick inside skin (reserve skins for later filling.) Saute garlic in 2 tablespoons of the butter until golden. Remove and discard garlic. Break sausage meat up into butter. Saute until pork is brown. Drain excess fat. Remove from heat, cool and stir in parsley. In another pan saute mushrooms in oil and a pinch of salt. Into a mixing bowl sieve potato removed from skins. Stir in sausage, cooked mushrooms and truffles. Season with a pinch of salt, pepper and nutmeg and mix until ingredients are well blended. Fill potato skins with this mixture, heaping filling high. Sprinkle with bread crumbs and remaining butter, melted. Arrange in a shallow baking dish or on a baking sheet and bake in preheated oven for 15 to 20 minutes or until lightly browned. Serve immediately.

Torta tarantina

Potato tart with cheese Taranto style

Serves 4
Difficulty *
Time: 1-1/2 hours
Oven Temp. 375° F.

4 large potatoes
1/4 cup olive oil
Salt

1/2 lb. mozzarella cheese, sliced
1 can (1 lb.) Italian tomatoes, chopped
1 tsp. crumbled oregano

Boil potatoes in their jackets until tender but still firm. Drain, peel and slice 1/2-inch thick. Brush 2 tablespoons of the oil in a 1-quart baking dish and arrange potato slices in bottom. Sprinkle with salt to taste. Place mozzarella slices over potatoes and spoon over tomatoes. Sprinkle oregano over tomatoes and sprinkle with remaining oil. Bake in a hot, preheated oven for 20 minutes and serve.

Spinaci alla lombarda

Spinach Lombardy style

Serves 4
Difficulty *
Time: 1 hour
Oven Temp. 400° F.

3 lbs. spinach
1/2 cup (4 oz.) butter
1/2 cup grated Parmesan cheese
4 eggs
Salt

Cook well washed spinach in a very small quantity of salted water until tender. Drain well and saute for several minutes in 3 tbsp. of the butter. Grease a 1-quart casserole with butter. Place spinach in casserole, sprinkle with grated Parmesan cheese and 3 tbsp. of the butter, melted. Bake in a preheated oven for 15 minutes or until brown. Fry eggs in remaining butter, season with salt and pepper and serve on top of each serving of spinach.

> Spinach is not one of the many vegetables which go back to antiquity in Italy. The ancient Romans did not know it, for it only reached Italy from the Middle East after the Crusades. But Florence used it so plentifully during the Renaissance that in France to this day any dish described as *à la florentine* is almost certain to contain spinach. It seems dated as of Renaissance times by the name given to spinach omelets in Florence, *ova affrittellate alla Medici.*

Spinaci alla romana

Spinach Roman style

Serves 4
Difficulty *
Time: 1 hour

2 lbs. spinach
2 tbsp. lard (or oil)
1 clove garlic, chopped
5 strips fat and lean prosciutto crudo
2 tbsp. *each* pine nuts and Sultana raisins
2 tbsp. butter
Salt

Wash spinach and cook in very little salted water. Drain, press out all water, saute gently in lard (or oil) with garlic and prosciutto. After a few minutes add raisins and pine nuts. Add butter and stir until melted. Season to taste with salt.

Spinaci alla romana

Pomodori casalinghi ripieni

Stuffed tomatoes home-style

Serves 4
Difficulty *
Time: 1-1/2 hours
Oven Temp. 350° F.

8 medium tomatoes
Salt, pepper
1 small onion, chopped
9 tbsp. butter
3 cups soft bread crumbs
1/2 cup (2 oz.) grated Parmesan
A few basil leaves, chopped
6 sprigs parsley, chopped
2 anchovy fillets, rinsed with cold water and chopped
1/4 cup pine nuts, ground in a mortar

Cut a thin slice off the tops of the tomatoes. Scoop out seeds, then squeeze tomato cups slightly over a bowl to catch juice. Sprinkle tomato cups lightly with salt and invert them on a rack set over a pan. Reserve juice. Saute onion in 1/4 cup of the butter until golden. Combine onion and drippings, bread crumbs, grated Parmesan, basil, parsley, anchovy fillets and pine nuts. Sprinkle with salt and pepper and stir in reserved tomato juice. Mix well. Arrange tomato cups side by side in a buttered baking dish, stuff with filling. Dot with remaining butter and bake in a preheated oven for 20 to 25 minutes or until tomatoes are tender but still hold their shape.

Pomodori casalinghi ripieni

The tomato is so ubiquitous in Italian cooking that it is difficult today to imagine this cuisine without it; yet Italians got along without it for centuries. A native of America, it was not available to Europe until after the discovery of the New World, and even after it had reached Europe, it was not quickly accepted. The first known reference to it in Italian writings is dated 1554, but a half-century later it was still appearing only occasionally in Italian gardens as a curiosity, and it would be another 150 years before it became a common vegetable. Even so it was quicker to make its way to the table in Italy than in its native country, for many Americans still believed it was poisonous up to the end of the last century. In the end, it was the French and the Italians who taught Americans to eat their own vegetable, and the United States had to import from Italy new varieties of tomatoes developed there during the period when America was shunning this fruit.

Pomodori ripieni alla moda romagnola

*Stuffed tomatoes
Romagna style*

Serves 4
Difficulty *
Time: 1-1/2 hours
Oven Temp. 350º F.

4 large tomatoes
Salt, pepper
1 package (1 oz.) dried mushrooms, soaked, drained and chopped
1 celery stalk, chopped
6 sprigs parsley, chopped

1/2 onion, chopped
1/4 cup butter
2 dinner rolls soaked in milk
1/2 cup (2 oz.) grated Parmesan cheese
1 egg yolk
1/4 cup olive oil

Choose ripe but firm tomatoes. Cut a thin slice from top. Scoop out, discarding seeds, juice and a good part of the pulp. Salt and pepper lightly on inside.
Prepare filling as follows: Saute mushrooms, celery, parsley and onion in a saucepan with 2 tablespoons of the butter until wilted. Squeeze bread dry and break it up. Add to pan. Simmer filling over moderate heat for 2 to 3 minutes. Season to taste with salt and pepper. Remove from heat and stir in Parmesan and egg yolk. Stuff tomatoes, arrange side by side in a baking dish and pour oil over them. Dot with remaining butter and bake in a preheated oven for about 30 minutes.

Something like a quarter of a century ago, I won a prize at a Vermont county fair for the zucchini I had grown on my farm. It was not much of a triumph; nobody else entered any. Zucchini, a long green bludgeon-shaped summer squash (courgettes), was practically unknown to Americans, who have found out about it since then, for zucchini gives you a lot of squash for your money. Mine never passed two feet in length, but in Italy's Campania they may reach six. It is the favorite form of summer squash in Italy, often stewed together with kindred vegetables, like tomatoes or eggplant, or stuffed—economically in Genoa with its own flesh, cottage cheese and mushrooms; more expensively in Rome, with chopped meat, tomatoes and grated cheese.

Zucchine piccanti

*Zucchini
with hot sauce*

Serves 4
Difficulty *
Time: 30 minutes

1 cup soft bread crumbs
2 tbsp. wine vinegar
8 zucchini squash (courgettes)
1 tbsp. capers, chopped

1 tbsp. chopped parsley
2 anchovy fillets, chopped
1 tbsp. chopped chives
7 tbsp. olive oil
Salt, pepper

Sprinkle bread with vinegar. Cut ends off zucchini and cook them whole in lightly salted boiling water until tender, about 20 minutes. Mix capers, parsley, anchovies and chives in a bowl. Squeeze bread dry and add to bowl together with oil. Season to taste with salt and pepper and beat well. Spoon sauce over drained zucchini.

Zucchini alla milanese

Zucchini Milanese style

Serves 6
Difficulty **
Time: 1-1/2 hours
Oven Temp. 350°F.

3-1/2 lbs. zucchini (12 small
or 6 large)
1/2 cup (4 oz.) diced cooked ham
2 tbsp. chopped parsley
1/4 cup chopped fresh basil
leaves
2 tbsp. dry bread crumbs, approx.
2/3 cup grated Parmesan cheese
2 eggs
Nutmeg
Salt, pepper
5 tbsp. (4-1/2 oz.) butter
1 tbsp. flour
1 cup milk

Cut ends off zucchini and cut them to same length. Wash and drain. Boil zucchini in lightly salted water for 10 minutes or until half cooked. Drain. Slice in half lengthwise and remove pulp, reserving it in a bowl. Reserve shells (1/2-inch thick.) Mix ham, parsley and basil with chopped zucchini pulp. Add bread crumbs, all of the grated Parmesan except for 2 tablespoons, eggs, freshly grated nutmeg and salt and pepper to taste. Mix these ingredients thoroughly and set aside. Melt 1/4 cup of the butter and stir in flour. Gradually stir in milk. Stir over low heat until sauce bubbles and thickens. Stir sauce into zucchini mixture. Add more bread crumbs if mixture is not thick enough to spoon. Using a spoon fill zucchini shells with mixture. Arrange them side by side in a buttered (use remaining butter) shallow baking dish. Sprinkle with remaining grated Parmesan and bake in a preheated oven for about 1/2 hour. Serve hot in baking dish.

Zucchini alla milanese

DESSERTS

Renato Giani was referring especially to Sicilian desserts when he wrote that in eating some of them, "you are, without realizing it, taking part in a rite, a sort of communion, a little as if you belonged to a secret sacrificial society, a sect of the initiated, of the dedicated." It is true that it is above all in Sicily, where deeply-rooted superstitions lie just beneath the threshold of consciousness, that consuming certain desserts is almost equivalent to casting a magic spell, for they were associated originally with ancient rites and possessed symbolic meaning. But everywhere in Italy, it is desserts which mirror most often the country's long history.

The ancient Roman cook's delight in deceiving banqueters by making one food resemble another is echoed today in the southern pastries decorated with colored frosting to look so much like fruit or vegetables or even fish that you might easily take them for the real thing unless you pick them up. You are reminded that the Saracens once ruled Sicily, and occasionally penetrated into the peninsula, by sweets so Oriental as to be almost cloying (torrone, zabaione), and that they contributed to the Italian menu a second time when the Crusaders returned from the Near East by ice cream, acquired first by Italy and then passed on by Italians to the rest of Europe and America (but nobody makes it better than Neapolitans or Sicilians). Many Italian pastries appear only on certain religious holidays, and no doubt once possessed a special significance which has been forgotten now. And at least one dessert, *cannoli*, is believed to go back to prehistoric times.

The richness of Italian desserts seems paradoxical, for when the average Italian family eats at home, the meal usually ends simply, with fruit or cheese. But when guests are invited, or whenever a holiday occurs—then there appear those unbelievably luscious melting cakes, drenched with subtle liqueurs, to be gulped down with gusto and utter disregard for the waistline.

A few years ago I undertook a month-long gastronomic tour of Italy which led me from Syracuse, Sicily, to San Polo di Piave, Veneto. I gained 22 pounds. It was not the pasta which did it, it was the *dolci*, especially those rich cakes doused in liqueurs which, while they are undoubtedly solids, seen to be quivering permanently on the edge of liquefaction, and, if they were any sweeter, would set your teeth on edge. I couldn't resist them, with or without marmalade-like fillings and creamy icings. No one can make such cakes better than the Italians, and while in most countries their production would demand the skill of a master pastry cook, in Italy the art seems to be within the reach of everybody. Deep in the provinces, in tiny hamlets where you are surprised to find any food on sale at all, you will come upon fantastically complicated pastry. It is taken as a matter of course.

Genoise

Genoa cake

Serves 6
Makes 1 9-inch round cake
Difficulty **
Time: 2 hours
Oven Temp. 350° F.

4 eggs
2/3 cup sugar
1 cup sifted all-purpose flour
1/2 cup butter, melted and cooled
Confectioners' (icing) sugar

With an electric mixer beat whole eggs and sugar in a rounded copper bowl. Set bowl over very low heat (to one side of the direct flame if you are using gas), and beat mixture until it has become slightly warmed and about twice the original volume. Remove from heat and continue to beat until it has cooled completely. Gently fold in sifted flour and butter. Pour mixture out into a buttered and floured 9-inch springform pan. Bake in a preheated oven 40 minutes or until cake feels firm to the touch in the center. Invert and turn out onto a serving dish. Cool. Sprinkle with confectioners' sugar.
This is a cake with a fine delicate texture and can be used in many types of cakes. Cut into thin layers and spread your favorite frosting or filling between them.

Panettone casalingo

Panettone family-style

Makes 1 9-inch round cake
Difficulty *
Time: 1-1/2 hours
Oven Temp. 350° F.

Genoise

It is curious to find a French name used in Italy for an Italian dessert—for what Génoise means, of course, is Genoese. Perhaps it underwent translation because the French appreciated the particular type of dough from which it is made more than the Italians, who bake so many luscious cakes that they could take this one in their stride. And, after all, why shouldn't the Genoese be called the Génoise in Genoa? French fried potatoes and the French horn are not called French in France, pork sausages are not called frankfurters in Frankfurt and chopped steak is not called hamburger in Hamburg—it is called American steak there.

3/4 cup sultana raisins
1/2 cup butter
1/2 cup sugar
2 egg yolks and 1 whole egg
2-3/4 cups sifted all-purpose flour
1 tsp. cream of tartar
1 tsp. baking soda
1 cup lukewarm milk
1/2 cup candied citron, diced
Grated rind of 1 lemon

Soften raisins in warm water. Butter and flour a 9-inch springform pan. In a bowl cream butter until fluffy. Add sugar and beat mixture until it is creamy. Beat in 1 egg yolk. Sift flour with cream of tartar and baking soda. Stir in some of the flour. Beat in second yolk, a little flour and then whole egg. Beat in warm milk. Beat in remaining flour. Continue to beat with an electric mixer for 15 minutes. Drain raisins and dry in a towel. Lightly sprinkle raisins and citron with flour and stir into cake batter. Stir in lemon rind. Pour into pan, smooth with a cake spatula and bake in a preheated oven for about 45 minutes. Let Panettone cool 10 minutes before removing from pan. Serve sprinkled with confectioners' (icing) sugar.

Panqiallo familiare di Natale alla romana

Pangiallo familiare di Natale alla romana

Roman Christmas cake

Makes 1 round loaf
Difficulty **
Time: 2-1/2 hours, plus time required for dough to rise
Oven Temp. 375° F.

2/3 cup sugar
2-3/4 cups sifted all-purpose flour
1 envelope active dry yeast
1/2 lb. almonds, coarsely chopped
1/2 lb. hazelnuts, coarsely chopped
1/2 lb. pine nuts
3 lbs. raisins
1/2 lb. candied citron and orange peel, diced
Spices: pinch of cinnamon, cloves, nutmeg, allspice
3 tbsp. oil

Over low heat dissolve 1/2 cup of the sugar in 1/4 cup water until syrup becomes clear. Put 2-1/4 cups of the flour in a bowl and mix it with the yeast dissolved in 3 tablespoons lukewarm water and with the sugar syrup. (The result should be a rather soft dough. Add a little lukewarm water if necessary.) Beat in almonds hazelnuts, pine nuts, raisins, citron and orange peel and a pinch of spices. Knead on a floured board until smooth and elastic. Shape this dough into a round loaf and let it rise uncovered in a warm place for about 12 hours on a buttered baking sheet.

Over moderate heat dissolve remaining sugar in 1 tablespoon water. Remove from heat, stir in remaining flour and 3 tablespoons oil and a pinch of cinnamon to make a thin batter the consistency of thick cream. Carefully spoon batter over round loaf and bake in a preheated oven for 45 minutes.

Rome is the city par excellence for pangiallo, which appears there as a Christmas treat. The name means, of course, "yellow bread"; actually it is a sort of fruit cake.

Panettone is almost a trademark of Milan. If you arrive there by train, as I always do, you will find the station noisy with vendors selling this greatest of all coffee cakes in all sizes; but the best time to become conscious of them is on leaving, when you can acquire one and thus carry away with you a morsel of Milan. I always take the largest I see; it has never yet had time to get stale before I have finished it. You will encounter panettone all year round, but it is particularly associated with Christmas. In the old days, the Duke of Milan used to cut three slices from a panettone at Christmas time, and each person present ate a bit of each piece for good luck; and in every household, the head of the family performed the same rite.

There is a story which attributes the invention of panettone to the fifteenth century, when an impecunious Milanese baker named Antonio was subsidized by a young man interested in marrying his daughter, so that he was able to buy particularly fine flour for his Christmas bread, to make it with much egg, and to add sugar, raisins and candied citron peel to convert it into cake. Antonio got rich, his backer got the girl, and panettone got its name—pan de Tonio, Tony's bread. It makes a nice story but, alas, the termination of the word has nothing to do with any Tony but is simply the suffix signifying bigness, of one kind or another—in this case, richness. Panettone is, prosaically, simply "enriched bread".

Colomba pasquale means "Easter dove"—in cooking, a cake made in the shape of that bird. As an Easter symbol, the dove requires no explanation, but in Milan and Pavia it gets one anyway. Milan's legend is connected with the battle of Legnano, when Milan and her allies of the Lombard League defeated the Emperor Barbarossa; two doves, the story goes, alighted on the altar of the Milanese war chariot during the battle, promising victory. The dove-shaped cake has been made ever since in memory of this incident. However, Pavia's tale represents it as already existing six centuries earlier. According to this story, Pavia angered Alboin, King of the Longobards, by withstanding for three years the siege he had leveled against the city. When he finally took it, he decreed that in punishment for its obstinacy, it would be pillaged. But as he entered the city gates, a pretty girl offered him one of the dove-shaped cakes, and, touched by the gesture, Alboin changed his mind and spared Pavia to serve as his capital.

Colomba pasquale alla modenese

Easter cake Modena style

Makes 1 9-inch round cake
Difficulty **
Time: 3 hours, plus time required for dough to rise
Oven Temp. 350°F.

For filling:

2-1/4 lbs. green apples, peeled and diced
2-1/4 lbs. firm pears, peeled and diced
1/2 cup sugar

For dough:

2 envelopes active dry yeast
1/2 cup lukewarm water
1 tsp. salt
1/2 cup lukewarm milk
1/4 cup sugar
5 tbsp. soft butter
3 eggs
3 tbsp. Marsala wine
Grated rind of 1 lemon
4-1/2 cups sifted all-purpose flour
1/2 cup Sultana raisins
1/4 cup pine nuts

For filling: Simmer apples and pears in a saucepan with sugar and 1/2 cup water until fruit is reduced to sauce consistency and liquid has evaporated. Press through a fine sieve, put into a pyrex baking dish and bake in preheated oven until compote has become the consistency of apple butter (be sure to stir occasionally) about 1 hour. Cool.

For dough: In a large bowl dissolve yeast in lukewarm water. Stir in salt, milk, sugar, butter, 2 of the eggs, wine, lemon rind, adding enough flour to make a thick dough. Turn out on a floured surface and knead until smooth and elastic. Let rise covered in a bowl in a warm place until double in bulk.
Soak raisins in water. Put dough on a floured surface, knead vigorously and divide into 4 pieces, three of them equal, one slightly larger. Use the largest piece to line the bottom and sides of a greased 9-inch pie pan or dove-shaped pan. Spread a little of the fruit compote over dough; follow this with a layer of some of the raisins and pine nuts. Cover with a second layer of dough and continue in this way until all the ingredients are used up, making top layer dough. Let rise 35 to 40 minutes in a warm place. Brush surface with remaining egg (beaten). Sprinkle with sugar and bake in a preheated oven for about 1 hour or until richly browned.

Dolce di frutta secca

*Italian fruit cake
with rum*

Makes 1 9-inch square cake
Difficulty *
Time: 1-1/2 hours
soak fruit-2 to 3 hours
Oven Temp. 350° F.

1/2 cup chopped dried figs
1/2 cup chopped dates
1/2 cup chopped dried apricots
1/2 cup raisins
1/2 cup rum
1-3/4 cups all-purpose flour

2 tsp. baking powder
1/2 cup butter
1 cup sugar
2 eggs
2/3 cup milk
1 tsp. vanilla

Marinate fruit in rum for 2 to 3 hours, stirring from time to time. Sift flour and baking powder. Cream butter until fluffy in a mixing bowl. Gradually beat in sugar. Beat in eggs one at a time. Beat in flour and milk alternately beginning and ending with the flour. Stir in vanilla. Drain rum from fruit. Fold fruit into cake batter. Pour mixture into a greased and floured 9-inch square pan. Bake in a preheated oven for about 40 to 45 minutes until firm to the touch in the centre. Cool in pan and then cut into squares to serve.

When I was a boy, one of our Christmas treats was dried figs, pressed into rectangular bricks; it never occurred to me then that I was being offered one of the oldest productions of the prepared food industry. I was not yet a reader of Aristophanes, who, in his *Peace*, exhorts his hearers: "Ah! Remember, men, the former life the goddess granted us, the bricks of dried figs,..." Not until I was 25 or so would I taste a fresh fig, and discover that it would have been impossible to predict its flavor from that of the dried fruit (this is less true for the apricot, successfully dried, as well as the fig, in Italy). Gastronomically speaking, fresh figs and dried figs are two different fruits, so there is no reason why a country where fresh figs are obtainable nearly all year round should not also produce desserts based on the quite dissimilar flavor of the dried variety.

Torta alla mandorla

Almond tart

Makes 1 10-inch cake
Difficulty *
Time: 1 hour
Oven Temp. 350° F.

6 eggs
1 cup superfine (caster) sugar
Grated rind of 1 lemon
1 tsp. vanilla

1 cup all-purpose flour
1 cup butter
1/2 cup sifted confectioners'
(icing) sugar
1 cup chopped toasted almonds

Grease and flour 10-inch layer cake pan, 2 inches deep. Beat egg whites until stiff. Gradually, 1 tablespoon at a time, beat in half of the sugar. Beat egg yolks until soft and fluffy. Gradually beat in remaining sugar. Fold egg yolks into egg whites. Fold in lemon rind and vanilla. Fold in flour and half of the butter, melted and clarified. Pour into pan and bake in a preheated oven about 35 minutes or until firm to the touch. Remove from pan and cool on a rack. Cream remaining butter until soft and fluffy. Beat in confectioners' sugar. Place cake on a platter. Spread top with a thin layer of butter cream and sprinkle with almonds. Garnish with whole almonds and candied cherries, if desired.

Torta di noci

Walnut cake

Makes 1 9-inch round cake
Difficulty *
Time: 1-1/2 hours
Oven Temp. 350° F.

20 walnuts, shelled
2-1/4 cups sifted all-purpose flour
1/2 cup butter
1 cup sugar
3 egg yolks

Grated rind of 1 lemon
2 tsp. baking powder
1/2 cup milk
1/2 cup Sultana raisins, soaked and drained

Butter a 9-inch springform pan and lightly flour. Shell walnuts, trying to keep 8 halves whole for decoration. Chop remaining walnuts coarsely and mix with 1 tablespoon of the flour. Cream butter in a bowl until creamy. Beat in sugar and egg yolks, one at a time. Stir in lemon rind. Alternately beat in flour mixed with baking powder and milk. Finally stir in walnuts. Pour mixture into pan. Top with reserved whole walnut meats and Sultana raisins. Bake in a preheated oven for 40 to 45 minutes. Remove from pan and cool on a rack. Serve cold cut into thin wedges.

Torta di noci

La pasta frolla

Short pastry dough

Makes enough pastry to line 24 tart shells, two 9-inch pie pans, or one 11-inch flan pan.
This recipe for short pastry dough can be considered basic for the preparation of an infinite number of home-made cakes, cookies, pies, timbales, etc.

2-3/4 cups sifted all-purpose flour
2/3 cup sugar
Pinch of salt
2/3 cup (5 oz.) butter
Grated rind of 1 lemon
1 egg

Mix flour with sugar and a pinch of salt, and make a well in the centre. Cut softened butter into small pieces and put it in the centre along with grated lemon rind. Break egg and slide it into centre of the well. Mix dough just long enough to combine ingredients. (The secret of tender dough lies in avoiding overheating it with one's hands.)

Form dough into a ball, wrap it in wax paper. Chill for at least 30 minutes. When ready to prepare the dessert, do not handle dough again but roll it out at once on a floured surface with a floured rolling pin to a 1/4-inch thickness. This can be used to line buttered cake pans, barquette or cookie molds. For small pastry shells the baking time for the dough at 375° F. is from 10 to 15 minutes. Large pastry shells take longer, about 20 to 25 minutes.

This is the classic procedure. However there are many variations which can be made depending on requirements. For instance, use 2 egg yolks instead of 1 egg. If desired, you can make the dough with 1/3 cup butter and 2 tablespoons oil. If you prefer a more delicate pastry, add 1/3 cup finely grated blanched almonds or 1 teaspoon vanilla or 1 tablespoon liqueur such as triple sec or anisette. To make a salted pastry dough, suitable for vegetable tarts or canapes, use the same proportion of ingredients but omit sugar and increase quantity of salt to 1/2 teaspoon. Follow the same procedure used for sweet pastry dough.

Dolce trentino

Fruit tart Trentino

Makes 1 10-inch tart
Difficulty **
Time: 2 hours
Oven Temp. 350° F.

For filling:

3 apples and 2 pears, peeled and chopped
1/4 cup sugar
Piece of lemon peel
Juice of 1/2 lemon
1 cup dry cake crumbs
2 cups chopped dried figs
1/4 cup Sultana raisins
1/4 cup pine nuts
1/4 cup chopped candied citron, diced
1/2 cup apricot preserves
1 egg, well beaten

For crust:

4-1/2 cups sifted all-purpose flour
1/4 tsp. salt
1 cup sugar

1 cup butter
3 egg yolks
Grated rind of 1 lemon
3 tbsp. white wine

For crust: Prepare crust, see La Pasta Frolla.

For filling: Put apples and pears in a saucepan and add sugar, lemon peel, lemon juice and 1/3 cup water. Simmer, covered, over moderate heat until fruit is well cooked, but not falling apart. Drain fruit and set aside for later use, reserving juice. Pour reserved juice into a bowl and add crumbs. Soften dried figs and raisins in a little warm water. When they are soft and slightly swollen, dry in a towel, then add to crumbs. Stir in pine nuts, citron and apricot preserves.

Roll out 2/3 of the dough into a sheet large enough to line an ungreased 10-inch pie pan. Roll it up on the rolling pin, then unroll it over pie pan. Press it down firmly with your hands, then trim off excess dough. Fill with an even layer of crumb mixture and cooked fruit. Knead trimmings and remaining dough into a ball. Roll out on a floured surface into a round large enough to cover the pie pan. Place over filling and pinch around edges to seal. Prick top of dough with a fork, brush with beaten egg and bake in a preheated oven for about 45 minutes or until richly browned.

Tortellini dolci fritti

Fried jam tarts

Makes 3 dozen
Difficulty **
Time: 2 hours

For pastry dough:

4-1/2 cups sifted all-purpose flour
Salt
1/2 cup sugar
2 eggs

For filling:

1/2 cup Sultana raisins
2 cups chestnut puree
1-1/2 cups plum or sour cherry jam (or any other rather tart jam)
3/4 cup apricot jam
1 tbsp. pine nuts
1/4 cup bitter cocoa

1/4 cup peach liqueur
Grated rind of 1 lemon
1 tsp. instant coffee
1/2 cup crumbled bitter almond macaroons (purchased amaretti or see recipe Amaretti alle mandorle)
Deep fat or oil heated to 380° F.

Prepare crust, see La Pasta Frolla.

For filling: Soften raisins in warm water. Drain. In a bowl mix chestnut puree, the 2 jams, raisins, pine nuts, cocoa, liqueur, lemon rind, coffee and macaroons.
Roll out one portion of dough on a floured surface into a sheet 1/8-inch thick. Dot surface with mounds of filling the size of a walnut and about 4 inches from each other. Roll out remaining dough the same size as the first. Place over filling. Press dough around each mound of filling. Cut into rounds or squares using pastry cutter or pastry wheel. Pinch edges of each individual tartlet. Fry in preheated fat until a golden brown, a few tarts at a time, about 2 to 3 minutes. Drain on absorbent paper. Cool and serve sprinkled with confectioners' (icing) sugar, if desired.

Nepitelle alla calabrese

Calabrian tartlets

Serves 4
Difficulty **
Time: 2-1/2 hours
Oven Temp. 350° F.

Crust:

3-1/2 cups sifted all-purpose flour
1/2 tsp. salt
1 tbsp. sugar
6 tbsp. vegetable shortening
2 eggs
Grated rind of 1/2 lemon

Filling:

5 tbsp. sugar
1 cup raisins, soaked and chopped
2 squares bitter chocolate, melted
Pinch of powdered cinnamon
1/3 cup blanched almonds, roasted and chopped
3 tbsp. hot grape juice

For crust: Prepare crust, see La Pasta Frolla. Roll dough out on a floured surface into a sheet slightly less than 1/2-inch thick, then cut out 4 4-1/2-inch circles. Reserve trimmings.

For filling: Mix sugar with raisins, chocolate, cinnamon, almonds and grape juice. Spread this filling over circles of dough and raise edges slightly, pinching to form little baskets. Re-knead trimmings, roll out and cut into 1/4-inch wide strips. Arrange strips of dough in a lattice on top of tarts. Arrange on a greased baking sheet and bake in a preheated oven for 20 to 25 minutes.

Nepitelle alla calabrese

Dolcetti al brandy alla ligure

*Almond pastry
Ligurian style*

Makes 1 8-inch square pan
Difficulty **
Time: 1-1/2 hours
Oven Temp. 350° F.

3/4 cup blanched almonds
6 tbsp. butter
2/3 cup sugar
3 eggs
1/2 cup sifted all-purpose flour
3 tbsp. brandy
Confectioners' (icing) sugar

Dolcetti al brandy alla ligure

Roast almonds in a frying pan over low heat until richly browned. Stir constantly. Chop very fine. Melt butter, stir in sugar and eggs, gradually stir in flour, almonds and brandy. Butter and flour an 8-inch square pan. Pour batter into it and bake in a preheated oven for 20 to 25 minutes or until lightly browned. Let it cool in pan. Cut into small squares or diamond-shaped pieces. Arrange them on a serving platter and sprinkle with confectioners' sugar.

Savoiardi

*Savoy biscuits
(Ladyfingers)*

Makes 6 dozen
Difficulty **
Time: 1-1/2 hours
Oven Temp. 325° F.

7 eggs, separated
1 cup superfine (caster) sugar

3/4 cup all-purpose flour
3/4 cup potato starch (or flour)
Salt

Beat egg whites warmed to room temperature until fluffy. Gradually beat in sugar until very stiff. Beat yolks until fluffy. Gradually fold egg yolks into egg whites. Fold in flour, potato flour and a pinch of salt mixed together. Fill a pastry bag with 1/2-inch diameter round nozzle with batter and press out to form ladyfingers on floured and buttered baking sheets. Bake in a preheated oven for about 15 to 20 minutes or until puffed and lightly browned. Remove while warm and cool on a rack.

Meringhe al brandy

Brandied meringues

Makes 20 meringues
Difficulty *
Time: 1-1/2 hours
Oven Temp. 250° F.

2 egg whites
1 cup confectioners' (icing) sugar
1 tbsp. brandy (cognac)

1 to 1-1/2 tbsp. butter
2 tbsp. flour

Warm egg whites to room temperature. Beat egg whites until stiff. Gradually beat in confectioners' sugar, 2 tablespoons at a time, until stiff and glossy. Fold in brandy. Put mixture in a pastry bag with a 3/4-inch in diameter round opening. Force out 3-inch lengths onto a heavily buttered and floured baking sheet 2 inches apart to allow for spreading. Bake in preheated oven until they are hard, about 40 minutes. Let cool on baking sheet. Remove carefully from baking sheet and arrange on a serving platter.

Meringhe con panna e marrons glacés

Meringues with whipped cream and marrons glacés

Serves 4
Difficulty **
Time: 1-1/2 hours
(if meringues
are baked at home)
Oven Temp. 250° F.

2 egg whites
1 cup sugar
5 marrons glacés
1/2 cup whipped cream

Beat egg whites until stiff and beat in sugar, 1 tablespoon at a time until stiff and glossy. Butter and lightly flour a baking sheet. Put meringue mixture in a pastry bag with either a smooth round or rosette tip. Make mounds the size of a plum directly onto baking sheet. Place into preheated oven for 40 to 45 minutes. Leave oven door ajar about 2 inches to allow steam to escape so meringues are dry and remain white. Place meringues into serving dishes. Grate or finely chop marrons glacés and fold into whipped cream. Spoon mixture on top of meringues.

Meringhe con panna e marrons glacés

Amaretti fritti

*Fried bitter
almond macaroons*

Serves 4
Difficulty *
Time: 30 minutes

3/4 cup dry Marsala wine	Milk	
1/4 cup brandy	Deep fat or oil, heated to 360° F.	
2 tbsp. sugar	1/2 lb. bitter almond macaroons	
2 eggs	("amaretti" see below)	
1-1/3 cups all-purpose flour	1/2 cup confectioners' (icing) sugar	

Mix Marsala and brandy in a bowl. Prepare batter for frying: In a separate bowl, mix sugar, eggs, 1/2 cup of the flour and enough milk to make batter the consistency of heavy cream. Heat oil for deep frying in an iron frying pan. Dip macaroons in the Marsala-brandy mixture, then in remaining flour, then immerse completely in batter, a few at a time, making sure that they are well covered. Drain and then deep-fry until golden brown, about 2 to 3 minutes. Drain macaroons on paper towels. Arrange on a serving platter and dust well with confectioners' sugar and serve hot.

> The macaroon, that delicious little dainty of almond paste, is supposed to have been invented in Italy during the Renaissance, possibly in Venice—the Venetian dialect word *macarone*, the same, of course, as macaroni, but which means there a particularly fine dough, is supposed to have given the macaroon its name. In that case, Venice may be pardonned for overdoing things by adding chocolate to macaroons, making them, in Venetian opinion, *bruti ma boni*—ugly, but good. Several other Italian cities are noted for the quality of their macaroons—Modena, which calls them amarelli or amaretti and exports them in large quantity; Pontelagoscura, in the province of Ferrara, an almond-growing centre; Salsomaggiore in Parma province, where they are fashioned in the same size and shape as the almonds which flavor them; and Oristano in Sardinia.

Amaretti alle mandorle

Bitter almond macaroons

Makes 16
Difficulty *
Time: 1 hour
Oven Temp. 325° F.

1-1/3 cups shelled blanched almonds	1 cup plus 2 tbsp. superfine (caster) sugar
4 bitter almonds	2 to 3 egg whites

Butter and flour a baking sheet. Grind almonds and bitter almonds in a mortar, using a pestle, or else grind them fine in a meat grinder. Put almonds in a bowl, add sugar and enough of the egg whites to make mixture the consistency of mashed potatoes. Beat until well blended. Using a teaspoon, put mounds of the paste the size of a large olive on the baking sheet. Be sure to keep them at least 2 inches apart since they will swell considerably while baking. If you wish, sprinkle with a bit of granulated sugar. Bake in a preheated oven for 30 minutes or until macaroons are pale brown. Remove from baking sheet immediately while still warm. Let cool completely on a rack before serving. These macaroons can be kept for a long time if well sealed in a glass jar. For a variation, use hazelnuts instead of almonds.

Cannoli, the pastry which perhaps more than any other is a trademark of Sicily, belongs to the group of Sicilian desserts behind which lurk ancient rites or superstitions, whose original meanings and magical uses have now been forgotten. Cannoli ("pipes") are indeed, as their name suggests, cylindrical; their sweet pastry envelopes contain creamy fillings whose exact ingredients vary from place to place. They were formerly called *cappelli di turchi*, which may have been a reference to the shape of the fez or to the fact that they were supposed to have been of Saracen origin—or both. The fillings may indeed have been Saracen; but to ascribe the pastry tube to Saracen times would be to rejuvenate it tremendously, according to students of ancient rites who say that the form of this sweet is very old, perhaps prehistoric, and that it is meant to suggest that of menhirs, the stone steles which were probably fertility symbols. The theory that cannoli stood for fertility is certainly not invalidated by the fact that they used to appear at weddings, nor by their later association with Easter, a feast of resurrection, which in all agriculturally-based religions is a symbol of the spring rebirth of vegetation. Nowadays cannoli is eaten all year round, but its association with Easter has not entirely disappeared.

Cannoli alla siciliana

Sicilian fried stuffed pastries "cannoli"

Makes 16
Difficulty **
Time: 3 hours

For dough:

2-3/4 cups sifted all-purpose flour
2 tbsp. sugar
1/4 cup butter
1 egg
2/3 cup white wine (or Marsala), about
1 egg white (to brush on dough)
Deep fat or oil heated to 380° F.

For cream filling:

1 lb. ricotta cheese
2 cups sifted confectioners' (icing) sugar
1/3 cup minced mixed candied fruits and cherries
2 oz. (2 squares) bitter chocolate, coarsely grated
Additional candied cherries

For dough: In a bowl mix flour and sugar. Cut in butter until particles are very fine. Add egg and wine gradually to obtain a thick dough. Knead on a floured surface until smooth, about 5 minutes. Cover and let stand for at least an hour.

For filling: Press ricotta through a sieve and mix with confectioners' sugar (reserving 2 tablespoons for later use), candied fruit and chocolate. Chill.
Roll dough into a paper-thin sheet on a floured surface. Cut into 5-inch rounds and wrap each round around a metal cylinder called a cannoli tube, brushed with olive oil. Seal ends by brushing with a little egg white. Deep-fry the cannoli, a few at a time in preheated oil until lightly browned. Drain on paper towels and cool for a while. Slide metal cylinders out carefully. When ready to serve stuff cannoli with cream filling using a pastry bag with a wide round spout. Put a half of a candied cherry at each end and dust with confectioners' sugar.

Struffoli alla partenopea

*Neapolitan
confetti cookies*

Serves 6
Difficulty **
Time: 2 hours

3 cups sifted all-purpose flour
3 eggs, well beaten
6 tbsp. sugar
2 tbsp. butter
1/2 tsp. each grated lemon
and orange rind
2 tbsp. minced candied
orange peel
1/2 cup minced candied citron
1 tbsp. brandy
Salt
1-2 tbsp. milk
Deep fat or oil, heated
to 360° F.
3/4 cup honey
3 tbsp. colored sprinkles for
decoration

Mix flour, eggs, 1 tablespoon of the sugar, butter, grated lemon and orange rind, candied orange peel, half of the citron, brandy and a pinch of salt. Add milk if necessary to make a stiff dough. Knead dough on a floured surface, shape it into a ball, wrap in a towel and let stand for about an hour. Pinch off pieces the size of a large olive and roll with the fingers into slender sticks the shape of a little finger. Join ends to form a ring. Drop into preheated hot oil. When they are golden brown, remove from pan with a slotted spoon and drain on paper toweling.

In a large saucepan mix honey, remaining sugar and 2 tablespoons water. Bring to a boil over moderate heat and simmer until syrup takes on a yellowish color. Lower heat and add "struffoli", stirring to cover them completely with honey. Drain and put them on a plate in a mound. Sprinkle with colored sprinkles. Garnish with remaining citron.

Struffoli alla partenopea

Budino al cioccolato profumato al caffé

Chocolate mocha pudding

Serves 4
Difficulty **
Time: 1-1/2 hours, plus time
required to refrigerate

3 egg yolks
1/2 cup fine (caster) sugar
8 squares (8 oz.) semi-sweet
chocolate
3/4 cup butter
1 tsp. instant coffee
1 cup sweetened whipped cream
4 coffee beans
2 tbsp. chopped pistachio nuts

Budino al cioccolato profumato al caffe

Beat egg yolks with 5 tablespoons of the sugar, beating mixture with a whisk until it is creamy. Grate chocolate into a saucepan. Melt over hot water. Let cool. Mix butter with remaining sugar in a separate bowl until soft and creamy. Stir in egg mixture, instant coffee and melted chocolate. Fold in whipped cream a little at a time. Pour the mixture into a 3-cup pudding mold and refrigerate for 3 to 4 hours. Shortly before serving dip mold into lukewarm water for a moment. Invert pudding onto a dessert platter. Garnish with coffee beans and chopped pistachio nuts.

Budino di crema alle noci

Cream mold with walnuts

Serves 8
Difficulty **

Time: 2 hours, plus time
required to refrigerate
Oven Temp. 400° F.

4 cups (1 quart) milk
1 cup heavy cream
1 cup sugar
1/4 cup walnut liqueur ("nocino"
or any other liqueur to taste)
1 cup semolina
3 cups shelled walnuts,
chopped
3 eggs separated

In a saucepan combine milk, cream, half of the sugar and walnut liqueur. Bring to a boil, then sift in semolina and cook, stirring constantly, until thickened. Add walnuts, let cool to room temperature. Stir in egg yolks, one at a time, and, last, fold in stiffly beaten egg whites. In a pan heat remaining sugar with 1 tablespoon water, without stirring over moderate heat until a golden brown syrup. Pour into a 1-1/2 quart pudding mold and tilt mold so syrup coats the inside of pan. Pour pudding mixture into mold and place on rack in a pan over hot (not boiling) water. Bake in a preheated oven for 35 to 40 minutes. Let stand at room temperature until cool, then chill for about 2 hours and serve.

Zuppa inglese

"English soup"

Serves 4
Difficulty **
Time: 1 hour
Oven Temp. 250° F.

**Genoise (1 Genoa cake
see p. 230) or 12 oz. package
sponge cake
2 cups prepared vanilla pudding ***
**Alchermes Italian liqueur
1 tbsp. chopped candied fruits
Rum
3 egg whites
6 tbsp. sugar
2 tbsp. finely chopped candied
orange peel
1 tbsp. sifted
confectioners' (icing) sugar**

* Vanilla pudding: Mix in a saucepan 1/3 cup
cornstarch, 1/3 cup sugar and 2 cups milk. Stir
over low heat until thick. Stir in 2 tsp. vanilla.
Cool.

Cut Genoise or sponge cake into 1/2-inch thick slices. Put pudding * in a bowl. Set aside 3 tablespoons. Stir in candied fruit. In a deep ovenware dish, about 8 inches in diameter, place first reserved 3 tablespoons pudding. Over this place half of the sliced sponge cake sprinkled with Alchermes liqueur. Cover with remaining pudding mixed with candied fruits. Add remaining sponge cake slices sprinkled with rum. Beat egg whites until stiff. Gradually beat in sugar 1 tablespoon at a time until stiff and glossy. Heap on top of dish. Sprinkle top with candied orange peel and confectioners' sugar. Bake in a preheated oven for 15 to 20 minutes or until meringue is very pale brown.

> Zuppa inglese, it has been remarked, is neither soup nor English. The first part of this observation can be ignored; *zuppa* here does not mean "soup," but "sop." As for the word "English," there are at least two possible explanations. The first takes the word *inglese* literally, assuming that the Italian dessert is a copy of the English trifle—sponge cake and custard—which is, obviously, very close to zuppa inglese. ("Trifle," incidentally, used to mean in England a dish of clotted cream). Italian zuppa inglese, however, seems not to need English inspiration; it is very much in tune with other southern, or especially Sicilian, desserts; from its nature, it ought to be Saracen. Hence a second explanation suggested is that the name may be a corruption of zuppa angelica, a very similar dessert, whose chief difference is that its cream is chocolate flavored.

Semifreddo di cioccolato

*Chocolate mousse
and ladyfingers*

Serves 4
Difficulty *
Time: 30 minutes, chill
2 to 3 hours

**1/2 cup (4 oz.) butter
1/2 cup sugar
2 egg yolks
1/4 cup cocoa
Milk**

**2 packages (3 oz. each)
ladyfingers
2 tbsp. chopped pistachio nuts
1/4 cup chopped toasted
hazelnuts**

Mash butter until soft and fluffy. Beat in sugar until creamy. Stir in egg yolks and, gradually, beat in cocoa. Stir in a tablespoon or 2 of milk until the consistency is like thick sour cream. Put a layer of ladyfingers in a 1-quart glass bowl. Spread with a little of the chocolate mixture. Sprinkle with some of the pistachio nuts, cover with another layer of ladyfingers and continue adding layers in this order until all the ingredients are used up, ending with cocoa mixture. Sprinkle hazelnuts over top and chill for 2 to 3 hours.

Spumoni al marsala

Spumoni cream mold with Marsala wine

1/4 cup Sultana raisins
3 tbsp. Maraschino liqueur
6 egg yolks
1 cup fine (caster) sugar
1 cup sweet Marsala wine
2 envelopes unflavored gelatin
1/4 cup chopped toasted almonds
1/4 cup grated semi-sweet chocolate
2 cups (1 pint) heavy cream, whipped

Serves 12
Difficulty **
Time: 1 hour, chill 4 hours

This dessert should be prepared as early as possible in the morning. Soak raisins in Maraschino liqueur 20 minutes. Prepare zabaglione (see Zabaione in piedi p. 248) using egg yolks, sugar and Marsala. Stir gelatin into 1/4 cup water. Stir gelatin into hot zabaglione. Let zabaglione cool, stirring from time to time. Chill until zabaglione is slightly thickened. Fold raisins together with Maraschino liqueur, almonds, chocolate and whipped cream into zabaglione. Pour mixture into 2-quart spumoni form or other 2 quart mold. Chill for 4 hours. When ready to serve, dip mold for a few seconds in a saucepan of lukewarm water. Tap to loosen and invert onto a serving platter. Garnish with cherries and pistachio nuts, if desired.

Zuccotto alla panna

Zuccotto with whipped cream

Serves 6
Difficulty **
Time: 1 hour, chill 3 hours

1 small sponge cake or 2 packages (3 oz. each) ladyfingers
1/2 lb. almond nougat ("torrone") available in Italian shops or see Torrone casalingo p. 263.

2 cups heavy cream
1/4 cup confectioners' (icing) sugar
1 tsp. vanilla
4 squares (4 oz.) semi-sweet chocolate, coarsely grated
1/2 cup Triple Sec liqueur
1 tbsp. cocoa

Slice sponge cake into 1/4-inch thick slices. Chop almond nougat ("torrone") fairly fine. Whip cream. Fold in confectioners' sugar, vanilla, grated chocolate and nougat. Sprinkle some of the sponge cake slices with some of the liqueur and line a 2-quart round bottom bowl with them. Pour half of the cream mixture into lined bowl. Stir cocoa into remaining cream and spoon over first layer. Cover top with remaining slices of sponge cake after soaking them lightly in remaining liqueur. Chill. After 3 hours, loosen edges and invert mold. Turn out the contents onto a serving dish.

Crema fritta alla veneta

Fried custard Veneto style

2 cups milk
1 tsp. vanilla
1/2 cup sugar
1 cup sifted all-purpose flour
Salt
4 eggs and 4 egg yolks
5 tbsp. butter
Dry bread crumbs
Deep fat or oil heated to 360° F.
Confectioners' (icing) sugar

Serves 4   Difficulty **   Time: 2 hours

Bring milk to a boil, remove from heat, add vanilla and let stand for 15 minutes. In a saucepan mix sugar, flour, pinch of salt, 2 whole eggs and 4 yolks. Mix well and gradually beat in warm milk. Stir constantly over moderate heat until smooth and very thick. Remove from heat and beat in 2 tablespoons of the butter. Mix well and pour into an 8-inch square pan to make a layer 1/2-inch thick. Melt remaining butter and pour over cream. Chill and then cut into 1-1/2-inch squares or diamond-shaped pieces. Beat remaining eggs in a bowl. Dip custard pieces into egg, then into bread crumbs. Deep-fry, turning pieces to brown evenly on all sides. Drain on absorbent paper and sprinkle with confectioners' sugar and serve very hot.

Dolce di crema di uova sode

Dolce di crema di uova sode

Ladyfinger cream mold with hard-cooked egg yolks

Serves 6
Difficulty *
Time: 1 hour,
plus time required
to refrigerate dessert

1/3 cup brandy
1/3 cup Aurum (orange-flavored Italian liqueur from Abruzzi)
2 packages (3 oz. each) ladyfingers
1 cup (8 oz.) soft butter

8 yolks of hard-cooked eggs
1/4 cup sugar
1 cup heavy cream whipped with 1/4 cup confectioners' (icing) sugar and 1 tsp. vanilla

Mix brandy and Aurum. Quickly dip ladyfingers into mixture. Use them to line 1 quart round bottom bowl. Mash butter until light and fluffy. Mash egg yolks and stir into butter with sugar. Fill mold with alternating layers of creamed butter and whipped cream. Cover with a layer of ladyfingers dipped in brandy mixture. Cover and chill for 12 hours.

Zabaione in piedi

Zabaglione with ladyfingers

Serves 6
Difficulty **
Time: 1 hour,
chill several hours

1/4 cup apricot liqueur
1 envelope gelatin
3 eggs plus 5 egg yolks
1 cup sugar
1/2 cup dry Marsala wine
1/2 cup white wine
2 packages (3 oz. each)
ladyfingers

Moisten a 1 quart charlotte mold very slightly with liqueur, tilting the mold in your hands to distribute liqueur evenly. Soak gelatin in cold water. To prepare zabaglione, beat eggs with yolks. Gradually beat in sugar. Beat until thick and fluffy. Beat in Marsala and white wine. Place into the top part of a double boiler set over simmering water. Beat until mixture is foamy and thick like whipped cream. Remove zabaglione from double boiler and stir in gelatin. Mix vigorously and let cool very slightly. Line charlotte pan with ladyfingers on bottom and sides. Pour half zabaglione slowly into charlotte pan. Cover with remaining crumbled ladyfingers, add remaining zabaglione and chill. When ready to serve, turn the dessert out of the mold onto a serving plate. Garnish the edges of the plate with cookies of various kinds or with rosettes of whipped cream.

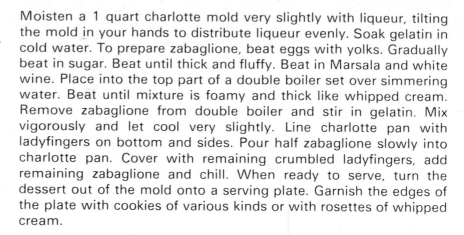

The nature of the rich creamy half-dessert half-drink called zabaione, known all over the world, would suggest a Saracen origin; and it seems almost certainly Sicilian, as far as Italy is concerned, despite occasional claims to its paternity from Rome and Naples. Yet certain etymologists declare that the word is of Illyrian origin, which seems unlikely, and that it was originally an Illyrian drink made from grain, which seems wildly unlikely. The mystery of the name need deter no one from enjoying this luscious mixture of wine (preferably Marsala), egg yolks and other ingredients which vary slightly, with the place where it is made, and sometimes with the imagination of the individual cook.

Granita di limone

Lemon ice

Serves 12
Difficulty *
Time: 30 minutes

12 cups crushed ice
Juice of 12 lemons
6 tbsp. sugar, about
12 lemon slices for garnishing

Fill sherbet glasses with the crushed ice. Place in freezer until ready to serve. Mix lemon juice and sugar to taste. Stir until sugar is dissolved. Pour over ice. Serve at once garnished with lemon slice.

The usual translation for granita is sherbet, but outside Italy what I understand by sherbet is usually quite smooth in texture, sometimes even creamy. The granita I have eaten so often on the sidewalk terraces of the Via Vittorio Veneto in Rome is more like shaved ice; possibly it is different in Sicily, where it is popular too, but I have never sampled it there. In Rome, for some reason, it is *infra dig.* to order granita in the afternoon; it is strictly a morning confection, I don't know why. However, ignorant foreigners will be served later in the day without the slightest indication of disapproval, if they choose to ignore tradition. The favorite flavor is lemon, but I have also tasted strawberry, coffee and chocolate. There are certainly others.

Coppa tutti frutti

Tutti frutti
ice cream

Serves 4
Difficulty *
Time: 30 minutes, plus time
for marinating fruit

1/2 cup mixed candied fruits
1/4 cup kirsch liqueur
1/4 cup maraschino liqueur
1 cup *each* lemon sherbet,
strawberry and pineapple
ice cream

Dice candied fruit, reserving 4 cherries intact, and marinate in kirsch and maraschino liqueurs mixed together. Drain candied fruit and put it in the bottom of 4 parfait glasses. Alternate lemon sherbet, strawberry and pineapple ice cream to fill cup. Top with reserved cherries and serve. Spoon over liqueur drained from fruit.

Italians are today undoubtedly the greatest ice cream makers in the world. Sicily leads in ice cream excellence, followed closely by Naples (it was a Sicilian who introduced ice cream into France, a Neapolitan who introduced it into the United States). Sicily was presumably where Italian ice cream started, for sherbet is supposed to have been first produced there by the Saracens; whether they had yet added cream, or milk, to their frozen desserts I do not know. In any case it has been added now. The most elaborate temples of frozen desserts I know are Sicilian ice cream parlors; I recall one in Acireale which tempted me to sample everything in the place, a task for a lifetime.

Coppa Venus

Venus ice cream cup

Serves 4
Difficulty *
Time: 30 minutes

1 pint vanilla ice cream
4 halves of canned peaches

1 cup hulled strawberries
1/2 cup heavy cream, whipped

Divide ice cream among 4 glasses and garnish with peach halves, strawberries and whipped cream.

Coppa Montecarlo

Ice cream with
wild strawberries

Serves 4
Difficulty *
Time: 30 minutes

4 small scoops vanilla
ice cream
1 cup heavy cream, whipped
1 cup wild strawberries,
hulled and halved
4 coconut macaroons
1/4 cup finely chopped
pistachios

Place ice cream into glasses. Top with whipped cream mixed with wild strawberries and crumbled macaroon cookies. Top with chopped pistachios.

Coppa Venus   Coppa tutti frutti   Coppa Montecarlo

Dolce di ricotta al rum

Ricotta rum cake

1 9-inch sponge cake,
2-inches thick
(see Genoise p. 230)
1 lb. ricotta cheese
1/2 cup sugar
1 tsp. vanilla extract
2 tbsp. rum
1 package (6 oz.) chocolate
chips
1 tbsp. mixed diced
candied fruits
1/4 cup Sultana raisins,
soaked and drained
1/4 cup confectioners' (icing)
sugar

> A slice of cheese unadorned may very well replace dessert in the meal; but there are also a number of Italian cheeses which lend themselves to conversion into full fledged desserts by being combined with sugar, honey, jam or other sweet substances. Particularly adaptable to such treatment are ricotta, a cousin of cottage cheese, and mascarpone, a cream cheese eaten most often, precisely, as a dessert.

Serves 6   Difficulty *   Time: 1 hour and chill 2 to 3 hours

Cut sponge cake into three equal layers. Mix ricotta, sugar, vanilla extract and rum until smooth. Stir in chocolate chips, candied fruits and raisins. Place 1 cake layer on serving platter. Spread half of the ricotta mixture over sponge cake layer, cover with a second layer, spread second layer with remaining ricotta mixture and top with the third layer. Chill for 2 to 3 hours before serving. Just before serving, sprinkle top heavily with confectioners' sugar.

Palline
dolci di ricotta

Sweet ricotta balls

Serves 4
Difficulty *
Time: 1 hour

1 lb. ricotta   1 tbsp. flour
2 eggs   1 tsp. grated lemon peel
3 tbsp. sugar   Shallow oil or fat

Mash ricotta. Stir in eggs, sugar, flour and lemon peel. Shape little balls, about as big as a small walnut, then flatten slightly between your floured palms. Fry in oil 1/4-inch deep until brown. Turn and brown on other side.

Mascarpone
al gorgonzola

*Cream cheese and
Gorgonzola mousse*

Serves 6
Difficulty **
Time: 30 minutes, plus time
required to mash Gorgonzola
and to refrigerate

6 oz. sweet Gorgonzola
(about 3/4 cup)
2 tbsp. cognac
1 package (8 oz.) Mascarpone
or cream cheese
1 cup shelled walnuts, crushed
in a mortar
1/2 cup heavy cream, whipped

Crumble Gorgonzola into bits and sprinkle with cognac and let marinate for 5 to 6 hours. Mash Gorgonzola adding a little at a time Mascarpone and crushed walnuts. Gently fold in whipped cream. Spoon mixture into a lightly oiled 3-cup mold. Chill overnight. When ready to serve, dip mold into hot water for a few seconds and invert on a plate. Serve with bread or crackers.

Mascarpone al gorgonzola

Mozzarella fritta alla romana

Mozzarella fritters Roman style

Serves 4
Difficulty *
Time: 1 hour

1 lb. mozzarella cheese
Flour
2 eggs, well beaten

Oil (or vegetable shortening)
2 inches deep, heated to 360° F.
Superfine (caster) sugar
Cinnamon

Slice mozzarella, making slices about 1/2-inch thick and about 1-1/2 inches square. Coat pieces with flour. Dip in egg and fry in a large frying pan with oil. Fry until brown on both sides, about 3 to 4 minutes. Drain on absorbent paper when slices are golden brown. Arrange on a serving platter and sprinkle generously with superfine sugar mixed with a pinch of cinnamon.

Budino di ricotta

Ricotta pudding

Serves 4
Difficulty *
Time: 1 hour

1-1/3 cups ricotta
3 tbsp. sugar
1 egg yolk
2 tbsp. orange liqueur
2 tbsp. cocoa

1 tbsp. sugar
1 package (3 oz.) ladyfingers
1 tbsp. orange liqueur
1 tbsp. brandy

Cream ricotta with a spoon. Add sugar, egg yolk and liqueur. Divide this mixture into 2 equal parts. Add cocoa and sugar to one part and mix well. Spoon plain ricotta mixture into a serving bowl. Place ladyfingers on top and sprinkle with liqueur and brandy. Spoon over chocolate ricotta mixture. Chill until ready to serve. Alternatively, line an 8-inch springform pan with moistened ladyfingers and then put the two ricotta preparations in one at a time, first the light-colored one, then the chocolate-flavored one. Chill.

Cassata alla siciliana

Sicilian cheese cake

Makes 1
Difficulty **
Time: 1 hour

1-1/2 lbs. ricotta cheese, sieved
1 cup sugar
Triple sec liqueur
4 squares (4 oz.) bitter chocolate, coarsely grated
1/2 cup chopped candied fruits (citron, orange peel, cherries)
2 Genoise cakes (p. 230)
Cognac
Candied fruit

Mix ricotta and sugar until creamy. Remove 1/2 cup and set aside for top of cake. Add 1 tablespoon of liqueur to remaining cheese along with chocolate and candied fruits. Chill mixture for 30 minutes. Using a serrated knife, cut sponge cakes baked in round form into 1/2-inch thick slices. Take the baking pan and line with wax paper. Mix equal parts cognac and liqueur. Dip sponge cake slices lightly in mixture and line bottom and sides of baking pan. (Be careful not to oversoak cake, otherwise it will fall apart.) Pour in ricotta mixture, pressing it down and leveling it with a spatula. On top put a layer of remaining sponge cake moistened with cognac-liqueur mixture. Repeat. Chill for a few hours. When you are ready to serve, turn cassata out upside down on a plate; if it doesn't come out easily, immerse pan briefly in boiling water. Remove wax paper, cover cassata with reserved ricotta and serve, garnished with candied fruit.

Macedonia di frutta

Mixed fruit compote

Serves 4
Difficulty *
Time: 30 minutes,
chill 2 hours

2 small ripe cantaloupes
2/3 cup maraschino liqueur
2 peaches
2 pears
1 cup strawberries, hulled
1 cup pitted fresh cherries
2/3 cup sugar

Wash cantaloupe, cut in half horizontally, remove seeds and scoop out pulp, leaving a shell 1/2 inch thick. Chop melon removed. Moisten inside of melon shell with 2 tablespoons of the maraschino. Peel and pit peaches. Peel and core pears. Dice fruit into 1/2-inch cubes. Mix melon, peaches, pears, strawberries and cherries in a bowl and add remaining maraschino liqueur and sugar. Mix and chill for 2 hours. When ready to serve, spoon marinated fruit into melon shells and serve in a bowl filled with crushed ice. Garnish with fresh plum or apricot leaves. If you don't like maraschino flavoring, use orange juice or a mixture of half orange juice and half sparkling wine.

Macedoine of fruit is international; whether it is of Italian origin or not I have no idea. From its name, one might be tempted to ascribe it to ancient Greece; but the name was not given to it because it is assumed to be a dish of Macedonia. It is so called because this mixture of different fruits is put together from many smaller parts, as Alexander the Great united a large number of minor peoples under Macedonian rule.

Mele in gabbia

Apple strudel
Italian style

Serves 4
Difficulty ***
Time: 4 hours (if dough is prepared at home)
Oven Temp. 375°F.

For filling:

4 cooking apples, peeled, cored and sliced
6 tbsp. butter
6 tbsp. sugar
1 cup soft bread crumbs
7 tbsp. Marsala wine
Cinnamon
Grated peel of 1/2 orange
1/2 cup Sultana raisins
1/4 cup pine nuts

For sauce:

1 cup apricot liqueur flavored with 2 tbsp. maraschino

For pastry dough:

1-1/2 cups all-purpose flour
1/4 tsp. salt
1 tbsp. lemon juice
3 eggs, well beaten
2 tbsp. oil
Melted butter

Peel apples, core them and slice fairly thick; put them in a pan with butter (reserving 1 to 1-1/2 tablespoons) and sugar. Saute apples until tender. Cool and then mix in bread crumbs lightly sauteed in reserved butter. Mix Marsala, a pinch of cinnamon, grated orange peel, raisins and pine nuts. Let stand 10 minutes. Drain well. Stir in apples.

In a bowl mix flour and salt. Stir in lemon juice, 2 of the eggs and oil. This makes a soft dough. Knead hard on a floured surface until smooth, elastic and not sticky. Cover and let rest 30 minutes. Cover a table with a large cloth. Flour the cloth. Roll out dough to a 14-inch square. Brush top of dough with butter. With backs of the hands carefully stretch out dough from the center until it is paper thin. Brush dough with butter. Trim off thick edges of dough. Arrange filling in a strip along one side of the dough. Turn ends of dough over ends of filling. Use the cloth to lift and fold over the dough. Using the cloth, roll the dough to enclose the filling and keep rolling until dough is completely rolled around the filling. Roll onto a greased baking sheet. Brush with remaining beaten egg. Bake in a preheated oven for 40 to 45 minutes. Cut while warm into slices. Spoon over apricot sauce.

Bordura di mele guarnita

Apples with whipped cream and marrons

Serves 4
Difficulty *
Time: 1-1/2 hours

4 cooking apples
5 tbsp. sugar
1 cup water
1 tsp. vanilla

1 cup whipped cream
2 tbsp. confectioners' (icing) sugar
8 marrons glacés (4 chopped, 4 whole)

Peel apples and core them whole. Cut apples in half and put in a saucepan. Add sugar and water. Cook over moderate heat, stirring gently until apples are tender but still hold their shape. Stir in vanilla. Remove from heat and let cool in their own syrup. When ready to serve put apples into serving dish. Pour a little of the syrup over them. Whip cream with confectioners' sugar. Using a pastry bag, cover with rosettes of whipped cream. Sprinkle with chopped marrons glacés. Garnish with remaining whole marrons.

Mele alla ricca

Stuffed baked apples

Serves 4
Difficulty *
Time: 2-1/2 hours
Oven Temp. 350° F.

4 large cooking apples
Juice of 1 lemon
2 tbsp. butter
1/2 cup sugar
1/2 cup sweet Marsala wine
1/4 cup raisins
1/4 cup pine nuts
2 cups prepared vanilla pudding (see Zuppa inglese, p. 245)
1/2 cup chopped candied orange peel

Wash and core apples, making a 1-inch in diameter hole in apple. Squeeze lemon juice both inside and out to keep the apples from turning brown. Butter a baking dish, arrange apples in it and put a piece of butter into center cavity of each. Sprinkle with sugar and half of the Marsala and bake in a preheated oven for 40 minutes or until apples are tender but still hold their shape. Mix raisins, pine nuts and remaining Marsala. Let stand 1 hour. Drain and mix with vanilla pudding. Place apples on a serving platter and cool. Spoon over pan juices and fill with pudding mixture. Sprinkle with candied orange peel and serve.

Mele alla ricca

Albicocche meringate

Apricot meringues

Serves 4
Difficulty **
Time: 2 hours
Oven Temp. 275°F.

Apricots:

8 large ripe apricots
7 tbsp. water
1/4 cup sugar
Dash of vanilla

Rice with vanilla:

2 cups milk
1/2 lb. rice
2 tbsp. butter
5 tbsp. sugar
2 egg yolks
1 tsp. vanilla

Meringues:

3 egg whites
1 cup sugar
1/2 tsp. vanilla

Albicocche meringate

Apricots: Wash apricots, cut in half and remove pits. Heat water in a saucepan with sugar and vanilla until it comes to a boil. Add apricots to this syrup and simmer gently for 4 to 5 minutes. Remove from heat and let cool in the syrup.

Vanilla rice: Boil milk, remove from heat as soon as it reaches boiling point and let cool. Meanwhile drop rice into boiling water then drain immediately and wash with warm water. Drain thoroughly and transfer to a saucepan with melted butter. Stir until lightly browned. Add hot milk. Simmer stirring constantly until rice is tender, about 20 minutes, at which point the milk will have been completely absorbed. Remove from heat, stir in sugar and let cool. Add egg yolks one at a time and vanilla and mix. Pour mixture into an 8-inch layer cake pan. Spread rice evenly in pan. Let cool.

Meringue: Beat egg whites until stiff. Gradually beat in sugar, 2 tablespoons at a time until stiff and glossy. Fold in vanilla.
Drain apricots from syrup and place on top of rice. Using a pastry bag with rose tip, squeeze a rosette of meringue over each apricot, covering them completely. Bake in a preheated oven leaving oven door slightly open for 40 minutes. Meringue should dry and brown ever so slightly. Let cool and serve.

Ciliegie alla ricotta

Cherries with ricotta

Serves 4
Difficulty *
Time: 3 hours

1 lb. cherries
2 tbsp. sugar
1 cup skimmed milk

1/4 cup ricotta
2-inch piece of orange peel
(only colored part, no white underskin)

Put cherries in a saucepan and cover with water to which 1 tablespoon of the sugar has been added. Cook 20 minutes, remove from heat and refrigerate. Mix milk with ricotta and remaining sugar. Add piece of orange peel (a small piece) and chill. After 2 to 3 hours, remove orange peel and pour sauce over cherries and serve.

Fichi con panna montata al croccante

Figs with whipped cream and almond macaroons

Serves 4
Difficulty *
Time: 1 hour

**1 lb. fresh figs (or 2 large jars drained kadota figs if out of season)
1/2 cup Maraschino liqueur
1 cup raspberries
1/4 lb. almond macaroons (purchased Amaretti or see Amaretti p. 241)
1 cup heavy cream, whipped**

Put figs in a glass bowl, sprinkle with maraschino liqueur and chill for at least 1/2 hour. Press raspberries through a sieve (reserving 8 whole.) Crumble macaroons into fairly large bits and fold both puree and crumbs into whipped cream. Spoon cream over figs. Garnish with reserved whole raspberries. Set glass bowl into a larger one full of crushed ice and serve.

> In my opinion there is nothing better to be done with a fresh fig than to eat it just as it comes from the tree—at the beginning of the meal with a paper-thin slice of Parma ham if you wish, at the end with nothing but its rich self. It is one of the greatest fruits of the world and *the* greatest of the Mediterranean area. However, once in a while, for a change, a little elaboration on the fig is certainly permissible; it doesn't prevent anyone from eating them untouched the next time. They may be stewed for dessert, or treated in some other fashion—as in Bari, which does not exactly fry them, but heats them slightly, with a flavoring of almonds, fennel and bay leaves (the Basilicata leaves out the bay leaves and comes closer to really cooking them). Umbria stuffs white figs with walnuts and almonds. And, fresh or stewed, they can be combined to excellent effect with cream.

Banane alla maniera della nonna

Grandmother's baked bananas

Serves 4
Difficulty *
Time: 1-1/2 hours
Oven Temp. 400° F.

**4 ripe but firm bananas
4 baking apples
1/4 cup sugar
1 cup heavy cream
1/2 cup Kirsch
1/4 lb. bitter almond macaroons
1/4 cup (2 oz.) butter**

Cut off ends of bananas, then slit only the skin to divide it in half lengthwise. Remove banana from jacket and cut into slices. Reserve all 8 half skins. Peel apples, core and dice. In a saucepan, cook apples with 3 tablespoons water and sugar for 5 minutes. Puree apples into another saucepan. Mix with 1/4 cup of the cream and Kirsch. Simmer over low heat until thick. Stir occasionally. Use thick applesauce to fill banana skins. Top with banana slices. Sprinkle with macaroon crumbs. Spoon over melted butter. Place them side by side in a shallow baking dish. Bake in preheated oven for 8 to 10 minutes until surface is browned. Serve topped with remaining cream whipped until stiff.

« Banane alla maniera della nonna »:

Pesche capricciose allo zabaione

Caprice of peaches with zabaglione sauce

Serves 4
Difficulty **
Time: 1 hour, plus time
required to marinate fruit

**Zabaglione (see Zabaione in
piedi, p. 248, substituting
spumante wine for Marsala
and white wine)**
1 pint strawberries, hulled
2 tbsp. sugar
Juice of 1 orange
2 tbsp. Maraschino liqueur
4 large ripe freestone peaches
Juice of 1/2 lemon
2 pecan pralines, coarsely chopped
4 candied violets

A fresh peach strikes an Italian as an excellent dessert in its own right, and so it is; but adorned, stuffed or cooked peach desserts present themselves so naturally to the imagination that they were already present in ancient Roman times. It is possible that today's tastes might not accord particularly with those of the Romans. Modern times have not preserved the Roman dish in which peaches were cooked in a sauce of vinegar, wine, olive oil, honey, pepper, mint—and liquamen, a seasoner made from decayed fish! As if this had not already done enough violence to the peach, it was liberally peppered before serving. Modern Italy makes stuffed peaches with more respect for the fine fresh flavor of the fruit: in Piedmont a hole scooped out from the centre of a half peach is filled with its own pulp, mashed together with macaroons, egg yolk, butter and sugar; in Liguria, the stuffing is again some of the flesh of the peach, with candied citron and candied squash, the whole cooked in sugared white wine.

Prepare zabaglione omitting gelatin and chill. Put strawberries in a bowl. Mix with sugar, orange juice, and maraschino and marinate in refrigerator for 1 hour. Peel peaches, scoop out top and carefully remove pits, leaving peach whole. Place them in a bowl, sprinkle with lemon juice and chill. When ready to serve, drain peaches and spoon pralines into each cavity. Arrange peaches around the edges of serving bowl. Add strawberries with their juice in center. Spoon over cold zabaglione and put a candied violet on each peach.

Pesche in tegame

Baked stuffed peaches

Serves 4
Difficulty **
Time: 1-1/2 hours
Oven Temp. 350° F.

**4 large firm but ripe
peaches**
1/2 cup sugar
Grated rind of 1 lemon
2 tbsp. bitter cocoa
**1/4 cup blanched almonds,
chopped**

**4 or 5 bitter almond macaroons,
crumbled (purchased Amaretti
or see Amaretti p. 241)**
1 egg yolk
Peach liqueur
2 tbsp. butter

Peel peaches, split in half and remove pits. Scoop out some of the peach leaving a shell 1 inch thick. Put pulp removed in a bowl. Add half the sugar, lemon rind, cocoa, almonds, macaroons and egg yolk. Mix with enough liqueur to form a thick paste. Stuff peach halves with this filling, arrange them in a baking dish, dot with butter, sprinkle with remaining sugar and bake in a preheated oven for 25 to 30 minutes or until peaches are tender and still hold their shape.

Ricotta con le pere

Ricotta and pears

Serves 4
Difficulty *
Time: 1-1/2 hours

4 pears
1/2 cup sugar

2 tbsp. brandy
1 lb. ricotta, sieved
1/4 cup cocoa

Peel pears and cut each pear into 8 wedges. Remove core and cook pears in water to just cover with half of the sugar until tender, about 15 minutes. Remove pears and boil cooking liquid until it is thick and syrupy, about 30 minutes. Cool. Stir in brandy, sugar, ricotta and cocoa until smooth. Place pears into dessert glasses. Spoon over ricotta mixture and chill until ready to serve.

The pear, like the peach, is capable of serving as a dessert all by itself without complications—or one might serve with it a slice of pecorino, the fresh juiciness of the fruit and the sharpness of the cheese being admirably complementary. With such fine varieties as the Passacrassana of Ferrara, the Martin secco of the Valle d'Aosta, the cinnamon pear of Belluno, the Principe Umberto and the William at their disposition, Italians need elaborate no further on the pear. However, they do. Cooked pears range all the way from those simply stewed in great steaming kettles in the market of Venice and dished out for famished shoppers, to the *crostata di pere alla milanese*, a tart of pears set into a bed of apricot jelly and enlivened with a dash of rum.

Timballo con le pere alla piemontese

Deep-dish pear pie Piedmont style

Serves 4
Difficulty *
Time: 2 hours
Oven Temp. 375° F.

For filling:

6 large firm cooking pears
peeled, cored and diced
1/2 cup sugar
1/2 cup red wine
1 whole clove
Pinch of cinnamon

For pie crust:

1-3/4 cups sifted all-purpose
flour
Pinch of salt
1/2 cup yellow cornmeal

2/3 cup fine (caster) sugar
2/3 cup (5 oz.) butter
3 egg yolks

In a saucepan mix pears, sugar, wine, clove and cinnamon. Simmer for 15 minutes or until pears are almost tender. Cool.
In a bowl mix flour, a pinch of salt, cornmeal and sugar. Cut in butter (reserving 1 to 1-1/2 tablespoons) until particles are very fine. Stir in egg yolks and, if necessary, a little water to make a thick dough. Knead a few times on a floured surface until a smooth ball. Let it stand covered for 30 minutes. Roll out 2/3 of the dough on a floured surface into a sheet large enough to line the bottom and sides of an ungreased 8-inch pie pan.
Drain pears. Pour pears into lined pie pan. Roll out remaining crust and place over filling. Crimp edges to seal. Prick top. Bake in a preheated oven until well browned and crisp, about 35 to 40 minutes. Serve hot.

258

Pere al marsala

Pear-prune dessert with Marsala

Serves 4
Difficulty *
Time: 1 hour

4 ripe but firm pears, peeled and cored while whole
4 pitted prunes
1 cup water

1 cup dry Marsala wine
2 tbsp. sugar
2-inch piece of lemon rind
1 stick cinnamon

Use an apple corer to core pears. Stuff each core cavity with 1 prune softened in warm water for 15 minutes. Set pears upright in a saucepan. Pour in water and Marsala. Sprinkle with sugar. Add lemon rind and cinnamon and cook with the pan covered, turning pears from time to time, for about 20 minutes or until easily pierced and tender.

Delizie di pere ''gran duchessa''

Compote of pears à la Grand Duchess

Serves 4
Difficulty **
Time: 2 hours

For fruit:

8 firm pears
4 squares (4 oz.) semi-sweet chocolate, melted
1/4 cup sugar

2 whole cloves
2-inch piece cinnamon stick
2 cups dry white wine

For zabaglione with cream:

5 tbsp. sugar
2 egg yolks

1/2 cup heavy cream, whipped
1/4 cup dry Marsala wine

Peel pears and cook them whole with sugar, white wine, cloves and cinnamon until tender, about 20 minutes. Remove spices, let cool and cut 4 of the pears into wedges, removing core.
Prepare zabaglione (see Zabaione in piedi p. 248) omitting addition of gelatin, using egg yolks, sugar and Marsala. Chill and fold in whipped cream. Put pear wedges in a glass serving bowl. Cover with some of the pear cooking syrup. Spoon over zabaglione. Drizzle with melted chocolate. Place glass bowl on a large glass platter. Put whole pears around bowl on plate and pour remaining pear syrup over them.

Delizie di pere ''gran duchessa''

Susine sotto spirito

Plums in spirit

Serves 6
Difficulty *
Time: 30 minutes, 2 days
for marinating

2 lbs. plums (round or long, ripe but firm)	2 cups water
1-1/2 cups sugar	Vodka, about 1/4 cup
	Rum, about 1/4 cup

Wash plums thoroughly and dry carefully. In a saucepan mix sugar and water. Boil syrup for 20 minutes. Remove from heat and let cool until lukewarm. Add plums and reheat to a boil. Remove from heat and transfer fruit and syrup to a 1-quart glass container. Cool and fill jar with a mixture of vodka and rum in equal parts. Let stand 2 days before serving.

Susine al vino

Plums in wine

Serves 6
Difficulty *
Time: 30 minutes

2-1/2 lbs. red plums	5 cloves
1-1/3 cups fine (caster) sugar	3 cups dry white wine
Grated rind of 1 lemon	

Wash whole plums and put them in a saucepan with sugar, lemon rind, cloves and wine. Cook over moderate heat until plums are tender and syrup starts to thicken, about 30 minutes. Plums prepared this way are good either hot or cold. Serve plums with some of the syrup spooned over them. The extra plum syrup is good in a granita (i.e., poured over crushed ice – see Lemon ice, p. 248) or mixed with club soda for a refreshing drink.

Torta di fragole e ricotta

Strawberry and ricotta pie

Serves 6
Difficulty **
Time: 1-1/2 hours
Oven Temp. 400° F.
then 350° F.

6 tbsp. sugar	3/4 lb. ricotta
1/2 cup red wine	3 eggs, separated
1 pint strawberries, hulled	Juice of 1/2 lemon
1 cup zwieback crumbs	2 tbsp. flour
3 tbsp. butter, melted	1/4 cup plain yogurt
	Pinch of salt

Dissolve 2 tablespoons of the sugar in wine and chill for 2 hours. Place strawberries in a bowl and cover with sweetened wine. Mix crumbs with 1 tablespoon of the sugar and butter. Pour into a buttered 8-inch pie pan and press down firmly on bottom and sides. Bake in a preheated oven for 5 minutes. Let it cool. Press ricotta through a sieve into a bowl. Beat egg yolks and stir into ricotta. Stir in remaining sugar, lemon juice, flour, yogurt and salt. Beat egg whites until stiff and fold in carefully. Pour into pie pan and bake in a 350° F. oven for 1 hour. Cool. Drain strawberries and place berries on top of pie.

Fragole belvedere

Strawberries Belvedere

Serves 4
Difficulty **
Time: 1-1/2 hours

1 pint large ripe strawberries, hulled and halved
1/4 cup sugar
Juice of 1 lemon
3 tbsp. Cointreau
1 8-inch round sponge layer or yellow layer cake
(see Genoise, p. 230)

2 cups prepared vanilla pudding (see Zuppa inglese, p. 245)
1/2 cup heavy cream whipped with 2 tbsp. sugar and 1 tsp. vanilla
1/4 cup slivered almonds

Sprinkle strawberries with sugar, lemon juice and Cointreau and marinate for 1 hour. Cut sponge cake in half horizontally. Drain berries and sprinkle half of the juice over bottom half of cake layer. Spread with half of the pudding. Top with second half of cake. Sprinkle with remaining strawberry juice. Spoon over remaining pudding. Spoon cream in a border around edge of cake. Fill center with strawberry halves. Sprinkle with almonds.

Cremona claims that torrone, a sweet eaten especially at the Christmas season, was invented there in 1441 to be served as one of the desserts at the wedding by which Francesco Sforza astutely changed his status from condottiero to noble by marrying an illegitimate daughter of the Visconti family. The torrone made for this occasion was modeled in the form of Cremona's cathedral campanile, the highest in Italy, the Torrazzo—hence, torrone. But torrone is nougat, and nougat was probably a Saracen invention. Sicily claims it too, and its claim seems a little more solid.

Torrone casalingo

Italian home-style nougat

Makes 1 8-inch square pan
Difficulty *
Time: 1-1/2 hours, plus time for torrone to solidify

* Ostia is a milky white, edible wafer about the thickness of a sheet of paper. These wafers can be purchased in an Italian bakery or in a confectioners' suppy house.

2/3 cup honey
2 egg whites
1 cup fine (caster) sugar
1/2 cup water

1/2 cup toasted whole almonds
1 tsp. vanilla
Large squares of *ostia* wafer *

Boil honey until it reaches 290° F. on a candy thermometer. Beat egg whites until stiff. Pour in honey in a thin stream, beating constantly. Beat for 1 minute. Boil sugar and water until 290° F. on a candy thermometer. Beat into honey mixture. Stir in almonds and vanilla. Line the bottom and sides of an 8-inch square pan with *ostia* wafers, fill with candy mixture. Cover with *ostia* wafers, and set a weight on top. Let stand for 24 hours. Unmold and cut into 1 × 2 inches oblongs. Wrap each piece separately in wax paper or foil. Store in an air-tight container in a cool, dry place.

Fragole belvedere

Montebianco con marrons glacés

Mont Blanc with marrons glacés

Serves 4
Difficulty **
Time: 3 hours, plus time
required to refrigerate

2-1/2 lbs. chestnuts	Sugar
Milk	1 cup heavy cream, whipped
1 tsp. vanilla	Marrons glacés

Slit chestnuts and cover with water. Boil for about 30 minutes, drain and peel, removing shell and brown inner skin. Cover chestnuts with milk in a saucepan. Add vanilla and bring to boiling point. Cover and cook over low heat for about 45 minutes or until chestnuts are tender and mealy. Stir occasionally to prevent sticking. Drain, mash chestnuts in a food mill. Measure puree and add half the amount of sugar. In a saucepan set puree over moderate heat and, stirring constantly, cook until mixture becomes thick and pulls away from sides of saucepan, about 30 minutes. Remove from heat and let it cool completely. Put puree in a potato ricer and press chestnuts through, letting them fall in a mound onto serving plate. Cover this with whipped cream and garnish with marrons glacés. Chill until ready to serve.

Italy has two types of chestnut, both of which are often used in desserts. *Castagne* are small ones, which grow several to the pod; *marrone* are larger, with only one nut to the pod (those of Naples are particularly esteemed). Sometimes the whole nut goes into desserts, sometimes the first step is to grind it into flour, which can then be used to produce dishes like the chestnut pancakes (*necci*) of Lucca, which are filled with cottage cheese, or the chestnut cream which put an end to the illustrious Gallant family when its last surviving member, aged 12 at the time, died from a surfeit of it.

Composta di castagne alla crema

Chestnut puree with whipped cream

Serves 4
Difficulty *
Time: 2-1/2 hours, plus time
required for refrigeration
Oven Temp. 325º F.

2-1/2 lbs. chestnuts	7 tbsp. water
3 cups milk	1 tsp. vanilla
1 cup sugar	1 cup heavy cream, whipped

Place chestnuts into preheated oven for 20 minutes or until almost tender. Peel and place in a saucepan. Add milk and cook until tender. Mash with a potato masher or food mill and catch puree in a bowl. Put sugar in a saucepan, add 7 tablespoons water and cook at a boil until a thick syrup that forms a soft ball when dropped into cold water. Beat syrup into chestnut puree and stir in vanilla. If desired, stir in 2 tablespoons cocoa or 1 ounce (1 square) grated semi-sweet chocolate. Pile chestnut puree into a serving bowl and cover with whipped cream, adding enough to make a mound of whipped cream in the center.

INDEX